AF064502

Fragments of Colossae

Sifting through the Traces

Alan H Cadwallader

Copyright © 2015 with Alan Cadwallader.

All rights reserved. Except for any fair dealing permitted under the Copyright Act, no part of this book may be reproduced by any means without prior permission. Inquiries should be made to the publisher.

National Library of Australia Cataloguing-in-Publication entry

Creator: Cadwallader, Alan H, author.
Title: Fragments of Colossae : sifting through the traces / Alan H Cadwallader

ISBN: 978-1-925232-53-0 (paperback)
               978-1-925232-54-7 (hardback)
               978-1-925232-55-4 (ebook : Kindle)
               978-1-925232-56-1 (ebook : pdf)

Subjects: Cities and towns, Ancient--Turkey--Colossae (Extinct city).
               Colossae (Extinct city)--Antiquities.
               Colossae (Extinct city)--History.

Dewey Number: 939.2

An imprint of the ATF Ltd
PO Box 504 Hindmarsh
SA 5007
ABN 90 116 359 963
www.atfpress.com

Graphic Design & Layout: Lydia Paton
Font (Body text): Garamond (11.5pt)

Fragments of Colossae
Sifting through the Traces

Acknowledgements

This book seeks to furnish a resource for the avid reader of the history and archaeology of an ancient site, to provide insights for the rise of the early Christian movement and to gather together a little of the rich heritage of the peoples of Honaz and Denizli. Colossae has suffered from a lack of concerted scholarly attention for centuries and this work, the fruit of fifteen years of determined research, is possible only because of the warm support, encouragement and assistance of a large number of people, many of whom have become good friends over that time.

Preeminently, my debt to the Iyilikçi family continues to grow. The quality of food that Hafize endows me with during my visits does Turkey's culinary reputation proud. And Ismail has constantly shown detailed interest in my work and wrought new connections with people to ensure that I have the optimum possibilities of discovery. He has also, especially through his links with the Denizli Rotary and Rotoract Clubs, made it possible for preliminary results of research to be returned to those who live and thrive in this culturally and historically abundant area. Ismail's infectious enthusiasm has captured the assistance of his sons, Özgür and Önür, as well, who, along with their partners, Burcu and Neslin, have lavishly contributed their own insights with perceptive questions and comments, always cultivated by good food and relaxed settings. Bereketi üzerinize olsun.

Successive governors of Denizli, have graciously met with me on each of my visits to the area and encouraged my research in tangible ways, making possible new understandings and perspectives on ancient Colossae and Chonai. An official photographer, Hakan Kurt, has been most generous in granting me copies of his own photographs of the site, which have provided welcome supplements to this book. And the governor's personal assistant, Durmus Sevindlik, has made every visit friendly and supported. Sana çok teşekkürler.

The wonderful people of Honaz, from the farmers who have given me lifts on their tractors on a hot day to municipal officials who have refreshed me and looked for ways to help me, I am most grateful. There is always a human element to research, but I have learned dimensions of humanity and hospitality that I never would have anticipated when I began. Special thanks is due to the Mayor of Honaz, Turgut Devecioğlu, whose vision and plans for the municipality demand his constant attention but who is never too busy to welcome me, learn more of my work and ensure that I have chauffeurs (most especially Mustafa Ulutas) and refreshments to see me through my day's activities. Mehmet Bayrak, a local farmer has embraced me as his brother, and ensured that his son, Mustafa, unlocked the secrets learned from twenty and more years' playing and working around the site. In more recent times, I have had the delight of meeting Kemal Yalçın, one of Turkey's finest living writers. He grew up in Honaz and one of his novels, *Dowry on Loan*, is lifted from real life, unlocking a deeply personal dimension to the tragedies that disrupted the Turkish and Greek worlds after the First World War. Kemal, and his nephew, Deniz Canpolat, a Honaz businessman, clarified for me the old Greek quarter of Honaz and generously alerted me to new possibilities of research. Hepinize çok teşekkürler.

In the early days of research, I was introduced to some of the local archaeologists, either based at the *Denizli-Hierapoli Arkeoloji* Müzesi or working independently. Hüseyin Baysal, Ali Ceylan and Haşim Yıldız gave me particular insights into Colossae's place in the region and encouraged my work. Çok teşekkür ederim.

Stimulation for research and for shaping the right research questions, rarely comes from isolating oneself. I have benefited enormously from conversations with Prof Dr Ender Varinlioğlu, whose kindness and sharp intellect are such a rare combination. His permission given to me to publish previously unknown inscriptions has been the greatest boon for research on Colossae. Contributions and discussions with a number of others have also been immensely valuable. I am very grateful to Halak and Hatice Erdemir of the University of Manisa, to Ekaterini Tsalampouni of the Aristotle University of Thessalonike and Flora Karagianni of the Museum of Byzantine Culture, Thessalonike, to Greg Horsley of the University of New England, to Ismail Albayrak of the Australian Catholic University and especially to Celal Şimşek, Bilal Söğüt and Erim Konakçi of Pamukkale University. Each of these has made particular contributions through their comments and insights, though, doubtless, they will have their own independent views about the material presented herein. Special mention should be made of the research colloquium, *The Colloquium on Material Culture and Ancient Religion*, emanating from the University of Texas. The principals who organise this regular venture, Steven Friesen, Dan Schowalter, Christine Thomas and James Walters have provided an immense service to scholars through their meticulous organisation of field trips, engagements with specialists and their generous encouragement for individual research projects. Vobis omnibus gratia.

I wish also to express sincere thanks to those who have helped this project through to completion: to the late Julie Hooke for additional photographs; to Dr Peter Lewis for photographs of coins; to Rosemary Canavan not only for some additional photographs but also for kindly and generously contributing the chapter on Clothing in Colossae; to the Society of the Sacred Mission and the Australian Research Theology Fund for grants to enable aspects of the research and production of the book. Two universities with which I have been connected, Flinders University and the Australian Catholic University, have at times assisted with travel funding, and the latter afforded me the opportunity for a sabbatical in 2013 during which time much of this book was written. Otium quo plurimum studiis confertur; gratias.

Finally, I thank my wife, Robyn, who helped to adjust contorted sentences into something (hopefully) more readable, and also my family, whose curiosity about Colossae has not been dampened in spite of the occasional lengthy monologue that has followed a simple question. To Dan especially, who has unreservedly echoed the enthusiasm of discovery, albeit on the other side of the world, this book is dedicated.

Alan Cadwallader

Contents

Acknowledgements		*v*
Contents		*vii*
Introduction		*1*
Chapter 1	Barefaced Colossae...	*5*
	European efforts to find Colossae	*5*
	'Tograi Smith' and the first modern notice of Colossae	*10*
	The recovery of Colossae	*14*
Chapter 2	Stationing Armies at Colossae..	*29*
	Armies and their needs	*29*
	Colossae and the Persian presence	*30*
	Laodikeia and the relationship with Colossae	*34*
	Colossae's resources	*35*
	Colossae as a Roman and Byzantine station	*36*
Chapter 3	The Gods in City and Country...	*45*
	Gods and the natural environment	*47*
	The gods of water, earth and vegetation	*49*
	Cybele, the Great Mother	*50*
	Dionysos, the god of wine, theatre and new life	*53*
	Artemis the hunter	*55*
	Tyche of the Colossians	*59*
	Zeus the Thunderer	*65*
	The gods, heroes and mere mortals	*68*
Chapter 4	The Theatre..	*75*
	Choosing a site for a theatre	*75*
	The size and design of the theatre	*80*
	The theatre in ancient society	*82*
	Modifications to the theatre along Roman architectural lines	*86*
	Gladiators at Colossae	*87*
Chapter 5	The Fortress...	*97*
	The secrets of the Colossae höyük	*97*
	From the mound to the mountain—the medieval fortress of Colossae	*99*
	The role of the Byzantine fortress	*100*
	Features of the fortress area	*105*

CHAPTER 6	*WEAVING THREADS: CLOTHING IN COLOSSAE* by Rosemary Canavan...	*111*
	The context	*111*
	The textile industry: sheep and shepherds	*115*
	The textile industry: trade	*118*
	The textile industry: the workers	*120*
	The textile industry: the clothing	*127*
	The letter to the Colossians	*130*
CHAPTER 7	THE WATERS AND THE BATHS..	*135*
	The Persian presence at Colossae	*135*
	Colossae and its network of rivers	*138*
	Colossae and the harnessing of water	*141*
	The Roman baths at Colossae	*145*
CHAPTER 8	THE NECROPOLIS..	*155*
	The in-ground tombs	*155*
	The bomoi	*157*
	The necropolis in relation to city life	*160*
	The cliff tombs	*161*
	The tumuli	*163*
	A sarcophagus	*166*
	Funerary inscriptions	*169*
	Carved reliefs on epitaphs	*171*
	Protecting the graves	*172*
	The funeral industry	*173*
CHAPTER 9	THE MIGHTY ARCHANGEL...	*181*
	The sacredness of water	*181*
	The presence of angels through history	*183*
	The archangel Michael in Asia Minor	*184*
	The story of St Michael of Chonai	*185*
	The geography and history behind the story	*187*
	The waters and the search for ancient Colossae	*190*
	The story and the Roman Emperor Julian 'the Apostate'	*194*
	The story and the battle over icons	*197*
MAPS		*203*
GLOSSARY		*206*
INDICES		
	Ancient and modern place-names	*214*
	Ancient and modern persons	*218*
	Subjects	*222*

Plate 1a *The mysterious mound identified as the centre of ancient Colossae.*

Introduction

For more than 200 years, Colossae has suffered disdain from explorers and tourists and the neglect of scholars. Today, an occasional intrepid explorer takes a dolmuş whose driver will willingly stop to release a passenger at the base of a large mound. Even more occasionally a tour bus squeezes Colossae into an itinerary that boasts the remarkable sites of Hierapolis and Laodikeia, sites that have benefited from decades of detailed archaeological attention and scholarly reconstruction. Colossae boasts a guard's hut, a sign and a general brief map in what is largely an area of primary industry, although light industrial factories seem to be creeping closer from the north.

Colossae has never been surveyed or excavated. There have been cycles of calls to remedy this lack that go back to the beginning of the twentieth century. In the absence of any such work, Colossae has languished in research. Scholars have tended to repeat judgements, substantially negative, that developed in the nineteenth century that left Colossae as all but dead and buried in the first century, courtesy of an earthquake that carried aftershocks into written sources. But not only was Colossae deemed lost to any substantial existence; lost also has been scholarly investigation.

A turning point in the study of Colossae came with the publication in 2011 of a major collection of essays, *Colossae in Space and Time*. This technical, academic book heralded the realisation that even without a permit for a survey or excavation, there was much more material and textual evidence waiting to be sifted and appraised. From the diaries and journals of explorers since the seventeenth century, long hidden in museum and library archives, from new appreciations of the extent and longevity of the ancient site especially in analysis of pottery remains, has come the impetus for a revival in scholarly interest.

This book builds on the foundation laid in that collection but is designed to bring the most up-to-date research on Colossae to a broader audience. Accordingly, the usual scholarly paraphernalia of footnotes and surveys of multiple opinions have been dropped and a concerted effort to ensure that technical terms have been kept to a minimum or given explanations if it has been deemed necessary to retain them. There is, nevertheless, much new material in this volume that will be of interest to scholars as well. In order to assist academic engagement with this research, detailed bibliographies and indices have been added. It is hoped that scholars will find these additions a compensation for the lack of clutter, albeit valuable, that is usually expected.

For those who want to know more about Colossae from an historical, archaeological or religious perspective, it is hoped that the text and multiple photographs presented here will unlock something of

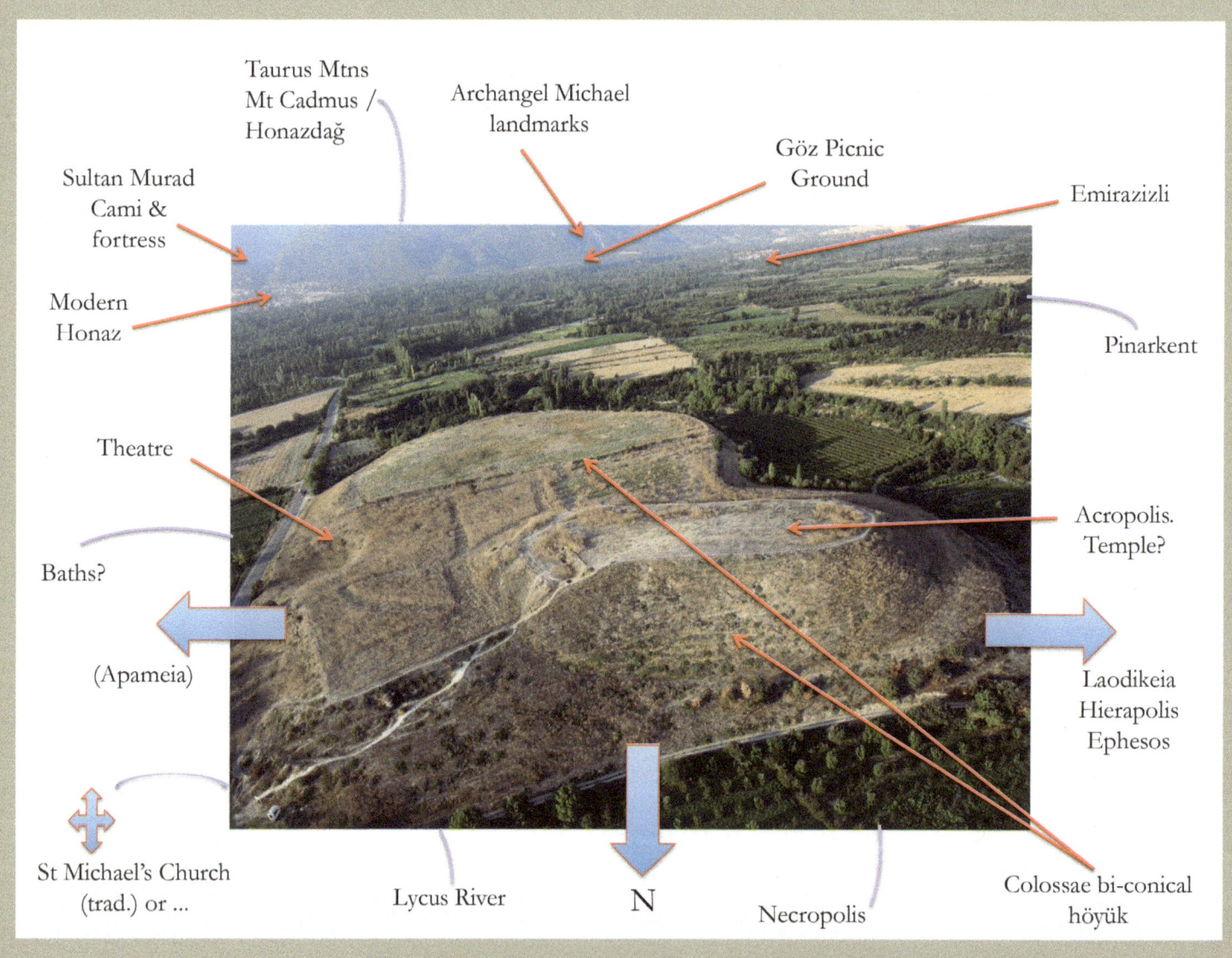

Plate 1b *The Colossae höyük (mound) in its wider geographical setting. The purple lines indicate features outside the photograph; the red lines indicate features within the photograph.*

the rich heritage of Colossae across three or more millennia. Certainly there is much included that has never been published elsewhere before, even though I am all-too-well aware that the detailed, meticulous calculations that accompany formally-authorised study of an ancient site, must await the future. Hopefully, Colossae will begin to be appreciated in a different light from the piecemeal or misconstrued conceptions of the past. Especially I hope that Colossae's name by which it became known in a later period of its history, that is Chonai, will unlock a rich seam of study, not only of ancient documents, but also of the landscape. Whilst the mound, the large höyük, rising above the surrounding landscape grabs the attention, perspective and imagination need to fan out southwest to the Göz Picnic Ground (the site, I hold, of the ancient healing spring of the archangel St Michael), west to neighbouring smaller mounds and other indications of settlement in the vicinity of Emirazizli and south to the remains of what is known as the 'Sultan Murad Cami' and the fortress that survey, from the slopes of the mountain, the modern town of Honaz. The interconnections between all these sites and the expanded territory they embrace will be critical for future study of the history of Colossae. Groundwork is laid in this book for a sense of Colossae that both interrogates the mound more deeply (especially its theatre and acropolis) and pushes attention beyond the mound, further afield than simply the northern vista of the extensive ancient necropolis.

The chapters within this book seek to explore why the site appears as it is today and what can be made of material that has been found. The arguments and conclusions presented here come from a combination of close attention to the evidence available (some items newly discovered), repeated meanderings around the site and the local area, and a comparison with material evidence from other places which may shine some light for the interpretation of Colossae/Chonai. Coins, inscriptions, artefacts, local knowledge, topography and the natural environment have all made their contribution.

One of Colossae's famous sons of the twelfth century, Nicetas Choniates, described Chonai as the city known of old as 'Colossae'. And he waxed lyrical, quoting Xenophon, an historian from more than 1500 years earlier, when he described Chonai as 'a large and prosperous city'. Nicetas may well have been showing off his literary credentials but it is clear (as his additional name suggests) that the Chonai of his day was a city to be reckoned with, just as it had been long ago. No doubt, like all cities, Colossae's fortunes waxed and waned. But Nicetas, in a sense, has issued an invitation to those who visit the site today and to those who read this book. He invites us to visualise a large city, a prosperous region, a crucial gateway to the Lycus Valley from the East.

Plate 1.1 *The bare höyük at lower left is the central focus of modern attention to the ancient city of Colossae. Behind the mound spreads the modern town of Honaz, nestled on the rise of the towering Honazdağ (ancient Mt Cadmus).*

CHAPTER 1
Barefaced Colossae

European efforts to find Colossae

Colossae is clearly marked on maps today, just to the north of the town of Honaz and east of the city of Denizli in south-western Turkey. But early European travellers into 'Asia Minor', as they often called it, were flummoxed in their search for Colossae because so little remained by which the ancient city might be identified.

One English adventurer, Robert Wood, made a note in his journal for September 1750 about some engraving of the name Colossae on a stone he had seen. He concluded, 'Probably thereabouts was situated Colossae'. Unfortunately he did not record the inscription. His position outside of Laodikeia was heading north on the road to Hierapolis (which he called by the local name 'Pambouk Kalesi', that is, 'Cotton Castle' after its white travertine steps). This suggests that the stone was a milestone telling how far to travel to reach a given destination. After all, Colossae lies some 15 kilometres *east* of Laodikeia.

It wasn't the first time Colossae had 'wandered'. The seventeenth-century German cartographer and historian, Christopher Cellarius, had published a map that pinpointed Colossae to the *west* of Laodikeia, almost directly south of Hierapolis,

Plate 1.3

Plate 1.2

Plate 1.2, 3 *Map of south-west Turkey by Sir Charles Fellows dated to 1852, with detail of the Colossae region. Fellows was uncertain of where Honaz and Colossae were — so he left them out! His identification of Mt Honaz, Denizli, Laodikeia and Hierapolis were not the most accurate either.*

Plate 1.4

at the junction of the Lycus (modern Çürüksu) and Maeander (modern Menderes) Rivers— that is, about 25 kilometres *west* of its actual location. By 1703, Cellarius' map had received an English edition that was to be repeated many times over the next seventy-five years. In an age when Turkish cartography was exceedingly difficult to find, any map was pored over for information, even if it proved none too reliable for European adventurers. Wood's journal note is probably an example of a map shaping perceptions so strongly that, when in the actual territory, the interpretation of a material fragment became constrained to a preconceived idea. And so Wood read the artefact, not as a travel marker, but as indicating that the city, otherwise invisible, was nearby.

Colossae has been the subject of many such preconceptions in pre-modern and modern interpretation. In the thirteenth century, Colossae had not only 'wandered'; it had sailed the high seas to end up on the island of Rhodes! In the attempt to make a word-play between its name, 'Colossae', and the famous 'Colossus' of ancient memory that towered above the harbor of Rhodes, some Byzantine high-culture writers made Colossae the alternate name for the island.

> *The golden Paul conquered the bronze Colossos*
>
> *Having been taken from earth to the third heaven*
>
> *And he shatters the monstrous by the sling-shot of his words*
>
> *Setting the foundation stone in their midst.*
>
> *Epigram Preface to the Epistle to the Colossians by Manuel Philes (1280–1330)*

Plate 1.4 *Detail of Christopher Cellarius' map of Asia Minor (1703) showing Colossae located to the west of Laodikeia. The small building symbols (castles) attached to such names as Hierapolis and Aphrodisias indicate that ancient ruins were known there. Significantly perhaps, both Laodikeia and Colossae lack the symbol.*

The letter to the Colossians was even re-named in some late New Testament manuscripts as 'the letter to the Rhodians'. It helped that the Knights of St John of Jerusalem had compounded multiple Colossian connections by migrating to Rhodes via Cyprus where, for a time, they occupied a site called 'Coloso' or 'Colossi'. (The medieval castle stronghold still exists.) When they moved to Rhodes they claimed their hospital was built on the foundation of the ancient Colossus and adapted their patron's name from St John of Jerusalem to 'St John Colossensis'. It was enough to ensure that metaphor had become a 'reality'.

Part of the explanation for this shift can be explained by the European loss of close connection with 'Asia Minor' consequent on the formation of the Ottoman Empire in 1299. By then Colossae was well under Selçuk control, shortly to be included within the Osmanlı empire. The severing of ties to the actual places esteemed in a Christian view of the world led to a combination of alternate constructions of reality—such as 'wandering Colossae'—and an evaporation of information about particular sites, churches and personnel.

Our earliest published and unpublished European reports of the area come in the seventeenth century, fully two hundred years after the cementing of Ottoman control through the taking of Constantinople in 1453 by the young Sultan Mehmet II. Of course, these give us the European perspective and one

Plate 1.5, 6 *The 1573 map of Abraham Ortelius which has 'Cosole' (a misspelling for Colose) at the onset of the peninsula on the southern extreme of Cyprus.*

CHAPTER 1 - BAREFACED COLOSSAE   7

needs to recall that the hallmark of all imperial governance—taxation—swung into operation from the beginning of the Ottoman period. Taxation records remind us that Honaz, along with adjacent towns, were operating quite prosperously through the period in which there were no European notices.

Perhaps inevitably, though regrettably, European characterisation of Turkey and its inhabitants was tinged by negative assessments. Turks, Greeks, Armenians and Jews—all were subjected to some unsavoury language, even when trade opportunities were beginning to unfold. When such predispositions were combined with first-hand experience of difficulties in travel, the reports that made their way back to Europe were hardly enticing to others to investigate further.

Attempts to discover Colossae or explore Honaz (the Turkish successor in name and location to 'Chonai') occurred at the beginning of European contact. This contact appears to have been led by the 'Franks' (as Europeans were called) stationed at Smyrna (=İzmir).

Plate 1.7

Plate 1.8

Plate 1.7, 8 *The Irishman, Daniel Pomarede, engraved this map of 'Turky in Asia' for the atlas of Thomas Salmon published in 1764. Salmon developed most of his work in Cambridge, where he ran a coffee house before making a world tour with George Anson. Pomarede's short twenty-three years of life (1742–65) never saw him leave Dublin. How much of 'Turky in Asia' Salmon himself actually saw is moot, certainly not enough to include Laodikeia and Hierapolis along with 'Colosses'. In this map (see the detail) Colossae is located on the Maeander not the Lycus River and stands alone as representative of the cities of the western half of the Maeander Valley, apart from Ephesos. He did include a Laodikeia—but this was Laodikeia Combusta in Pisidia, not Laodikeia ad Lycum in Phrygia. Nevertheless the subtitle of his publication claimed 'the geographical part is truly modern'. The map was repeatedly borrowed for other atlases right through the eighteenth century.*

FRAGMENTS OF COLOSSAE

Smyrna had long held an attraction to European states. It was ideally placed on the western seaboard of Turkey with flexible maritime connections across the Mediterranean. From early Ottoman times, it had maintained a secure line of communication with Constantinople. European nations recognised this connection quite early by appointing consular officials to both places. In England's case (which was far from the first European ambassadorial appointment), these officials were endorsed by Queen Elizabeth I, though, by and large, they were independent businessmen.

Ambassadors came with a coterie of assistants. Servants and bureaucrats all held, along with the ambassadors, the 'special protection' status that the Sultan afforded them. Included among these privileged foreigners were the 'chaplains' to the various commercial ventures. These were well-educated men, trained in Greek and Roman literature, in Christian writings and in the place that religion had in the life of the nations from which they came. The English Levant Company, the official commercial English entity established in Turkey, first appointed a chaplain to its staff in Constantinople in 1599 and in Smyrna in 1639.

Plate 1.9, 10 *The port of Smyrna, with the view of the city punctuated by mosques and their minarets. The sketch on the left by Thomas Allom (1834), shows the harbour at centre left and the medieval castle on the hill at upper right. In the foreground, a funeral procession is accented, watched by onlookers engaged in different pursuits—a carefully constructed orientalised view designed for the European consumer back home! At the right is a postcard collected by William Beamont on his tour of the seven churches in 1855 (conducted before the beginning of the construction of the Smyrna-Aidin railway in 1857). It accents the castle, the shoreline warehouses and fishermen at work, rather than the triple-masted trading ships in port.*

'TOGRAI SMITH' AND THE FIRST MODERN NOTICE OF COLOSSAE

The Reverend Doctor Thomas Smith became one of the most famous of these chaplains. He was the first to publish an account of his travels to centres that European values and education privileged in classical and Christian history. Like many of the chaplains who tried to maintain the religious practices of the Europeans in Turkey, Thomas Smith's appointment at Constantinople lasted only a short term (1668–1671). They were often eager to return home. But his intellectual ability and thirst for historical enquiry happened to coincide with a developing emphasis of the Levant Company at the time, and were encouraged. His travels in south-west Turkey were dependent on the arrangements that the then-ambassador, Sir Joseph Williamson, was able to make with the various Ottoman authorities. Williamson organised the necessary documentation that explained the purpose of the journey, authorised the acquisition of horses and provided letters of introduction to the various agas, or district governors, who controlled the regions they would visit.

Even though Smith is upheld as the first to write about the actual places of the 'Seven Churches', he had a few models to follow, such as those of John Covell and John Luke. Each of these earlier Levant Company officials kept detailed accounts of their journeys though both somehow avoided Colossae, even when enjoying the hospitality provided by 'Denizley', the Turkish city from which visits to Hierapolis, Laodikeia and Colossae could be organised. John Luke, however, did receive a communication that compensated for not actually visiting Colossae. A Greek living in Denizli provided him with the names of ten churches at Colossae, two of which were still operating, though the rest were in ruins. But the ruins John Luke did not see.

It seems that the Levant Company was already beginning to cultivate considerable good-will amongst Europeans by organising regular tours, for, as Smith noted, 'their practice and example have, for the most part every year since in the Autumn, been taken up and followed'. Autumn was the recommended season, as Europeans found the unraveling heat of late spring and early summer oppressive. It seems that the travel accounts that a number of people kept, were circulated and shared in the informal

Plate 1.11

Plate 1.11 *Elizabeth I (ruled 1558–1603), in a 1578 letter to the Ottoman Sultan Murad III (ruled 1574–1595), addressed him as 'the most renowned and Emperious Caesar, Sultan Murad Can, Emperour of all the dominions of Turkie....' A further consolidation of the political relationship followed in 1599 with the gift of a large chamber pipe organ to the next Sultan (Mehmed III, ruled 1595–1603). The present was as much 'a great and curious present' (as it was noted at the time), as intended to 'scandalise other nations, especially the Germans'. Clearly, there was competition among the European powers to court the favours of the Ottoman rulers. Engraving by the Dutchman, Crispin van de Passe the elder, adapted from a drawing by Isaac Oliver.*

gatherings in the 'Frankish' quarter of Smyrna. Thomas Smith's own published account has considerable overlap with the unpublished travelogue of Jerome Salter, a long-term commercial operator at Smyrna but neither Smith nor Salter acknowledges the other. It seems that whatever account we now possess from the seventeenth century is likely to be an amalgam! This may explain why certain phrases and assessments seem to be repeated, even into the early nineteenth century.

At first Smith aimed the account of his travels at a small, learned audience—by writing in Latin. But someone sensed a commercial advantage in bringing his work to a more popular readership and Smith was stirred to make his own translation from Latin into English. However, it was carefully noted in the preface to the new edition that Latin (the European language that marked learning) lay at the foundation of this new text, somehow bolstering its reliability and authority. Smith took the opportunity not only to supplement the material on the seven churches, but also to add a completely new section on Constantinople. Henceforth, Constantinople and the 'Seven Churches of Asia' were joined together in European texts, as if one needed to be understood in terms of the other. The book in English was a 'best-seller' in early publishing terms, going through a series of editions, even after his death.

Thomas Smith's particular intellectual capacity lay in languages and history. He had already established this reputation in England before he travelled east. Given that 'Smith' is such a common English name, the students and fellows at Magdalen College, Oxford University, nicknamed him 'Tograi' or 'Rabbi' Smith so he could be distinguished from all the other 'Smiths' at the University. He made a perceptive analysis of Turkish and Arabic words in use at the time. He gathered considerable information on the state and practices of the Greek Church at Constantinople and, perhaps most significantly for the intellectual appreciation of Turkey in England, he made a sweeping tour of a section of territory from Smyrna to Ephesos through the Denizli region. The journal of his tour, with notes on the materials he collected, was subsequently organised into writing with a full-blown title *Remarks upon the Manners, Religion and Government of the Turks. Together with a Survey of the Seven Churches of Asia as they now lye in Ruines: and a Brief Description of Constantinople*. So it was that existing roads, well-known to Turkish and Arab traders, began to be better known to Europeans wanting to explore the material remains of the 'Seven Churches'. These were the churches named by connection with a handful of cities of the Roman province of Asia in the

Plate 1.12 *An official companion to European tours of the Turkish interior, called a 'Janissary' is represented here in 'ordinary service uniform' according to the English consul, Paul Rycaut, who himself went on tour with the Levant Company chaplain, Reverend Doctor John Luke, in 1678.*

last book of the Christian Bible: the Book of Revelation, also called the 'Apocalypse'. Though Ephesos was named first in the list at the beginning of that book, the European base at Smyrna meant that this vibrant city assumed the privilege of being the first place to visit on the tour. Then, after Ephesos, the party of travellers set off for Pergamon, Thyatira, Sardis, and Philadelphia. Last of all, as well as at furthest remove from the coast and its associated European 'familiarity', came Laodikeia (ad Lycum, that is, on the river Lycus).

Colossae suffered by being linked with Laodikeia. It was assumed that the judgment on Laodikeia, which Smith described as 'the haunt of wolves and jackals and foxes' applied similarly to Laodikeia's neighbours—even if they were too infrequently visited to test the verdict. In any case, something happened on Smith's tour that curtailed subsequent contact with Colossae. His account is distinctly unfavourable about his local reception at 'Chonos' (Honaz). He assumed Honaz was 'Colosse', though the ancient höyük was some distance from the newer city-centre which lay close to the mountain fortress built on Mt Honaz. Regardless of the fact that Smith, like a number of subsequent travellers, carried the requisite travel and introductory documents, signed by the aga or governor of Denizli, these did not

Plate 1.13 *A lithocut drawing by Thomas Allom of the aqueduct ruins of Laodikeia that appeared in* Finden's Landscape Illustrations of the Bible *(1835), portraying the towering Babadağ of the Taurus Ranges to the south as its backdrop and the requisite camels and turbaned travellers to appeal to a European audience.*
Plate 1.14 (right) *A sketch by a later chaplain of the Levant Company at Smyrna, the Reverend Francis Arundell (chaplain 1822–1836). He, like his predecessor Thomas Smith, thought 'Khonos' as he spelt the name, was the same as 'ancient Colosse', even though he seems to have ridden through the site of the ancient ruins, three kilometres to the north.*

seem to cut any influence in neighbouring Honaz. What went unnoticed in Smith's caustic comments on Turk and Greek inhabitants alike was that relations between Honaz and Denizli were frequently 'tense', an inherited pattern that stretched back into Hellenistic and Roman imperial times. The lack of harmonious relations had been bolstered in the early Byzantine period in disputes over the St Michael healing spring and pilgrimage shrine.

Honaz, especially with its large mountain fortress, became a haven for those resisting the official local and regional government authorities, and the occasional bandit as well. Two such rebel movements were noted by visitors to Denizli: that of Inge Morad in the 1670s and that of Soley Bey Ogle in the 1730s. The result was that Europeans were primed in advance either to avoid a visit to Honaz altogether or to expect a negative encounter if they did venture forth. Richard Chandler in 1765 opted for avoidance, adding the comment, 'It is natural to wish for a speedy removal from a country in which we had been exposed to so many dangers.' A few hardy adventurers, such as the Englishman Richard Pococke, the Italian Antonio Picenini and the Frenchman Pitton de Tournefort did proceed further east from Denizli at different times but their records are sparse. Picenini noted that after passing a river just out of 'Chonos' (Honaz), his party saw pieces of columns, ruined inscriptions and other remains 'for the space of a mile'. Nothing however was copied or written down. Given the keen interest of Smith in inscriptions, as evidenced by his recording of some at Hierapolis and Laodikeia, it is unfortunate that his response to Honaz was to drive him away—and generations of travellers after him. So, regardless of how much ancient material was actually present during his and Picenini's tour, Colossae remained bare, at least in the recording of its remains for prosperity.

Plate 1.15

Plate 1.15 *The threat of bandits and rebel outbreaks was increasingly real as the Ottoman Empire experienced a marked decline in the nineteenth century. Europeans sought to support the government, even if they operated from a significant amount of self-interest, including the desire for ancient artefacts. Here, a sketch from the London magazine,* The Graphic, (1st October, 1885) *portrays the 'good Turk' as committed to the defence of the English travellers, though indicating this in terms of a master-servant relationship.*

Plate 1.16

The recovery of Colossae

European interest in exploring ancient connections began to explode in the early nineteenth century. Various countries—Russia, France, Germany and England in particular—competed with one another for the honour of new discoveries, especially those that might end up in their national museums. Indeed, France offered the newly re-established nation of Greece (released from Ottoman control in 1829) a substantial monetary loan that could be repaid in artefacts! At least this was the report of Colonel William Leake (himself an avid archaeological explorer and collector). The weakening of Ottoman power encouraged Europeans to explore, sometimes with little regard for the newly passed Turkish laws governing antiquities. But also, attitudes were changing. A certain 'Mahmouz Effendi' wrote extensively of the attractions of Turkey in English magazines in the mid-nineteenth century. And Sir Charles Fellows, the 1840s adventurer famous for his arrangement for massive mausolea being shipped from Xanthus (=Kınık) in the south of Turkey to the British Museum, had marked the turn-around in European attitude towards travel in Turkey by admitting that his own prejudice had been completely removed.

> It will be gathered from my Journal that at the time of my arrival in the country I was strongly biased against the Turks; and it will be seen in the course of the narrative how this unfavourable idea of the Turkish character was gradually removed by a personal intimacy with the people.
>
> *Charles Fellows, 1840.*

But one hundred and fifty years of potential recording had been lost for Colossae. During that time, the site had continued to be a virtual quarry, yielding up its slabs for new building projects, agricultural implements and even the burning of stone for the production of lime. When the Reverend Francis Arundell came to the area in 1826 he was struck by 'the multitude of fragments of marble pillars almost upon every terraced roof, where they are used as rollers'.

Nearly a century earlier (in 1737), Richard Pococke had noted the gleaming white marble building called an ak-han or caravanserai, built in the thirteenth century by Karasungur bin Abdullah between Honaz and Denizli. More particularly, he saw various 'spolia'—a head of a statue, a Medusa's head and a relief on it of two dragons. Even the undifferentiated stone used in the walls he took to be blocks from 'some antient ruin'. Richard Chandler had observed that a similar re-use had occurred at Smyrna, with stones from the theatre being deployed to build both the market and the vizir-khan.

Plate 1.16 *Two of Arundell's 'rollers' at the Çinaraltı Restaurant, a few kilometres from the site of Colossae.*

Such recycling of stone has a long history. The Byzantine fortress high above the village of Honaz grabbed existing materials for its various buildings—one foundation was made with a Roman column laid on its side. Before this particular recycling, one lengthy piece of hellenistic-style architrave was turned upside down and carved with an inscription, probably as part of a dedication for the church of St Theodore, one of the ten churches of Colossae/Chonai listed for John Luke in 1669. The inscribed part of the older architrave can be dated to about the fifth century. When William Calder, the English surface archaeologist found it, in 1933, it was being re-used again, this time as part of a step into a house at Honaz! The stone had survived through a succession of lives, but it did so by being constantly moved.

Plate 1.17

Another inscription on a pedestal from Colossae (no longer extant) was set up by a third-century mother, Ammiane, in memory of her son, Herakleon (whose age is not given, though he is called a 'hero'). She provided a bequest granted for an annual garlanding in his honour. The yearly remembrance apparently didn't last much beyond the death of the mother and father, Karpio, because, within fifty years or so, the stone had been grabbed for a dedication in honour of the three co-regnant Roman emperors, Constantius I, Diocletian and Maximian, at the turn of the fourth century. The stone was simply re-inscribed on its bare side and no doubt turned in the direction where the optimum view could be given to passing spectators.

Plate 1.18

Plate 1.17 *An elaborately carved entablature section (with dentil incisions, acanthus leaves and palmette ornamentation) that managed to escape the general harvesting for other purposes. It still lies at the site of Colossae.*
Plate 1.18 *The inscription reads 'for the one well-named from the divine gifts', a fairly standard pun on the name of Theodore. St Theodore was a popular warrior-saint and patron of many Byzantine churches, especially after he was said to have appeared to thwart some of the pagan ravages of the Emperor Julian the Apostate (361–363 CE) in Constantinople. The spectre of Julian also had its impact on Colossae, so it is not surprising that a church was dedicated there to Theodore. Sometimes, Christians expressed the triumph of Christ over paganism by re-using stones from pagan temples but placing them upside-down as an indication of victory.*

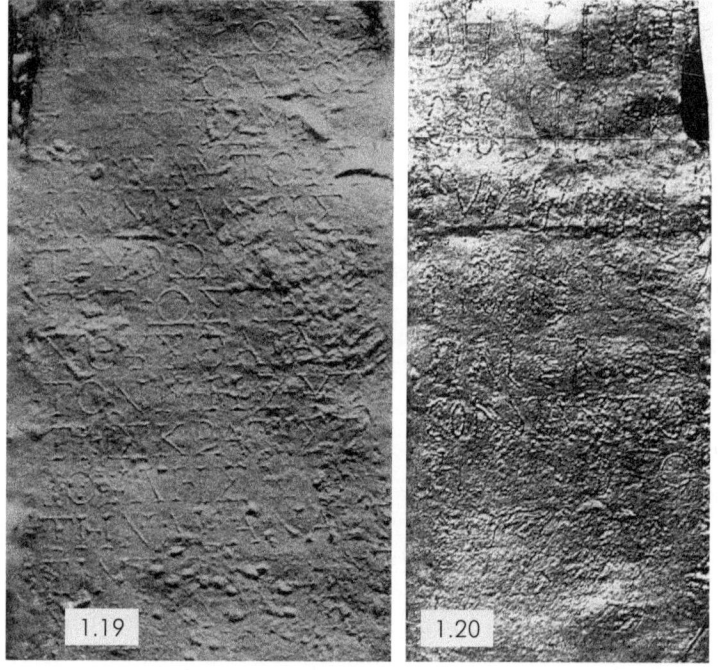

Plates 1.19, 20 *Two different inscriptions on the same pedestal, only available to us now from the filter-paper impressions (called 'squeezes') taken by William Calder in 1933. The first on the left is in Greek letters memorialising Herakleon and dated somewhere between 215 and 250 CE. The second, on the right, is in Latin and is a dedication to the emperors Constantius I, Diocletian and Maximian, dated somewhere between 293 and 305 CE. At different times, each was the 'front' of the stone.*

By the time the more detailed reports of artefacts and inscriptions began to emanate from European writers in the nineteenth century, Colossae had already yielded up tonnes of its stones to other uses: khans, fortress, walls. Even in quite recent times, the surrounds of animal pens come from its stones.

The famous early Greek archaeologist and nationalist, George Lampakis, in 1909 visited the main church being used by the Greeks in Honaz. His photograph of the congregation outside the church reveals Byzantine capitals upside down acting as column bases for the forecourt of the church. The forecourt no longer exists, but the column bases have been retained in the grounds of the mosque that succeeded the church as a holy place around 1926. One contains the cross familiar in Byzantine-carved capitals.

Sir Charles Fellows had noted in 1838 that contemporary 'cutters of gravestones … have quarries of white marble wherever the remains of a temple are to be found', recognising at the time of his 'excursion' (as he called it) that re-use of stone was common. George Lampakis saw one grave where an inscribed stone slab had been reused as part of the side of a tomb, though the wording was too abraded for him to decipher.

The recycling of such stone had a number of consequences. Firstly, after a millennium of constant re-appropriation of the stone of Colossae's Persian, Greek, Roman and Byzantine buildings, little was left visible for Europeans to marvel at. During the nineteenth century especially, European travellers, archaeologists and tourists wanted monuments—big, expansive remains that testified to the magnificence

Plate 1.21 *A heavily-damaged Corinthian capital was for a time on view (placed on top of a pillar base) just outside the guard-house at the foot of the Colossae höyük; it had been converted to a mortar bowl some time in its distant past.*

Plate 1.22, 23 *An animal pen to the north of the höyük, constructed from blocks of stone from the surrounding site of Colossae. Possibly some of the stones came from the remains of a nearby wall that marked the boundary between the city proper and the necropolis.*

Plate 1.24 *Detail of one block that shows the lead-pour, dowel-hole with the escape channel for excess designed to fix in place blocks, columns or sometimes large statues cut with a base.*

of their predecessors. Europeans consoled themselves that *they* were not decaying like the Greek and Roman past; nevertheless, they continued to imitate that past in their architecture and ideas. Indeed, this is precisely the reason behind the Society of Dilettanti sending out Richard Chandler in the eighteenth century.

But Colossae was a singular disappointment to such desires. Macmillan's *Travel Guide* of 1908 effectively discouraged visits to the site, though for reasons different from those advanced by the Rev'd Dr Thomas Smith two and a half centuries previously. The guidebook dismissively stated, 'There is nothing much to see'. Since that time, very little systematic investigation of the remains of the site has occurred. William Calder, who is responsible for the largest collection of inscriptions from the site (and this is not 'large'—13 only) spent less than two days in 1933 following his epigraphical nose around the Colossian necropolis and 'Honas' houses. Colossae similarly was visited inside a day by James Mellaart in search of pre-classical pottery sherds (he found some) in the early 1950s; a certain 'JMB' did the same in early 1963, depositing 24 pieces of pottery and one piece of glass in the 'Pottery Room' of the British Institute in Ankara, but without identifying where on the site the items were found. The Turkish Byzantinist, Ebru Parman also lead a day's foray around the höyük recording Byzantine architectural fragments in the late 1990s.

The most concerted attention to the site has been by Celal Şimşek, Director of Archaeology at Pamukkale University, who lead a team to excavate and analyse the tumuli in the necropolis in 1997. There has also been a systematic pottery survey in 2005 conducted by Bahadır Duman and Erim

Plate 1.25, 26 *Occasionally, identifiable architectural elements have been pushed from agricultural land into the river. On the left, a fluted column has become 'embalmed' by the famous Lycus River calcification process. On the right, a pedestal with an inscription honouring Markos, the head translator and interpreter for the people of Colossae. Within a year, spring floods along the river had swept away the pedestal.*

Konakçi, again from Pamukkale University. But there has been no overall survey of the site and its surrounding area and no excavation; neither has there been a permit granted for these archaeological pre-requisites for a deeper understanding of Colossae.

Secondly, the reaction of some Europeans was to move from disappointment to disparagement of Colossae. Instead of recognising that the barrenness of the höyük and its surrounds was an indication of continuous occupation of the area where stones were in a constant process of recycling, Colossae was declared to have been inconsequential, at least from the mid-Hellenistic period. The French biblical scholar and archaeologist, Ernst Renan, was particularly harsh in his assessment, 'The ruins of Colossae are of a very second-rate town…the tombstones are bizarre, without inscription … Colossae never recovered [after the earthquake in Nero's time]; she disappeared from the company of the churches … She has no imperial coins.' He has been proven wrong on every score. His English equivalent, Joseph Barber Lightfoot, was more reserved, but Colossae's 'comparative insignificance', he wrote, 'is still attested by its ruins, which are few and meager … without doubt Colossae was the least important church to which any epistle of St Paul is addressed'. Again the judgement is

Plate 1.27 *Photograph of the upturned capitals of the forecourt structure of the church at Honaz in 1909, by George Lampakis.*
Plate 1.28 *Two upturned Corinthian capitals in the mosque, which, although set into the pavement, appear to be identical to the front capital in the Lampakis photograph. They support a stone bench upon which is laid the body of the deceased (in the coffin provided by the mosque for the period of a funeral service, before burial). The new inscription on the front of the bench slab reads 'May God have abundant mercy upon him' (a prayer said for someone who has died). The colour green has particular significance as a Moslem identity marker. During the Ottoman period, Greeks (regarded as synonymous with Christians) were prohibited from wearing clothing that was coloured green; here it is the colour associated with death and new life. A green cloth is also draped over the coffin containing the deceased.*

misleading, if not incorrect, but in a century and a half since they wrote, this scholarly degradation of Colossae's importance has more than matched the despoliation of the material remains of the ancient site by successive waves of the local population.

The third issue flows from this appropriation of remains still to be found in various places around Honaz, in public and private settings. The advantage of the preservation of such artefacts (sometimes as part of an exchange between people that acts as a strengthening of the bonds of friendship) has to be set against the loss of more encompassing and specialised analysis. No record of where such remains were found—their 'provenance'—is generally kept. Many such 'removed' items, whilst held for a period, have an unfortunate propensity to disappear. The *bomos*—a grave pedestal common at Colossae—photographed in 1907 at the railway station-master's house in Appa by the English archaeologist, Gertrude Bell, was reliably reported as having been taken from the site of Colossae. The railway line at that stage ran past Colossae though Bell was too ill to venture to the site on her travels, much to her annoyance. She felt compensated by seeing the *bomos* at Appa, but it has since disappeared (see Chapter Eight, *The Necropolis*).

When the relocation of artefacts is combined with the inherited axiom that Colossae was not a significant city in the first century and beyond (often underscored by the equally misplaced assertion that the earthquake of 61 CE that hit the Lycus Valley spelt the end of Colossae), Colossae is made even more 'bare'. Items that are gathered for storage and recording at the Denizli Museum (at the site of Hierapolis) are, by default, assigned to Laodikeia when no indication of provenance (its original location)

Plate 1.29 *A Byzantine capital upturned and acting as a plant pot support, also in the mosque.*
Plate 1.30 *A tumulus (grave mound) in the upper section of the necropolis at Colossae, showing the entrance into the outer chamber.*

Plate 1.31 *'Spolia' or fragments of architectural elements, in this case column bases and drums, sitting atop a courtyard wall of a house in Honaz.*
Plate 1.32, 33 *An inverted palmette capital and a pedestal pillar base at a house in Pinarkent, a village near Colossae.*
Plate 1.34 *The squeeze of an inscribed round section of a larger (lost) epitaph that had become a feature of a bank building (now replaced) in Denizli. The stone itself, when the modern building was replaced, was moved to the Denizli Museum and was credited to Laodikeia.*

can be found. Colossae's supposed insignificance is contrasted with Laodikeia's great importance and this drags items of unknown provenance to be classified as 'from Laodikeia'. When Hasan Malay, a renowned Turkish epigrapher, credited some epitaphs of unknown provenance to Laodikeia, Colossae was not even considered. Similarly, the epigrapher, Thomas Corsten, included one fragment of a funerary inscription with the collection of Laodikeian inscriptions on the basis that it was found 'near Laodikeia'. A squeeze (paper impression) of this inscription is in the 'Squeeze Collection' of the British Institute in Ankara, with the added note that the location of the stone (when the squeeze was taken) was at the (old) Ziraat Bankasi (the Agricultural Bank) in Denizli. It was far from the first time that a stone had moved from an unknown location to become a featured part of a modern building.

Occasionally this has lead to conflict over attribution. The smooth statue of the Egyptian god Horus that stands proudly in the Denizli Museum at Hierapolis is designated as from Laodikeia on its public notice but a personal communication from Ali Ceylan when he was Assistant Director of the Museum, indicated that it had in fact been found at Colossae.

The loss of materials through constant re-appropriation, through destruction for the production of lime, through re-assignment to another city has combined with a lack of interest in visiting the site.

Plate 1.35 *The very still statue of the Egyptian god Horus that yet has been quite mobile, moving from Colossae to Laodikeia in the scholarly attribution of its provenance.*
Plate 1.36 *Signs of digging into the höyük in search of coins and other artefacts valued on the antiquities market.*

Plate 1.37, 38, 39 *Limestone foundation stones and wall blocks to the north of the höyük. As each year passes the number and the arrangement of such stones changes. At the centre is a bollard, and at the right a curved simple capital. These were both photographed in 2005, but have since disappeared.*

When the narrow perspectives that favoured monumentalism were combined with flawed interpretations that dismissed Colossae's importance, Colossae became even more 'bare'. Each year, artefacts that may have been seen previously, move or disappear and there is, unfortunately, some evidence of looting. It is worth pondering that out of the approximate 190 coins from the Colossian mint of the Hellenistic and Roman imperial period, only one has been expressly identified as found at the site of Colossae and only six are housed in Turkish museums. The murky waters of the antiquities market have supplied both a demand for items and a loss of detail that hampers further archaeological research.

This is not a new handicap. Early European travellers, like Richard Pococke, were eager to add items to their own 'cabinet', some even using their private collections as a retirement benefit, selling them at auction in Europe. Little wonder then that today, Colossae appears 'bare-faced'.

However, the evidence in the photographs in this chapter suggests that if one takes the time to walk slowly across the site, small pieces of the jigsaw of Colossae can be seen. Sometimes they can be quite rare—a fragment of a fresco, a piece of glass, a sherd of pottery from one of the great epochs of Colossian history.

Until a survey and excavation permit is granted to responsible authorities, the best that can be done is to capture such fragments by photograph, leaving the discoveries to lie where they were found.

Plate 1.41, 42, 43 *A fragment of a fresco, Roman glass and a potsherd from the Colossae höyük.*

Select Bibliography - Chapter One: Barefaced Colossae

British Institute of Archaeology, Ankara, 'Pottery Collection, Region 20'; 'Squeeze Collection, Region 20'.

Cellarius, C, *Notitiae Orbis Antiqui: Sive Geographia Plenior ... et Notitia Tabulis Geographicus*. Canterbury: John Owen, 1703.

Constantinus Porphurogennitus *On the Themes*.

Miller, E (ed), *Manuelis Philae carmina ex codicibus Escurialensis, Florentinis, Parisinis et Vaticanis*. 2 Vols; Paris: Imperial Printers, 1855–57, I.23 (§44)

Monumenta Asiae Minoris Antiqua [*MAMA*] *Vol VI: Monuments and Documents from Phrygia and Caria*. Edited by W Calder and W Buckler; Manchester: Manchester University Press, 1939, §§38, 42, 49.

Theodoret of Cyrrhus *Commentary on Philemon*.

William Leake-Lord Aberdeen Correspondence, British Library Ms Cotton Tiberius D. IV.

Allom, T, *Constantinople and the Scenery of the Seven Churches of Asia Minor Illustrated*. London: Fisher & Son, 1838.

Anderson, SP, *An English Consul in Turkey: Paul Rycaut at Smyrna 1667–1678*. Oxford: Clarendon Press, 1989.

Beamont, WJ (Jnr), 'Journal of a Visit to the Seven Churches of Asia, 1855', Warrington Museum and Archives Ms 706.

Bell, G 'Gertrude Bell Archives' University of Newcastle-on-Tyne.

Bent, JT, *Early Voyages and Travels in the Levant: 1. The Diary of Master Thomas Dallam 1599–1600 II Extracts from the Diaries of Dr John Covell 1670–1679*. Hakluyt Society; New York: Burt Franklin, 1893.

Cadwallader, AH, 'Revisiting Calder on Colossae', in *Anatolian Studies* 56 (2006): 103–11.

—'The Reverend Dr John Luke and the Churches of Chonai', in *Journal of Greek, Roman and Byzantine Studies* 48.3 (2008): 319–338.

Cadwallader, AH and M Trainor, 'The rise and fall of the European recovery of the Ancient site of Colossae', in *International Symposium on the History and Culture of Denizli and its Surroundings* Denizli: Pamukkale University, 2007, Vol. 2, 73–79

—'Colossae in Space and Time: Overcoming Dislocation, Dismemberment and Anachronicity', in *Colossae in Space and Time: Linking to an Ancient City*. Edited by Alan H Cadwallader and Michael Trainor; Göttingen: Vandenhoeck & Ruprecht, 2011, 9–47.

Ceylan, A and T Corsten, 'Inscriptions from Laodikeia in the Museum of Denizli', in *Epigraphica Anatolica* 25 (1995): 89–92.

Chandler, R, *Travels in Asia Minor and Greece or An Account of a Tour made at the Expense of the Society of Dilettanti*. London: J Booker, 1817.

Chishull, E, *Travels in Turkey and Back to England*. London: W. Bowyer, 1747.

Conder, J, *The Modern Traveller: A Description, Geographical, Historical and Topographical, of the Various Countries of the Globe*. 2 vols; London: James Duncan, 1824.

Erder, LT and S Faroqhi, 'The Development of the Anatolian Urban Network during the Sixteenth Century' in *Journal of the Economic and Social History of the Orient* 23 (1980): 265–303.

Fellows, C, *A Journal Written During an Excursion in Asia Minor 1838*. London: John Murray, 1839.

Heubeck, A, 'Zu einigen kleinasiatischen Ortsname', in *Glotta* 63 (1985): 115–36.

Hocaoğlu, MC, 'Gertrude Bell' in 1907 Yılı Batı Anadolu Seyahati (İzmir'den Isparta'ya)', in *Sosyal Bilimler Dergisi (SDU)* 29 (2013): 57–72.

Horne, TH, *Finden's Landscape Illustrations of the Bible, consisting of Views of the most remarkable places mentioned in the Old and New Testaments* ... London: John Murray, 1835.

Joint Library of the Hellenic and Roman Societies (University of London), *The Wood Collection* Vol 6. Fols. 66, 67.

Lampakis, G, *Οἱ ἑπτὰ ἀστέρες τῆς Ἀποκαλύψεως*. Athens: 1909.

Lightfoot, JB, *Saint Paul's Epistles to the Colossians and Philemon*. London: Macmillan, 9th edition 1890.

Macmillan & Co, *Guide to Greece, the Archipelago, Constantinople, the Coasts of Asia Minor, Crete and Cyprus*. London: Macmillan, 1908.

Malay, H, 'New Inscriptions from Phrygia [in the Denizli Museum]', in *Arkeoloji Dergisi* 2 (1994): 173–83.

Mellaart, J, 'Preliminary Report on a Survey of Pre-Classical Remains in Southern Turkey', in *Anatolian Studies* 4 (1954): 175–240.

Mills, S, 'The Chaplains of the English Levant Company: Exploration and Biblical Scholarship in Seventeenth- and Eighteenth-Century England', in *Die Begegnung mit Fremden und das Geschichtsbewusstsein*. Edited by J Becker and B Braun; Göttingen: Vandenhoeck & Ruprecht, 2012, 243–66.

Moralee, J, 'The Stones of St Theodore: Disfiguring the Pagan Past in Christian Gerasa', in *Journal of Early Christian Studies* 14 (2006): 183–215.

Özdoğan, M, 'Ideology and Archaeology in Turkey', in *Archaeology Under Fire: Nationalism, Politics and Heritage in the Eastern Mediterranean and Middle East*. Edited by L Meskell; London / New York: Routledge, 1988, 111–23.

Özgüç, T, *et al*, 'Recent Archaeological Research in Turkey', in *Anatolian Studies* 14 (1964): 21–37.

Parman, E, *Ortaçağda Bizans döneminde Frigya ve Bölge Müzelerindeki Bizans taş eserleri*. Eskişehir: TC Anadolu Üniversitat, Edebiyat Fakültesi Yayınları, 2002.

Pearson, JB, *A Biographical Sketch of the Chaplains to the Levant Company maintained at Constantinople, Aleppo and Smyrna 1611–1706*. Cambridge: Cambridge University Press, 1883.

Picenini, A, 'Travel Diary, Asia Minor' (1705) British Library, Add Ms 6269.

Pocock, R, 'Travels Journal' (1737) British Library Add Mss 22997, 22998.

—*Description of the East and Some Other Countries*. 2 vols; London: W Bowyer, 1745.

Renan, E, *Histoire des origines du Christianisme*. 6 vols; Paris: Michel Lévy Frères 1863–79.

—*L'Antechrist*. Paris: Michel Lévy, 1873.

Rycaut, P, *Account of the Greek and Armenian Churches*. London: 1679.

Salmon, T, *A New Geographical and Historical Grammar, wherein the geographical part is truly modern; and the present state of the kingdoms of the world is so interspersed, as to render the study of geography both entertaining and instructive*. London: William Johnston, 1764.

Salter, J, 'A Brief Relation of the Travels of Jerom Salter', Oxford: Bodleian Library, Eng. Msc. e. 218 (1668–1680).

Schneider Equini, E, *La necropoli di Hierapolis di Frigia: Contributi allo studio dell'architetturo funeraria di età romana in Asie Minore*. Rome: Accademia Nazionale dei Lincei, 1972.

Schönborn, A, 'Communication from Professor Schönborn of Posen relative to an important Monument recently discovered by him in Lycia', in *Museum of Classical Antiquities* 1 (1851): 43.

Seal, J, *Meander: East to West Indirectly, along a Turkish River*. London: Bloomsbury Press, 2012.

Şimşek, C, 'Kolossai' in *Arkeoloji ve Sanat* 107 (2002): 3–17.

Skilliter, SA, *William Harborne and the Trade with Turkey 1578–1582: A Documentary Study of the First Anglo-Ottoman Relations*. Oxford: Oxford University Press, 1977.

Smith, T, *Remarks upon manners, religion and government of the Turks. Together with a survey of the seven churches of Asia as they now lye in their ruines and a brief description of Constantinople*. London: Moses Pitt, 1678.

Spon, J and G Wheler, *Voyage d'Italie de Dalmatie, de Grece et du Levant*. Lyon: Antoine Cellier, 1678.

De Tournefort, P, *Relation d'un Voyage du Levant*. 2 vols; Paris: L'imprimerie Royale, 1717.

Wheler, G, *A Journey to Greece*. London: Cademan, Kettlewell and Churchill, 1682.

Wood, AC, *A History of the Levant Company*. Oxford: Oxford University Press, 1935.

Yıldız, H, 'Denizli Müzesi Müdürlüğü Lykos Vadisi Çalışmaları', in *Müze Kurtarma Kazıları Semineri* 9 (1999): 247–62.

Whitehead, D, 'From Smyrna to Stewartstown: A Numismatist's Epigraphic Notebook', in *Proceedings of the Royal Irish Academy* (1999): 73–113.

Wilson, M, 'Smyrna: the open door to the archaeological rediscovery of the seven churches', in *Ekklesiastikos Pharos* 89 (2007): 75–87.

Plate 2.1 *A coin from Colossae minted by the authority of the strategos of Colossae for Zosimos.*

CHAPTER 2
Stationing Armies at Colossae

ARMIES AND THEIR NEEDS

Armies are often presented as efficient, fluid, fighting units. But in the ancient world, some minimal requirements had to be met if an army was to live up to this description. These requirements were as basic as serviceable roads, a ready supply of wood and food, a reliable source of water, and of course, space for soldiers to bivouac. These happen to be the stock elements for the growth and maintenance of a city as well. So the 'extra' needed to attract or tolerate the stationing of an army demanded a city surplus of these items, which would then be held in reserve for when the military arrived. Once the need to billet occasional military visits was recognised, cities could negotiate a semi-permanent surplus and the infrastructure to compile extra resources quickly, should they be required. Some places (such as Appia = modern Pınarcık) are on record as mounting complaints against these exactions; other places, such as Pessinous (=Ballıhisar) become noteworthy in military terms for Roman authors (eg Livy) precisely because of their lack of trees. But Colossae seems to have accommodated regular hostings of military contingents. The abundance of natural resources and an efficient civic infrastructure are precisely what qualified Colossae for such provision over a long period of time. The region of Phrygia was renowned as the 'nursing-mother of pines' (according to Alcaeus of Messene, a poet of the late third century BCE)—Colossae no doubt contributed to this reputation, possibly even using the Lycus River for the export of timber products beyond its region.

Plate 2.2

Plate 2.2 *Part of the remains of the Byzantine fortress high on the edge of the slopes of Honazdağ.*

One inscription of the second century (CE) from Colossae refers to the holding of surplus grain and its sudden distribution for relief of the city as well as for imperial requirements (probably soldiers returning from campaigns on the Eastern front) during a period of famine. The person responsible for organising this supply held the office of *pareskon* (something like a superintendent of the agricultural board). Unfortunately, when the inscription was recorded by the French scholar, Ernst Renan, the stone was fragmentary and the honorand's name was missing. However, coins from Colossae of about the same time do name a famous citizen. His name was Zosimos and he is described as a patriot, a 'lover of the fatherland'.

Perhaps this Zosimos was the *pareskon*, the 'comptroller of grain'. He was responsible for inventories, acquisition of grain, storage, importation, the supportive bureaucracy and final sale and disbursement. Sometimes this office was held in conjunction with other civic duties—quite a list of offices is found in the inscription—but the importance of the office of *pareskon* was so valued that it lay, even when dormant, as an on-going responsibility of the city-state of Colossae, both as a safeguard for its own citizens and for the supply of imperial requisitions.

COLOSSAE AND THE PERSIAN PRESENCE

Colossae had a long history of temporary and semi-permanent military presence. In the Achaemenid period (550–330 BCE), the Royal Road was a crucial element of Persian communication and the imperial network of control. This road ran through Colossae. Trade benefits to the city flowed along this thoroughfare that stretched from Sardis on the Mediterranean coast to Susa in the east. The march for this entire length took three months.

But the Persians also had adapted an elaborate relay system first used by the empires of the Assyrians and Babylonians before them. The Persian kings maintained official quarters for couriers and stables for horses along the roadway. Herodotos (484–425 BCE), the Greek historian of that period, marvelled that these officials could do the journey (about 2700 kilometres) in a week: 'There is nothing in the world that travels faster than these Persian couriers' he wrote. But, along with the benefits of travel and communication that accrued to cities, came regional responsibilities for local maintenance of the roads, supply of accommodation and fodder at stations along the roadways and a preparedness to support official needs.

Plate 2.3

Plate 2.3 *Section of a stele from Sardis, now in the Archaeological Museum Istanbul, showing traders from the East.*

Colossae also featured in a further support for the huge infrastructural requirements of the Persian Empire—the spot-fire communication system that astounded the Greek philosopher Aristotle (384–322 BCE). It was claimed a message could thereby cross the empire in a day. Signal towers using mirrors and fire would rapidly bounce a message beacon to beacon from west to east. The high mountain ridges that arc around Colossae and which hold a liberal supply of timber were ideal places for these vigilance posts that supported a flaming transfer of information.

Soldiers were stationed in the areas where these signal towers were located, bringing a more permanent military operation to an area that, because of the presence of noble estates in the area, was doubtless quite familiar with the presence of soldiers anyway. The satraps (commanders) who owned these estates were the ones also responsible for raising cohorts of soldiers for military campaigns when needed (and sometimes, in the case of insurrections, when *not* wanted by the king).

Plate 2.4 *Persian soldier standing guard—section of a frieze from Persepolis now in the Louvre.*
Plate 2.5 *The rugged lines of Mt Honaz, also home to vast tracts of forest below—ideal combinations for spot-fire towers, even though frequently under snow in winter.*

CHAPTER 2 - STATIONING ARMIES AT COLOSSAE

The Royal Road was not the only highway through Colossae of importance to armies. Another main highway travelled south, linking Colossae with the Bay of Phineka. This route seems to have been crucial to the movements of Alexander the Great as he swept through Persian Asia Minor from the south-west.

Alexander brought a rapid Hellenization of Asia Minor in his wake, though a 'making-Greek' that wisely incorporated many of the characteristics of the administration set up under Persian rule.

Intimately connected with army supply and location in the Achaemenid period was the award and holding of royal estates. These provided an encouragement and reward for Persian satraps to reside at long distances from the hub of empire in the east (Susa) and to be key players in preserving the secure network that enabled the central authority to maintain control, especially over Greek cities in eastern Asia Minor constantly wanting to assert their autonomy. From these estates frequently came the foot-soldiers and calvary that would fill the ranks of armies when needed. Cyrus the Younger (died 401 BCE) appears to have encouraged a considerable reorganisation of estates and networks in the west in an effort to enhance efficiency and acceptance, no doubt as part of his ambition (ultimately futile) to take the throne from his brother, Artaxerxes.

Plate 2.6

Colossae was the site of at least one such vice-regal estate. If a letter from Darius I (550–486 BCE) to Gadatas (probably the steward of the estates) at Magnesia-on-the-Maeander (near modern Tekin) indicates a general policy, then there was an expectation that Persian-style gardens (*paradises*) would be duplicated in Asia Minor. This included the planting of seedlings brought from the region of the Euphrates.

These estates provided not only the basic concentration of Persian power in the area but the necessary structures for education and training, especially in military expertise. Colossae was endowed with space, water, timber and provided hunting all year round, just as in a neighbouring Persian viceregal estate called Kelainai (or Apameia, modern day Dinar). A satrap or army general would provide from his estate for family, an array of courtiers, bureaucrats and a small army. The ease of

Plate 2.7

Plate 2.6 *Coin portraying Alexander the Great as a clean-shaven Herakles (Hercules), with a lion pelt trailing from the back of his head.*

Plate 2.7 *The pass through the mountains to the south of Honaz.*

access to resources can perhaps be gauged by the size of the Persian army that swelled to over thirty thousand during its seven-day refurbishment at Colossae when Cyrus the Younger was moving east for the fateful Battle of Cunaxa in 401 BCE. A further 1500 Greek mercenaries joined them. Even if Xenophon (431–355 BCE), the Greek historian who accompanied the Persian pretender, exaggerates the size of the Persian juggernaut to heighten the heroism of the Greeks (even in a battle that was lost), this was no small company of soldiers to entertain. Colossae apparently was considered quite able to deliver the requisite support. As the historian Xenophon portrayed it, Cyrus always wanted to get to where there were water and fodder. Colossae fitted this bill precisely.

Two particular figures seem to have held estates in the Colossae region: Tithraustes and Ariaios. Both were key leaders in the Persian hierarchy and both were involved in one of the most famous assassinations of the period—that of the Persian general Tissaphernes who had become embroiled in a palace intrigue that was considered destablising to the king, Artaxerxes. The conspiracy cost him his life (in 395 BCE), at Colossae. The story is told by a number of early writers (for example, Diodorus Siculus and Xenophon).

It appears that part of the reward for Tithraustes and Ariaios was gaining control of some of the enormous holdings that Tissaphernes had held around Colossae. But fortunes can quickly change and within forty years, Tithraustes' son or grandson found his newly inherited estates overrun by the Greek general Chares (in 356–55 BCE), although it would not be until Alexander the Great that Persian control of the area was permanently lost. In the aftermath of Alexander's death in 323 BCE, his empire was divided between his generals, and this brought further adjustments to Colossae's role in the area.

Plate 2.8 *A second-century CE Greek copy of the letter of Darius I to Gadatas displayed at the Louvre, Paris.*
Plate 2.9 *Persian coin bearing the head of Tissaphernes.*

Laodikeia and the relationship with Colossae

Laodikeia re-founded as a new city in the 250s BCE) assumed much of the primacy from Colossae along this section of the Royal Road, but Colossae still possessed a rich agricultural hinterland. Here various crops, fruit-trees, sheep and pigs were farmed; it had an abundant supply of water from three rivers and many freshwater springs and heavily forested lower reaches of the southern mountain range. All these riches continued to provide a ready resource for the movements and supply of armies and imperial entourages. Indeed it is likely that Colossae served as a supply base on two occasions when revolts against republican Rome occurred. Twice Laodikeia became the protective refuge for embattled Roman officials and was subjected to sieges.

Plate 2.10

Plate 2.11

The first siege, by Mithridates VI of Pontus against the Roman general Quintus Oppius, occurred in 89 BCE, a crucial event in the last great revolt against Roman rule in Asia Minor that lead to a deliberate massacre of thousands of Romans throughout the province in the following year. Fifty years later, there was a second siege lead by the Parthians (the descendants of the Persians) joined with the ambitious rebel Roman Labienus against Ventidius, one of Mark Antony's commanders, in 39 BCE. In order to maintain the sieges, control of the surrounding region was essential—Colossae was doubtless one of the many cities that were harnessed for the supply of the troops locking down Laodikeia. In the aftermath, we hear of Laodikeia along with Aphrodisias (=Geyre), Stratonikeia (near Eskihisar) and Miletos (near Balat), being honoured by the Romans. Laodikeia became the centre of the assize district of Kibyra, and received considerable notice in Latin literature. No such honours are recorded for Colossae. Laodikeia had certainly caught Roman attention and favour, and Roman writers from Cicero to Tacitus recalled it approvingly. Colossae, given the sudden hiatus in its own mint's production, with coins only appearing again in the time of Hadrian, may well have suffered some penalties for a lack of resistance to

Plate 2.10 *A coin of Mithridates VI, with luxuriant hair tied by a* taenia.
Plate 2.11 *The upheaval wrought by earthquake is in evidence in the southern necropolis at Hierapolis where graves have been tipped to right angles from their natural state.*

these threats to Roman republican control. Its appearance in Roman literature is notably impoverished. Indeed, when the Lycus Valley was rocked by a massive earthquake in 61 CE, Laodikeia is praised for its self-funded recovery by the Roman historian Tacitus. But no mention is made of Colossae even though it too, according to a recently discovered inscription, relied on its own citizens for provision of the resources necessary to rebuild city infrastructure such as the baths and water conduits (see Chapter Seven, *The Waters and the Baths*).

COLOSSAE'S RESOURCES

The coins of Colossae bear a tangential witness to the rich supplies of a region well able to support both the stationing and movement of army contingents. The river Lycus is honoured through the personification of the river god as well as through the emblem of the wolf (*lykos* means wolf) in coins coming from the time of the emperors Hadrian (ruled 117–138 CE), Antoninus Pius (138–161 CE) and Commodus (180–192 CE).

Other Colossian coins display the goddess Artemis the hunter in various postures: in one she is riding a chariot and with her arrow about to strike a wild boar (see Plate 3.30); in another she stands as an archer on the ground; and here (Plate 2.13), she is in preparation, hard into the chase.

Plate 2.12

Plate 2.13

There is a number of coins that extol the prosperity of the city through the symbols of grain baskets, cornucopia, the intact walled city and the general portrayal of Tyche, the goddess of good fortune. The inscription honouring the grain storage superintendent mentioned above, specifically singles out Tyche for honour alongside the official (perhaps named Zosimos). Prosperity was very much within Tyche's portfolio and she was frequently seen in connection with multiple cities, as in this relief. Thus Laodikeia, Hierapolis and Colossae could all claim her, though for the local residents the associations and content of her bounty might vary. Occasionally these variations might be reflected in the motifs accompanying her representation.

Such elements are fairly standard for a city wanting to promote a positive view of itself. However, Colossae seems to have enjoyed a prosperity much-celebrated by its own citizens. On one pedestal that records many names of the leading members of the city at the end of the first century CE, a hunting

Plate 2.12 *The river god portrayed on a Colossian coin from the time of Commodus.*
Plate 2.13 *Artemis in full flight, preparing her arrow, whilst in her biga drawn by two deer. The coin is from the time of the emperor Commodus (180–92 CE) and is heavily laden with a legend giving the authorisation of the chief magistrate of Colossae for the coin on behalf of Zosimos IV, who is declared a patriot.*

dog is carved as well as a branch bearing a fruit that is strongly suggestive of cherries or figs.

Even allowing that there may have been some gap between reality and representation, it is clear that Colossae felt justified in signalling the extent of her resources. Suggestions of the importance of hunting at Colossae also reinforce the perception of the ongoing ability of Colossae to sustain an army presence, something which it would have made a matter of civic pride (just as we know Ephesos did from an inscription that that city executed).

Colossae as a Roman and Byzantine station

Certainly, all Colossae's resources were called into service during the pan-hellenic tour of the Emperor Hadrian in 129 CE, which began in Athens and swept through the Eastern part of the Empire. An inscription from the Royal Road just outside central Colossae indicates that the massive military, administrative and courtly train was, at least in part, welcomed and maintained by the city.

Plate 2.14

The inscription reads, 'To the Imperator Caesar Trajan Hadrian Augustus Olympios. Loukios (Statios) Makedo the military tribune (dedicated this).' It not only honours Hadrian in full imitation of his Olympic pretensions but would have been placed on the main road into the city by a tribune of the Praetorian Guard, either for Hadrian's benefit, or, more likely, as a sign of Colossae's willing and faithful endorsement of imperial control and Hadrian's rule. Doubtless Macedo and members of his military entourage (probably

2.15

Plate 2.14 *A relief of the three Tyches, originally from the Via Appia outside Rome, now in the Louvre Museum in Paris. Whilst there is a clear similarity between each of the Tyches—seen in the clothing, the head piece of city wall and laurel wreath—there are subtle differences: the lekythos wine jug, the sprig of olive leaves and the matronly veil of the leading Tyche. It is dated to the second century but the grouping of three Tyches is relatively common. Even so there is no evidence yet discovered that would group Laodikeia, Hierapolis and Colossae in simlar fashion.*
Plate 2.15 *Inscribed relief of a hunting dog and 'cherry twig' on the pedestal honouring Korumbos.*

the ninth cohort) drew considerable benefit from the city's enthusiastic efforts to gain imperial favour during Hadrian's time, just as the city was more than prepared to be linked with the tribune. One epitaph, still to be found in the necropolis at Colossae, records a 'leatherworker' by the name of Dion, a name closely built on that of Zeus (*Dis*). His range of products would no doubt have been eagerly sought by the military entourage and his name was particularly apt to attract business during Hadrian's visit.

It may be significant that just a few years prior to this visit, Colossae had her ability to mint coins restored to her. This was almost certainly tied to expressions of loyalty to the Roman imperial machine.

There is every reason to recognise that the military presence in Colossae as elsewhere in the empire, provided many images for everyday thinking. In the New Testament letter to Philemon (who lived at Colossae), St Paul uses the metaphor of 'fellow-soldier' to describe another member of the household, one Archippos (verse 2). Philemon, with a woman named Apphia along with Archippos, seem to have sponsored a Christian congregation in their house. In addition, the Letter to the Colossians (2:5) pictures the members of the church as eagerly lined up like a military cohort.

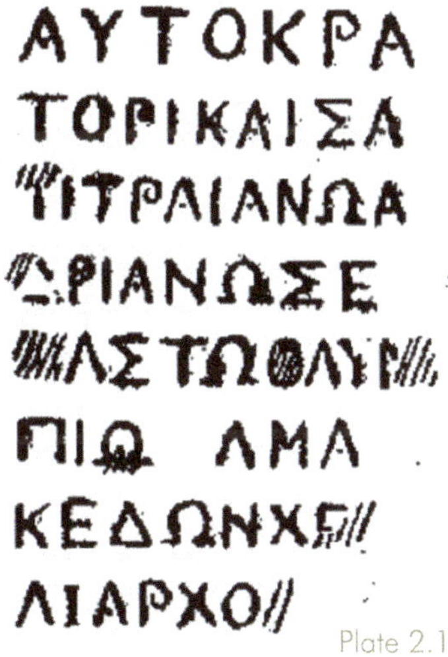

Plate 2.16 *The inscription honouring Hadrian as copied by the surface archaeologist JCG Anderson in 1897 and described by him as found 'in a field near the ruins'.*
Plate 2.17 *The toppled epitaph stone (a* bomos*) for Dion the leatherworker.*

Colossae's importance for imperial interests continued into the early Byzantine period. It is continuously mentioned in lists of bishops and political leaders, such as that compiled in 530 CE by the early Byzantine chronicler, Hierocles. The shift of the name of the city from Colossae to Chonai began to find mention in official lists from this time—a shift of name more than a shift of place. This did not diminish the city's military importance. In fact, with the upheavals in the Byzantine empire resulting from the unpredictable and destructive raids by Arab forces from the east in the seventh century, Colossae/Chonai moved from being a temporary military station in Hellenistic and Roman times to a permanent defence base. As the leading Byzantine historian, Clive Foss, has recognised, Ephesos is all but useless to the defence of the Maeander-Lycus Valleys when the main threat comes from the south and the east, not the west. With the Taurus mountain range made the new defensive border under the Byzantine Emperor Heraclius (610–41 CE) against encroachment through Cilicia from the west, Colossae was ideally placed to meet this threat, far more than Laodikeia, the long-standing Roman metropolis. Colossae not only had the requisite supplies for an army; it had an ideal position for strategic defence.

The massive reaches of Mt Cadmus (Honazdağ) could harbour a preemptive vision of the valley running east to west and deliver an early warning of any insurgence descending from the south through the pass. It is quite probable that this use of the towering Honazdağ stemmed back to Persian times and earlier. Signals could readily be sent, not only east and west but even down to the city centre on the plain.

Plate 2.18

Plate 2.18 *The höyük of Colossae in the valley below the mountain fortress.*

Today the remains of what was an imposing fortress still watch over the life of the plain. Colossae/Chonai became so important in this military positioning that, with the reorganisation of the administrative structure of the Byzantine empire, Chonai was made, if not the capital, then what the great surface archaeologist, William Ramsay, calls a *tourma* (pivotal garrison) or *topoteresia* (administrative mission). It was certainly the key defensive post of the new Byzantine province of Thrakesion, a province that commanded 10,000 troops, the second most heavily armed province in the eighth and ninth century empire. We hear also of an exarch—a military commander/governor—based at the city in the ninth century. In part the rise in ecclesiastical status of Chonai (from bishopric to archbishopric to metropolitanate all within a century) reflects the increase in importance of the city to the empire. Chonai—which gives the modern day name of Honaz—had become crucial to the defence of the troubled Byzantine empire. Accordingly, Chonai attracted even more attention not only with the supply of imperial funds and support for its barracks, but also with the interest of Turkish invaders and Greek usurpers. (See Chapter Five, *The Fortress*.) Significantly perhaps, the region still retained considerable prosperity—the Anatolikon theme to the north-east continued to import supplies of olives, wine, wheat and wood from cities in Thrakesion. Doubtless, this included Colossae.

Plate 2.19

Even after the final collapse of the Byzantine empire in 1453, Colossae continued to support the movements of armies. The siege of Rhodes in 1522, consequent on a misguided attempt from European powers to position themselves against one another and against the Ottomans, brought the journey south of the Ottoman Sultan, Suleyman the Magnificent (sometimes called Suleyman the Lawgiver) with his army.

Plate 2.19 *A section of the walled fortifications of the fortress on Mt. Cadmus (Honazdağ).*

A two-day refreshment at Chonai was followed by a single day's stopover at Denizli—perhaps an indication of the relative size and importance of these two cities in this period.

Subsequently, the stability of the Ottoman empire meant that much of the military appropriation of resources was transferred into mercantile interests, with Honaz primarily viewed as a revenue source through taxes. However, the garrison and the rugged terrain continued to be a prime attraction for competing forces in the region. In the early eighteenth century, the fortress was still enormous, covering almost the entire ridge on the mountain. The visiting French explorer, Pitton de Tournefort, left a sketch of the fortress in 1717 and it indicates a vibrant expanse of interlocked buildings, including the main garrison and a mosque.

This fortress shortly became the protected base for the insurgency lead by the rebel aga (governor) Soley Bey Ogle, from which he launched incursions as far as Smyrna. When he was finally defeated in 1739, 4000 of his men were slaughtered with him, again underlying the ability and importance of the area to resource and sustain military forces.

Colossae appears as an attractive site for armies to be based for more than two and a half thousand years. And if, as some observers think, the mound of Colossae was originally an artificially constructed hill fortress dating from Bronze Age times, the period for military presence could be even longer.

Plate 2.20 *A heavily-worn oil press beside a farm road near the former Greek quarter outside Honaz.*

Plate 2.21 *Sketch of the fortress at 'Chonac or Couleisar' made for de Tournefort's book.*

Select Bibliography - Chapter Two: Stationing Armies at Colossae

Alcaeus of Messene *apud Greek Anthology*, Book 16, Epigram 8.

Appian *History of Rome: Mithridatic Wars* 16–20.

Aristotle *On the Universe* 398a.

Aulock, H von, *Münzen und Städte Phrygiens*. Tübingen: Ernst Wasmuth Verlag, 2 vols, 1980, 1987.

Constantine VII *On the Themes* 3.36–37.

Ctesias Persica 53, 59, 68–69

Diodorus Siculus 14.80.6–8; 16.22.1–2.

Fragments of Greek History [FGrH] 105,4.

Greek Anthology 16.8.

Hellenica Oxyrhynchia 11.2–13.3.

Herodotos *Histories* 8.98.

Inscriptiones Graecae ad res Romanas pertinentes [*IGR*], Volume IV. Edited by R Cagnat, *et al*; Paris: E Leroux, 1927, §§869, 870.

Die Inschriften von Ephesos. Edited by H Wankel; Bonn: G Habelt, 1979–84, §4330.

Leo of Synnada *Epistle* 43.

Livy 38.18.4.

Nepos *Conon* 2.2; 3.1–2; 4.1.

Polyaenus *Strategems of War* 7.16.

Sylloge Inscriptionum Graecum [*SIG*]. Edited by W Dittenberger; Leipzig: S Hirzel, 1915–24, §22.

Tacitus *Annals* 14.27.

Xenophon *Anabasis* 1.2.6; 1.5.5; *Hellenica* 3.4.21–25; *Cyropaideia* 8.6.10

http://www.vcoins.com/ancient/tomvossen/store/viewItem.asp?idProduct=2746

Ainsworth, WF, *Travels in the Track of the Ten Thousand Greeks; being a Geographical and Descriptive Account of the Expedition of Cyrus and of the Retreat of the Ten Thousand Greeks as related by Xenophon*. London: JW Parker, 1844.

Anderson, JGC, 'A Summer in Phrygia II', in *Journal of Hellenic Studies* 18 (1898): 81–128.

Benjamin, AS, 'The Altars of Hadrian in Athens and Hadrian's Panhellenic Program', in *Hesperia* 32 (1963): 57–86.

Birley, A, *Hadrian, the Restless Emperor*. London / New York: Routledge, 1997.

Briant, P, *From Cyrus to Alexander: A History of the Persian Empire*. Winona Lake, IND: Eisenbrauns, 2002.

Cadwallader, AH, 'A New Inscription, a Correction and a Confirmed Sighting from Colossae', in *Epigraphica Anatolica* 40

(2007): 109–118.

—'Honoring the Repairer of the Baths: a New Inscription from Kolossai', in *Antichthon* 46 (2012): 150–83.

Elton, H, 'Military Supply on the South Coast of Anatolia in the 3rd century AD', in *Patterns in the Economy of Roman Asia Minor*. Edited by S Mitchell and C Katsari. Swansea: Classical Press of Wales, 2005, 289–304.

Foss, C, *Survey of Medieval Castles in Anatolia*. Oxford: BIAA, 1986.

—*Survey of Medieval Castles of Anatolia II: Nicodemia*. Oxford: BIAA, 1996.

Gibson, McG and RD Biggs, *The Organisation of Power: Aspects of Bureaucracy in the Ancient Near East*. Chicago, ILL: Oriental Institute of the University of Chicago, 1987.

Haldon, JF, *Byzantium in the Seventh Century: The Transformation of a Culture*. Cambridge: Cambridge University Press, 1997.

Halfmann, H, *Itinera principum: Geschichte und Typologie der Kaiserreisen im Römischen Reich*. Stuttgart: Steiner, 1986.

Hannestad, L, 'Timber as a Trade Resource of the Black Sea', in *The Black Sea in antiquity: regional and interregional economic exchanges*. Edited by V Gabrielsen and J Lind. Aarhus: Aarhus University Press, 2007, 85–99.

Højte, JM, (ed), *Mithridates VI and the Pontic Kingdom*. Black Sea Studies 9; Aarhus: Aarhus University Press, 2009.

Kreitzer, LJ, *Striking New Images: Roman Imperial Coinage and the New Testament World*. Sheffield: Sheffield Academic Press, 1996.

Kührt, A and S Sherwin-White, 'The Transition from Achaemenid to Seleucid Rule in Babylonia: Revolution or Evolution', in *Achaemenid History VIII: Continuity and Change*. Edited by H Sancisi-Weerdenburg, A Kuhrt and MC Root; Leiden: Nederlands Instituut Voor Het Nabiya Oosten, 1994, 311–27.

Magie, D, *Roman Rule in Asia Minor: To the End of the Third Century after Christ*. 2 vols; Princeton, NJ: Princeton University Press, 1950.

Meiggs, R, *Trees and Timber in the Ancient Mediterranean World*. Oxford: Clarendon Press, 1982.

Miller, MC, 'Town and Country in the Satrapies of Western Anatolia: The Archaeology of Empire', in *Kelainai-Apameia Kibotos: Développement urbain dans le context anatolien*. Edited by L Summerer, A Ivantchik and A von Kienlin. Bordeaux: Ausonios, 2011, 319–44.

Osiek, C and D Balch, *Families in the New Testament World*. Louisville KY: WJKP, 1997.

Pflaum, H-G, *Les Carrières Procuratoriennes Équestres sous le Haut-Empire romain* Paris: P Geuthner, Vol 1, 1960.

Ramsay, WM, *The Cities and Bishoprics of Phrygia*. Oxford: Clarendon Press, 2 vols, 1897.

Robert, L, 'Inscriptions', in *Laodicée du Lycos: le Nymphée, Campagnes 1961–1963*. Edited by J des Gagniers *et al*; Quebec: L'Université Laval, 1969, 247–389.

Sekunda, N, 'Changing Patterns of Land-holding in the South-Western Border Lands of Greater Phrygia in the Achaemenid and Hellenistic Periods', in *Colossae in Space and Time: Linking with an Ancient City*. Edited by AH Cadwallader and M Trainor; Göttingen: Vandenhoeck and Ruprecht, 2011, 48–76.

Treadgold, W, *Byzantium and Its Army 284–1081*. Stanford: Stanford University Press, 1995.

Plate 3.1 *The Medusa, the sinister, threatening deity covered with snake-hair had the reputation for turning to stone anything that looked upon her. Justinian's cistern in Istanbul has two giant heads of the Medusa used as bases for columns—one is turned upside-down, the other sideways as a sign of Christian triumph. But, prior to Christianity, her image was frequently used on funerary reliefs probably as a warning against any interference with the grave. This is a section of a mid-second century sarcophagus from Colossae, now in the Denizli Museum at Hierapolis.*

CHAPTER 3
The Gods in City and Country

There is no large statue of a god among the known remains of Colossae. We currently have a 60 centimetre figure of the Egyptian god Horus in the Denizli Museum at Hierapolis but where it comes from is highly contested (Laodikeia or Colossae). The eighteenth century English traveller, Richard Pococke, saw reliefs of a Medusa's head in the Ak Khan between Honaz and Denizli and what he called 'two dragons' (though these may have been the umbilicus or omphalos circle creatures still visible at the portal). These, along with the basic building blocks, have a probable claim on a Colossian provenance.

It is certain that Colossae participated in the worship of a multitude of gods; a mixed pantheon of deities is to be expected across every city in Asia Minor and beyond, interwoven with every aspect of life. When the New Testament Letter to the Colossians speaks of 'elemental spirits of the universe' (Col 2:8), the 'thrones or dominions or rulers or powers' (Col 1:16), the 'festivals and new moons' (Col 2:16), even the injunctions 'Do not handle, do not taste, do not touch' (Col 2:21), it may be doing no more than recognising the multidimensional religious landscape within which Colossians, along with others, operated. The worship of angels (Col 2:18) is a particularly expressive pointer to the religious environment of Colossae (see Chapter Nine, *The Mighty Archangel*); such beings were readily incorporated into a wide range of devotional practices, Greek, Roman, Persian as well as Jewish. The issue then is to seek out indications of Colossae's gods and perhaps to discern any particular

Plate 3.2

Plate 3.2 *The Ak Khan caravanserai between Denizli and Honaz, now fully restored to its 'white han' (=Akhan) glory and is a UNESCO heritage-listed treasure. The court and covered ways were completed by 1254 according to inscriptions found in the building. It was built under the orders of the governor of the Selçuk Germiyan region, Seyfettin Karasungur bin Abdullah. It covers an extensive 1100 square metres. If one looks closely, many signs of earlier use of the stones can be seen, including a lion's head, inscriptions and decorative panels from different periods.*

accents or expressions that characterised Colossae and its environs. After all, Hierapolis had Apollo and Laodikeia had Zeus Aetophoros as their specific patron gods. (Indeed Laodikeia was at one stage known as Diospolis, the city of Zeus.)

Specific, civic, cultic activities connected with these gods marked out each of these cities even though they had many gods and cults in common and could easily recognise one another's practices. There also were carry-overs from ages and customs prior to the advent of Hellenism and Roman influences which either by synthesis or by tenacious appeal survived the influx of new religious expressions. Mên Karou for example, the Phrygian god Mên in healing mode, had a rural sanctuary closely within Hierapolis' orbit.

The sources from which we can begin to discern the gods of Colossae are therefore either inferential or minimalist. They range from the suggestiveness of the area's topographical features to the iconography and legends on coins, from the names of Colossian citizens to the occasional figures and decorations on isolated artefacts. These need to be weighed against the comparative material which we know in greater measure from other places, especially those cities with which Colossae is likely to have interacted through proximity, trade or provincial obligations.

Plate 3.3

Plate 3.3 *Some coins in Roman Asia Minor were struck to express special ties between cities, often in competition with a major city that had received a special honour from the Emperor, such as the guardian (neokoros) of the imperial temple. But these coins, called homonoia or concord coins, also accented that the cities were not so jealous as to cause trouble in the Empire. They held to a key imperial value: concord. This homonoia coin shows the reverse side, with the patron god of Laodikeia, Zeus Aetophoros (eagle-bearer), with the patron god of Hierapolis, Apollo Citharœdos (cithara player), each turned to the other. The front (obverse) side of the coin has an image of the bearded emperor, Hadrian. The coin was probably minted around 134–138 CE, in the period following the completion of the second imperial temple awarded to Ephesos ('twice neokoroi'). The legend around the edge of the coin proclaims, 'The concord of the Laodikeians and the Hierapolitans'.*

Gods and the natural environment

Colossae was fed by a number of rivers, streams and springs. Because water was so crucial to the life of a city it became invested not merely with a host of regulations governing its use, but also a sanctity and numinous quality, as a host of writers, such as the fourth century Latin poet and rhetorican Decimus Magnus Ausonius, show. Here was a province of the gods and the means by which purity might be attained in order to approach the gods with reverence and safety. In some ways, these natural features carry a memory of sanctified associations—of stories, myths, gatherings and ritual practices—that predate as well as inspire the textual references.

> *Hail, O river, farmlands give praise, farmhands give praise, … O river, whose hills are lush with Bacchus' aromatic vines, O river of most verdant verges …*
> *Hail, O fountain: source unknown, sacred, nurturing, bountiful, lustrous, caerulean, unfathomable, rumbling, shady and unsullied. Hail, guardian deity of our city, of whom we may drink health-giving draughts … a fountain added to the role divine.*
>
> Ausonius, *The Moselle*, and *The Order of Famous Cities*

Plate 3.4 *The setting of the Colossae höyük—mountains, rivers, caves, chasms, forests and lush fertile plains—all that is needed to provide places for the gods, apart from the devotion of worshippers.*

Plate 3.5 *The beautiful shaded course of the Lycus River to the west of the höyük. The river appears much tamer than when it flowed before the construction of an artificial water channel just to the north of the necropolis in 2003–4; this syphoned off much of the river's volume.*

CHAPTER 3 · THE GODS IN CITY AND COUNTRY

The association of the river with numinous beings was probably more diverse than simply gods. The leafy green coolness that banked the river was certainly, as elsewhere, to be connected with nymphs for both hydraulic work and pleasurable play.

> *Cease from grinding, ye women who toil at the mill; for Demeter has ordered the Nymphs to perform the work of your hands, and they, leaping down on top of the wheel, turn its axle, which with revolving spokes, turns the heavy concave Nysarian stones …*
>
> Antipater of Thessalonike

An indication of the importance of the River Lycus to the city is given in civic coins. Two different types incorporating the river are known. One (from the time of the Roman emperor, Hadrian, 117–38 CE) features the river god of the Lycus, and a second, from the time of the Roman emperor Antoninus Pius, 138–61 CE) personifies the name Lycus in the figure of a wolf (*lykos* is the Greek word for 'wolf').

The river god was repeated in a coin from the time of the emperor Commodus (around 178–182 CE) that had the head of Crispina, his wife on the front. Clearly the river exercised a powerful grip on the imagination of the Colossians and even though no statue of the river god has yet been found, it is likely that such a form of representation would have been placed within the city.

Plate 3.6   Plate 3.7

Plate 3.6, 7 *The front ('obverse') of the coin features the bust of the goddess Athena and the back ('reverse') contains the wolf symbol of the Lycus River on a coin from the time of Antoninus Pius.*

Plate 3.8

Coins featuring the river god frequently added additional features designed to affirm some particular identifying mark of the city. Of course, the reclining god evokes the symbolics that is associated with banqueting or simply food offered at a tavern. The river god also sometimes holds a reed, as if to accent the fecundity of the river and can be portrayed as reclining on a cloak (called a 'chlamys') which is laid over a rock or a jar, the symbol of the springing source of the river. These symbols were fairly standard stereotypes found on the coins of various cities. Laodikeia, for example, in one of its coins proclaiming itself 'neokoros' under the emperor Caracalla (198-217 CE), laid claim to the river gods of both the Lycus and Kapros rivers. Hierapolis on the other hand had other symbols connected with its river god—he held a poppy and an ear of wheat. Even so, in the second and third centuries, Colossae was asserting for itself that the city and the regions it controlled were flourishing, an assertion that is backed up by some of the inscriptional evidence. All in all, the presentation at Colossae is one of prosperity that is associated with the river, whether through agriculture or other pursuits for which the gods were seen as ensuring good fortune.

THE GODS OF WATER, EARTH AND VEGETATION

In such a rich and geologically diverse region, gods that had strong connections with the environment naturally came to figure prominently in the life of the Colossian populace. The earlier Phrygian gods such as 'Great Mother' Cybele and Mên, the lunar and agricultural deity, remained

Plate 3.9

Plates 3.8, 9 *The reverse side of a Colossian coin that represents the Lycus River as a reclining river god.. Below is a full-size statue of the river-god, displayed at the Archaeological Museum in Istanbul, reclining on a cloak-covered jar.*

extremely powerful in the imagination of Greeks and Romans even with the passing of Phrygian governance. Mên is known from Colossae's coins and a rural healing sanctuary was located just north of Hierapolis.

Cybele, the Great Mother

The Greeks allied Cybele with the Earth goddess, Gaia (along with Rhea and Hera), an equation that goes back to the oldest papyrological record found in Greece, the fourth century (BCE) Derveni Papyrus. Rome turned to Cybele in 204 BCE for rescue from the threat of the Carthaginian general, Hannibal. Rome's first emperor, Augustus, cultivated the connection between Cybele and Rome's heroic founder Aeneas. Hence, yet another Eastern deity was harvested for Roman interests, even if the Asian fervor and eunuchs associated with her cult brought disdain from some Romans.

More than half a millennium later, Cybele enjoyed a huge revival of fortunes under the Roman emperor Julian (ruled 361–363 CE)—usually dubbed 'the Apostate' because he dumped his early Christian upbringing in favour of the array of gods of the past. He gave particular prominence to Cybele, even writing a lengthy didactic philosophical hymn in her honour and pouring funds into the rejuvenation of her sanctuaries and priesthoods across Asia Minor. Whilst there is no specific mention of Colossae in his writings, he does write of Phrygia generally and the cult-centre at Pessinous (modern Ballıhisar), located 250 kilometres to the north-east of Colossae. Julian ties aspects of her mythology to natural features: her consort Attis is left beside a flowing stream, growing like a flower; he enters a cave to pursue a nymph, then scorns the goddess—for which he paid with emasculation which was symbolised annually by the cutting down of a sacred tree.

Significantly perhaps, Colossae did become caught into Julian's revival of Cybele through a Christian story that seems to have come into literary existence shortly after

Plate 3.10 *The head of the god Mên, in the Archaeological Museum in Ankara, displaying the horns of the crescent moon and his Phrygian cap, central symbols of his identification.*

Plate 3.11 *A stele at the Museum of Archaeology in Istanbul shows a relief of the Great Mother, Cybele. As with many such representations throughout Asia Minor, she is flanked by lionesses as mistress of the animals, and holds a loud-sounding tambor in her left hand and patera of sacrifice in her right. But this relief also indicates her 'net of prophecy' in the interlocking lines of the folds of her clothing between her covered legs.*

FRAGMENTS OF COLOSSAE

Julian's early death. In the prelude in the Story of St Michael of Chonai, the Great Mother is mentioned as the object of supreme devotion by 'the Greeks' (a veiled reference to Julian and his supporters) in conjunction with the goddesses Echidna and Artemis, all of whom are opposed by the Christian apostles Philip and John (see Chapter Nine). No earlier reference to Cybele has yet been found at Colossae, though it is hard to imagine a site replete with water, vegetation and mountain having no influence from her power. There is however a mysteriously-clothed woman on one funerary relief erected by an association called 'The Friends'.

Beneath her *trimitos* over-garment, the woman is dressed in a chiton that is woven so distinctively as to create shapes that may be designed to evoke the form of a net. John Clarke is an art historian with particular expertise in the paintings of Pompeii, the elite coastal resort smothered by the eruption of Mt Vesuvius in 79 CE. He has noted that one of the symbolic features attached to Cybele, sometimes in the presentation of her clothing, is 'the net'. This interlocking of diagonal lines represents the ability to capture insights, oracles of benefit to devotees. Such an ability to capture and deliver prophecies was shared with a number of deities, notably Dionysos and the famous patron of oracles, Apollo.

Plate 3.12 *A statue of Attis, the consort of Cybele, held at the Denizli Museum. Like Mên, Mithras and the 'rider god' of Phrygia, Attis wears a Phrygian cap, defined by the rounded peak that curves forward.*
Plate 3.13 *Detail of a funerary epitaph for Gluko. If the relief of these two people (both adopting the familiar Hellenistic 'arm-sling' posture in their clothing) is in some way designed to represent the deceased then he is at the right, though the name could be Glukona and hence of the figure at the left who appears to be a woman. She wears very distinctive clothing, giving a religious connotation that fills out the inscription that records that the epitaph was erected by 'The Friends'. It may indicate, as often happened in ancient associations, that a religious practice was one of the main activities of this group.*

Plate 3.14 *Apollo, twin of Artemis, born of Leto, was honoured throughout Asia Minor, most famously at the oracular sanctuary at Klaros. Colossae joined in such honours combining, as in this Hellenistic coin, his connection with Helios, the sun-god and with the cithara, a symbol of his prodigious musicality and his role as dispenser of oracles. The radiate head recurred as a light-giving motif for the political body of Colossian citizens, the demos, which was combined with a variety of images: the healing deities Hygeia and Asclepeios, the stag of Artemis, Zeus Aetophoros, the rivergod, and Tyche. During Byzantine times, the image emerged to be a representation of Christ.*

Although the priestly caste serving the cult of Cybele was infamous throughout the Mediterranean world as self-emasculated eunuchs (in imitation of Cybele's divine consort, Attis) there were also women involved in the conduct of the cult. Indeed the foundation of the cult in Rome was headed by a priestess named Claudia. Diogenes the fourth century (BCE) tragic poet of Athens noted 'the turban-wearing women of Asia Cybele' who were responsible for the manic playing of percussion instruments 'celebrating her who is the wise minstrel of the gods and healer as well.' Strikingly in the relief in plate 3.13, both figures appear to be wearing head-dresses. This strengthens the possibility of an association connected in some way with or supported by Cybele.

Plate 3.15 *Mt Cadmus, modern Honazdağ, towers above the site of Colossae to the south of the city. Cadmus (or Kadmos) was the father of a beautiful daughter named Semele, with whom the father of the gods, Zeus, slept and from whom Dionysos was (re)born and preserved from the blazing thunderbolt of Zeus. Zeus was the god proclaimed in ancient hymns as the one from whom all things have their being.*

DIONYSOS, THE GOD OF WINE, THEATRE AND NEW LIFE

There is a long-standing connection between Cybele and another god, nurtured in their sharing of the natural features of the landscape and the mania of their worship. Dionysos (also known as Bacchus) flourished where there were mountains, caves, springs, lavish vegetation—all offered by Colossae and its surrounds. Indeed, it would be difficult to imagine a mountain named Cadmus not having a Dionysian cult connected with it, since the god figures prominently in the stories related to the ancient hero.

> *You of many names, pride of the Cadmeian maiden and offspring of the deep-thundering Zeus.*
> Sophocles *Antigone*

And throughout the region, Colossae boasts a range of caves that could be guarded by Dionysos' officials (called *antrophulakes*) especially those caves bordering river-courses.

Some Colossians recorded in inscriptions were named after the god. The variety of images of Dionysos on coins demonstrate that he was a key god in the religious city-scape and land-scape of Colossae. From the coins we see key symbols of the god: the laureate vine leaves, the accompanying panther, the thyrsos (a long staff wrapped in ivy and vine leaves

Plate 3.16, 17, 18 *A little to the west of the höyük of Colossae are a number of caves in the gorge wall of the Lycus River, which show leveled floors and pottery remains indicating intentional use. Plates 17 and 18 are from a further line of caves near another stream, the Aksu, that flows into the Lycus from the south. Here, evidence of ancient presence is to found in and around the grottos that lie within easy walking distance from the Colossae höyük. The caves were favourite drinking venues for those participating in the Dionysian cult.*

CHAPTER 3 - THE GODS IN CITY AND COUNTRY

with a cone as its apex). Sometimes a musical instrument is added; sometimes wine is poured from a kantharos; sometimes simply the wreathed head is given. These features crop up as adornments to honorific inscriptions and gravestones, frequently capturing the mysterious connotation of the god with revival, new life, new birth. Because of these connections, Dionysos was often connected with Demeter, another goddess of agriculture (also known on the coins of Colossae) and Persephone, the dark maiden of unmentionable name who haunts the underworld where she had been snatched by the god Hades. Persephone rarely occurs on coins; even more rarely is she named, for fear of being caught into her realm.

We have one inscription from Colossae that seems to refer to a priest or priestess of Dionysos. The reconstruction of the inscription by Wilhelm Quandt suggested that a key benefactor of the city of Colossae in the first half of the second century set up either a statue of Dionysos or for a priest of Dionysos. It is likely that there were special, secret initiations into higher levels of the cult of Dionysos, though in such a rich natural environment, most gods at Colossae probably had a 'mystery cult' practice connected with their observance, something strongly hinted at (albeit antagonistically) in the New Testament Letter to the Colossians (2:18).

Plate 3.19, 20 *At the left is a detail from the honorific pedestal to Korumbos, the repairer of the baths at Colossae. It shows a large ivy leaf and may flag the revival of Colossae's fortunes indicated in the restoration of a crucial centre of civic life. At the right is the worn remains of a pine cone carved on the side of a bomos gravestone from the necropolis at Colossae.*

Associations of Dionysos are known throughout Asia Minor and beyond, particularly in connection with acting guilds—Dionysos was the patron god for actors. There was likely such a group connected with the theatre at Colossae, even though we know of acting troupes who plied their craft from city to city, often relying on the hospitality of a local Dionysian association during their visits.

A connection between bearing the name of the god in some fashion and actually offering some sacrifice or devotion to Dionysos is seen in a small altar dedicated by a certain Thallos whose father's name was built on the name of the god: (probably) Bacchulis. The altar inscription seems to carry a brief prayer to Dionysos (Bacchus) and mentions the bestowal of a wreath. The altar may be pre-imperial but would doubtless have been part of the welcome to the emperor Hadrian on his visit in 129 CE, given that one of the titles that Hadrian adopted was 'New Dionysos'.

ARTEMIS THE HUNTER

Even more prolific on the coins of Colossae is the goddess Artemis. One can readily understand that the form of Artemis of Ephesos (Artemis Ephesiaca) grabbed the attention of the Colossians just as it did with most of the cities of the Roman province of Asia. After all, Ephesos was the province's capital and decorated twice with the title *neokoros* or imperial temple keeper. The huge statue of Artemis standing tall and heavily decorated above worshippers at her shrine had a huge impact on all who visited Ephesos.

Plate 3.21

Plate 3.22

All cities worship Artemis of Ephesos, and individuals hold her in honour above all the gods. The reason is ... the extreme antiquity of the sanctuary, the size of the temple, the eminence of the city of the Ephesians and the prominence of the goddess that dwells in the city.

Pausanias Travels

Plate 3.21 *Relief of Dionysos from the Naples Museum, displaying the symbolism of the cult: the wreath around the head, the panther, the drinking, the thyrsos.*

Plate 3.22 *The small altar of offering set up by a certain Thallos. The stone is now in the mosque at the local village of Pinarkent, having been taken there from somewhere on the site of Colossae. Unfortunately it has received a coat of hard cement on one side of the cylindrical stone which has covered part of the inscription. Photograph courtesy of Erim Konakçi of Pamukkale University.*

CHAPTER 3 · THE GODS IN CITY AND COUNTRY

Even the late first-century Christian book, the Acts of the Apostles, preserves the cry of devotees, 'Great is Artemis of the Ephesians … (whom all of Asia and the world worship)' (Acts 19:27–28). It is likely that the multi-officed Colossian citizen mentioned in a damaged second-century Colossian inscription (we shall call him Zosimos even though his name is missing) represented Colossae in the annual honours given to the Emperor and to the city of Ephesos. The inscription states that Zosimos 'joined in the sacrifices at the second temple' which is likely a reference to the provincial gathering in Ephesos, the city twice-honoured as guardian of the imperial cult. Part of the requirement attached to this high honour bestowed on Zosimos was to report back to the city's council, the *boulê*, on return.

The major collation of the coins of Colossae by Hans von Aulock yielded 153 coins. Allowing for subsequent finds, corrections and further coins catalogued in museums and listed on auction sites, Colossae's known coins now number 190, all but six coming from Roman imperial times. Of these, almost one-third feature Artemis in some manifestation. Clearly Artemis figured prominently in the city's religious observances.

Plate 3.23, 24 *At the left is the only Colossian coin known from the time of the Emperor Geta (co-ruled 209–11 CE), featuring the head of the emperor on the obverse and Artemis Ephesiaca with hinds at left and right on the reverse. The obverse of the coin is countermarked with a stamp from the city of Sardis (modern Sart), indicating the trade connections of Colossae across the province of Asia as well as the relative value of Colossian money in regional markets. The image of Artemis Ephesiaca is found in many places and in various media but seems ultimately to have been derived from one of the stock images found at Ephesos, as seen in the indented relief on a pedestal in the provincial capital.*

FRAGMENTS OF COLOSSAE

Plate 3.25

The memory of Colossae's fascination with Artemis was tenacious. Artemis cropped up in the story of St Michael of Chonai (see Chapter Nine, *The Mighty Archangel*) in the late fourth to early fifth century. But five hundred years later, her connection with Colossae was still being recalled in a lavishly illustrated collection of briefly described saints' days (called a synaxarion, though this book is often mis-named a 'menologion'). The book, or 'codex', had been commissioned by the Byzantine emperor Basil II, 'the Bulgar-slayer' (ruled 976–1025 CE). In this work, there is a feast-day on 23rd November for a certain Archippos. He is the Archippos mentioned in the Christian apostle St Paul's letter to Philemon (verse 2) and in the New Testament letter to the Colossians (4:17). Archippos shared a house with two others mentioned in the first letter—Philemon and Apphia—and these two are also included in the summary of his feast-day in the 'Menologion of Basil II'. They are said all to have been martyred during the time of the Emperor Nero (ruled 54–68 CE). The story relates that there was a feast-day for Artemis at her temple in Chonai (the later name for Colossae). When the three refused to offer sacrifice to the goddess, the 'idolatrous Greeks' dispatched the three to Androcles, supposedly the Roman prefect in charge of the corn-supply at Ephesos, where they met their end.

Plate 3.26

> *Archippos was flayed and then thrown into a cistern where he was submerged up to eye-level. Then he was initially impaled repeatedly in the whole of his body by the styluses of vagrant children and finally he was stoned.*
>
> Menologion of Basil II, 23rd November

The story has little historical substance and seems to be a collage of disparate curios from the past. But it does indicate a remembrance of how important Artemis was in the religious cityscape of Colossae and, with it, the tie to Ephesos, both of which are indicated in the coins.

Plate 3.25, 26 *This coin of Artemis with a stag is from the time of the emperor Commodus (177–92 CE) though the image appears under other emperors as well. The relief at the right is from Philippi and shows Artemis on the hunt, with a dog attacking a deer.*

However, the coins reveal something more. The dominant imaging of Artemis at Colossae is not Artemis of Ephesos, which attracts 17 coins, but the Artemis of nature— the hunter and the mistress of the deer. 43 Colossian coins are given to Artemis in her connection with nature.

Even though the images are familiar elsewhere, the preponderance and artistry of the coins points to a valuing of the natural environment and the hunt to an extent that harks back to Persian pastimes. This is particularly apparent in a series of Colossian coins that simply have a stag on the reverse side and a god on the front, the obverse. The god may be Artemis but the same iconographic structure can find, at Colossae, alternately the god Mên, or Dionysos, or the sun-god Helios. It is as if the animal life of Colossae's nearby forests is esteemed by the populace, or at least the elite speaking the values that they wanted the city to hold.

If Artemis is not commanding the stags and hinds, she is taking up her bow, either on foot or in her biga drawn by a pair of stags. Of particular note in one rendition of the motif, Artemis has actually shot an arrow that plummets into a wild boar. The image is particularly significant because one mythical foundation story for the city of Ephesos (as told by Creophylos, a chronicler of the sixth century BCE)

3.27

3.28

Plate 3.27, 28 *The stag, this time connected with the sun-god Helios, on a coin from Colossae dated to the time of the emperor Hadrian. At the right is a relief of Helios on a small altar in the Amman Museum, Jordan.*

FRAGMENTS OF COLOSSAE

Plate 3.29

involves just this animal. The eventual founders of Ephesos, initially inhabiting a tough landscape, sought a divine oracle about where they should live and were told 'wherever a fish should show them and where a wild boar shall show the way'. By an incredible coinciding of sea and land animals, the boar was eventually speared and where it fell, a temple of Athena was built and the city was settled beneath its vista, with a further temple to Artemis overlooking the marketplace and another to Artemis' brother Apollo. But here in a coin of Colossae, no human-thrown javelin brings down the boar (some ancient historians name the hunter as Androcles), but Artemis herself.

One modern historian, Stanley Cook, has noticed the difference in emphasis between the Ephesian Artemis and the dominant emphasis in Colossae. He named the Artemis hunter as specially characteristic of Colossae, even though Artemis the hunter is frequent at Ephesos as well (understandable given the huge estates that were there demarcated as Artemis' sacred territory). His classification of one type of Artemis as Artemis Colossensis may be a little extravagant but it was not the only time that Colossae laid claim to a special relationship with the gods. In the early third century, Colossae minted a coin that claimed that the city enjoyed a 'concord with the gods', a claim unmatched, to my knowledge, in Asia Minor. This too may seem a little extravagant! But it does show the level of competition and civic pride that gravitated around religious observance in the ancient world, even when images and stories frequently overlapped.

Plate 3.30

Tyche of the Colossians

One particular symbol accents the much-sought-after prosperity of overflowing provision—the cornucopia. The symbol is often given to the goddess of favour and fortune, Tyche, who holds the trumpet-basket filled with fruit and vegetables. There is one worn coin, featuring Tyche, that appeared recently on the numismatic auction market and may claim a Colossian provenance.

Plate 3.29 *This coin comes dates to the time of the emperor Severus Alexander (222–235 CE), pictured on the obverse but employs a frequently-used image of Artemis effortlessly reaching for an arrow whilst riding in her chariot (a 'biga') drawn by two stags.*
Plate 3.30 *Artemis slays a boar on a coin from the time of the emperor Septimus Severus (193–211 CE).*

The coin is dated to the early second century BCE. This would indicate that Colossae, like other Greek cities including its neighbours, esteemed Tyche as a patron. Nevertheless, Colossae's pre-eminent city patron, Zeus, fronts the coin thereby tying the prosperity of the city symbolised in the figure of Tyche with the protection afforded by the ruler of the gods, Zeus. It is a combination known in a number of places and forms, such as at Dionysopolis (near modern Ortaköy about 24 kilometres to the north of Colossae) where a votive relief of Zeus and Good Tyche standing together was raised 'for the benefit of the people'.

Although Tyche began as little more than an innocuous sea-nymph (according to the classical Greek writer Hesiod) she became, by the end of the classical age, one of the most powerful deities, precisely because of her association with the prosperity or decline of a city. She held both possibilities in her hand and was therefore to be appeased through lavish honours, invocations and deference. In the fourth century BCE, Athens erected a number of statues to *Agathê Tuchê*, 'Good Tyche', making an appeal for her positive devotion to the fortunes of the city. This appeal to Tyche that things might go well became ubiquitous in the ancient world, heading public documents such as wills through to private solicitations in protective spells, even when there may be explicit offerings being made to other gods. It was far more than simply a breath on the hand and a toss 'For good luck'.

3.31

3.32

Plate 3.31 *The obverse and reverse of a Hellenistic coin thought to come from the Colossian mint. It features the wreathed ('laureate') head of Zeus, ubiquitous in almost all the known coins of Colossae from the Hellenistic period. Tyche appears to be holding an ear of wheat, a link with the goddess Demeter, for whom wheat is also a prominent symbol. The usual cornucopia is all but abraded away. A similar coin replicating the images, though accenting Tyche's rudder, occurs in the reign of Antoninus Pius (138–61 CE).*
Plate 3.32 *A section of a larger-than-life-size statue of Fortuna (the Latin equivalent name for Tyche) at the Louvre in Paris.*

> *Give me all favour, all success, for the angel bringing good, who stands beside Tyche is with you. Accordingly render profitable success to this house.*
>
> Greek Magical Papyrus from Egypt

One notable appeal 'To Good Tyche' heads a pedestal that goes on to honour one of Colossae's most famous benefactors of the late first century, a citizen named Korumbos. The public recognition for Korumbos followed his extensive financing of repairs to the baths at Colossae and restructuring of substantial parts of the city's water infrastructure (see Chapter Seven, *The Waters and the Baths*). It is likely that these repairs were necessary after the destructive earthquake that hit the Lycus Valley in about 61 CE. Both the destruction and the restoration of a key indicator of prosperous city life were ample demonstrations of the power of Tyche. No wonder, then, that the pedestal begins with a devotional acknowledgement and appeal to her 'good side'.

Plate 3.33

Plate 3.33 *The top two lines of the inscription honouring Korumbos for his repair of the baths at Colossae. The top line is carved in the largest letters of the whole inscription. Though damaged at the right hand side, it can be readily reconstructed as ΑΓΑΘΗΙ Τ[ΥΧΗΙ] 'To the Good Tyche'.*

CHAPTER 3 - THE GODS IN CITY AND COUNTRY

A similar appeal seems to have been made less than a century later. Colossae was hit by the ravages of the combination of a crop shortage and the outbreak of an epidemic brought by diseased soldiers returning in 166–67 CE with more than they wanted from yet another war against the Parthians, this time led by the co-emperor Lucius Verus. The inscription previously mentioned that unfortunately has lost the name of its honorand (our Zosimos?) mentions as one of his claims to honour, that during 'the grain shortage, he supplied wheat at favourable rates'. The main purpose of the inscription is to record the erection of a statue of the 'goddess Tyche for the fatherland'. It seems that once the crisis had passed, Tyche was again honoured for having restored the city, this time in close association with another wealthy Colossian citizen.

There was no fatalistic shrug involved in the recognition of Tyche, in spite of detractors such as Cicero and Pliny who occasionally threw up criticisms for honouring Tyche in her bad manifestations. Rather, as the words of the old Greek proverb had it, 'To the one Tyche gives, let that person take'. Accordingly, festivals were held in her honour, where wine flowed, instruments pounded out the celebrations, and dancing filled the streets. Not to join the festivities was tantamount to refusing the good that Tyche brought—and who could survive after such an insult? Because Tyche, through her favour, could bring about changes in life's direction, she was sometimes given the epithet, Protogeneia — the Tyche of new possibilities, initial beginnings. One gem stone from Hellenistic Colossae, now lost, was engraved with the words 'Tyche Protogeneia of the Colossians'. This Tyche could receive offerings for everything from women seeking fertility for

Plate 3.34

Plate 3.34 *The youthful personification of the Colossian civic assembly, the 'demos' appears on the front of the coin, identified by the legend. On the reverse of the coin Hieronomos is named in the legend as the one who took responsibility for the minting of the coin which displays Tyche crowned with a city-model headpiece (a Roman emphasis), carrying a cornucopia in her left hand and steering the rudder with her right. The coin die is modeled closely on the cistophoric (silver Imperial not provincial city) coins with Latin legend and Hadrian's head on the obverse minted at Ephesos. Hieronomos is known as authorising other coin-types from the period of Hadrian. It is clear that fidelity to the Empire was being expressed in these coins.*

child-bearing to generals offering thanks for changed fortunes in war. At Praenesta, about 35 kilometres east of Rome, a temple to Fortuna Primigenia (=Tyche Protogeneia) was fed with water channeled from a natural spring. It was used not only for the purification of devotees but as a symbolic reminder of her ancient connection with water and hence of a continued association with mercantile ventures. Colossae may well have had something similar, if less grand, given the lavish provision of water in the area.

Another ancient proverb associated with Tyche was 'A divinity guides each person's tiller'. The rudder was one of the common symbols associated with Tyche, largely promoted by the maritime associations of the goddess, seen especially in the large and influential statue of Tyche at Antioch on the Orontes River. The Hellenistic coin that we have seen already (allowing that it is from Colossae) did not have this emblematic identification, possibly because Colossae was so far from the sea (approximately 180 kilometres from Ephesos to the west, 140 kilometres from Telmessos [modern Fethiye] to the south). However the rudder did appear in Tyche's right hand in a succession of Colossian coins from the early imperial period—from the rule of the emperor Hadrian, his successor Antonius Pius, Severus (193–217 CE) and Elagabalus (218–222 CE; this coin has Tyche linked with the Ephesian Artemis). By this time, the rudder had not only taken on an even more ubiquitous sense of 'guidance' but, in a noteworthy shift, Roman emperors, following the example set by Julius Caesar, had tied themselves closely to Fortuna (the Roman parallel to Tyche). Indeed, the first action of Octavian when he returned to Rome in 19 BCE after victory over Mark Antony at the Battle of

Plate 3.35 *A return to the Zeus pairing with Tyche occurs on this coin from the time of Antoninus Pius (138-61 ce). This time the coin names a certain Claudius Sacerdos as the governor. Claudius Sacerdos is also named on other Colossian coins that bear the images of Zeus and Sarapis (where he is named more fully as Tiberius Claudius Sacerdos). His cognomen (last name" may be an indication of a long-held function at Colossae, that is as a priest—which is what the word means in Latin. Perhaps he was a priest of the imperial cult of Roma; the cult was common throughout the cities of Asia Minor and indicated loyalty to the emperor.*

Mark Antony at the Battle of Actium was to construct an altar to Fortuna Redux. Plutarch, the prolific Greek writer of the late first century, even described Tyche as having ventured from the East in order to take up residence in Rome. Tyche was being claimed as the patron of a new age of prosperity.

Emperors wanted cities of the empire to believe that their future prosperity depended on the emperor's beneficence, not to mention their own civic loyalty. Tyche in the East readily absorbed some of the new developments in the Fortuna cult and her display became one of the indications that cities in Asia Minor supported the new political realities.

At Hyrkanis (modern Saruhanli) a bilingual inscription connects Tyche with Juno, often seen as a person's particular divine inspiration and thus retaining a sense of Tyche's accessibility to individuals. But another bilingual inscription from Iconium (Konya) appears to equate Fortuna with Tyche, though the wording

Plate 3.36

Plate 3.36, 37 *The pediment of the Temple of Hadrian at Ephesos dedicated by Publius Vedius Antoninus Sabinus. The capstone of the arch carries the bust of Fortuna.*

Plate 3.38

is damaged. The connection is not necessarily blending the Roman and Greek goddess absolutely. Indeed, the first visual identification of the goddess Roma (the divine personification of the imperial city) was as Tyche. But it was not the only time or the only instance where the Hellenistic (and Phrygian) gods of Asia Minor were appropriated and adapted to condone Roman rule. The persons charged with the authority to mint local coins at Colossae walked a narrow path of maintaining local civic pride yet deferring to Roman control. Subtle shifts in the iconography therefore are likely to indicate shifts in imperial power relations. As we shall see, Colossae appears to have got the balance wrong at least once in its history of dealings with Rome. *Mala Fortuna*, 'bad Fortune', could exercise an exacting toll.

Zeus the Thunderer

All of the gods mentioned thus far are inextricably connected with the ruler of the gods, Zeus. Zeus is well-known, of course, as the patron god of nearby Laodikeia. Sometimes the link is so strong that Zeus is called Zeus Laodikeus, though this is partly a misnaming of Zeus Aetophorus— Zeus the eagle-bearer—which is the standard representation of Zeus at Laodikeia. Colossae certainly adopted this representation of Zeus when it was first licensed under the emperor Hadrian to be able to mint its own coins in the imperial period. Certain Greek cities in the East of the Empire were permitted to mint their own coins, mostly bronze. The imperial

Plate 3.39

Plate 3.38, 39 *This coin of Zeus Aetophoros from Colossae comes from the time of the emperor Antoninus Pius, who succeeded the emperor Hadrian, during whose time Colossae resumed minting its own coins. The head of the coin is also intended to evoke Zeus but here it is with the influence of the Egyptian god Sarapis. Sarapis often appears with a wheat basket (a* modius) *on his head, a symbol of the fertility of agriculture. Sometimes the Egyptian connection was made even more strongly, with Sarapis and the goddess Isis combined on the faces of a single coin. Isis was often blended with the wife of Zeus, Hera, though could also be linked with Artemis and Aphrodite, even Hecate, another goddess of the underworld. At the right, to make the coin die impression clearer, is a broken hand section of a large statue of Zeus Aetophoros, displayed at the Allard Pierson Museum in Amsterdam.*

economy substantially relied on these small currency coins in the East to enable small commercial transactions to be negotiated (such as a cup of wine at a tavern!), so this meant two complementary types of currency were operating in Rome's eastern provinces: imperial coinage and coins minted by nominally autonomous city-states. When a city was granted the license to mint, it was a recognition that she had a measure of independent control over her own affairs. For Colossae to gain such permission was a substantial gain in status and a matter for civic pride.

But the minting of Zeus Aetophoros was a marked change from the dominant representation of Zeus that is found on the majority of coins minted at Colossae during the Hellenistic period before direct Roman control. These coins do not accent Zeus and the eagle but Zeus and his thunderbolt—Zeus Bronton, the thunderer.

The accent on Zeus the Thunderer with his thunderbolt can probably be interpreted as providing the backdrop to the way of portraying Michael the Archangel in the Christian story of St Michael of Chonai (see Chapter Nine *The Mighty Archangel*). There is little doubt that such synthesising derived from the popularity of the god in this form amongst the Colossian populace.

We see the image carved on the side of a grave-stone (a 'bomos') in the necropolis at Colossae. And we know of a priestess to Zeus in Colossae at the beginning of the second century (one Apphia, daughter of Herakleon) who erected a honorific pedestal to the emperor Trajan (98-117 CE). The inscription is unfortunately damaged but probably named Zeus as 'Zeus of the Colossians'. The remains of a temple on the top of the Colossae höyük identified by Georg Weber at the end of the nineteenth century could well belong to the temple of Zeus, surveying the surrounding fertile regions from the lofty height of the upper mound.

Plate 3.40 *The Hellenistic coin from Colossae of the laureate head of Zeus and his key Colossian identifier: the thunderbolt. If one looks closely at the centre of the thunderbolt, eagle's wings can be seen.*

> *Zeus is the head, Zeus the middle and from Zeus are made all things.*
>
> From a fourth century BCE hymn to Zeus found in The Derveni Papyrus.

Not only would this be a strong indication that Zeus was being claimed as the patron god of Colossae but that he was named in such a way as to distinguish Colossae's Zeus from that of Laodikeia. Moreover, in yet another indication of the interweaving of imperial politics and provincial piety, the pedestal honouring Trajan probably carried a statue of the emperor portraying Zeus-like features (perhaps with an eagle at his feet, or, as in Roman army standards, with an eagle atop a long staff).

The adoption of the 'Laodikeian' Zeus, that is, of Zeus Aetophoros, on the first imperial coins minted at Colossae is therefore to be seen as somehow politically motivated. Colossae's mint appears to have gone into a hiatus between the late Hellenistic period and the time of Hadrian. By comparison, Laodikeia retained its local minting right through this period. The single most significant event in this period is the war of Mithridates VI of Pontus against the Romans, a war in which Laodikeia appears to have provided a measure of resistance against his rebellion. Given that Mithridates laid siege to

Plate 3.41, 42 *The thunderbolt on the side of a damaged bomos from the Colossian necropolis. A similar motif is found on the side of an altar to Zeus Ktesis Patrios ('Zeus protector of one's property') now on display in the grounds of the Denizli Museum.*

Laodikeia, it is highly likely that Colossae, with its long history of support for resident armies (see Chapter Two, *Stationing Armies at Colossae*), provided supplies willingly or unwillingly. Rome, in both republican and imperial modes, readily punished cities for making wrong choices by, amongst other things, withdrawing the license to mint. Exactly this happened for the region of Achaea, west of Corinth in Greece, following its failure to support the campaign to make Vespasian emperor in 68 CE. Somewhere between 123 and 128 CE Hadrian licensed Hierapolis and Laodikeia to begin minting imperial ('cistophoric') coins, in addition to their own civic bronze coins. It appears that as part of Hadrian's recognition of the loyalty of the cities of the Lycus Valley, favour was dispensed, with Colossae finally re-gaining its license to mint, though not cistaphoric coins. The mark of this loyalty was to portray the emperor in connection with the over-arching god, Zeus, and to do so in the form clearly endorsed by Laodikeian loyalty: Zeus Aetophoros.

The gods, heroes and mere mortals

The list of gods for which we have evidence at Colossae from coins, inscriptions and texts is quite long and doubtless could well be extended once excavations are authorised. The list now has the names of: Zeus, Apollo, Artemis, Asclepios, Hygeia, Tyche/Fortuna, Demeter, Cybele/Great Mother, Dionysos/Bacchus, the Dioscuri brothers (Castor and Pollux), Mên, Helios, Selene, Athena, Echidna, Medusa, Nike, Sarapis, Isis and the 'river god'. Not all have been given extended treatment—the chapter is long enough already!

But there is one indication, frequently overlooked, which may indicate the presence of other gods and heroes at Colossae—people's names. To be sure, names are primarily a point of individuation even if the naming parents may aspire to something of a particular god's prowess for their newly born. But there are two factors which suggest that a study of the names known to be in use at Colossae might yield further indications of the gods honoured at Colossae. The first is found in the inscription on an altar in Plate 3.22 above. Here, an offering to Bacchus is made by Thallos son of Bacchulis, the father's name a derivative of the god. Something similar is found at Thessalonike in Macedonia where a priest named Hadaios makes an offering to the god Hades. The second is where we find that indigenous names (such as those of Phrygian, Scythian or Thracian origin) belonging to earlier generations give way to Greek names that are derived from Greek gods and heroes. The choice of such 'new' names indicates a desire to be seen in an identity favoured by the Greek and Roman elite, such as lived at Colossae. These factors do not guarantee that an alignment with a particular god was intended but it does remain suggestive.

And so, from the gods already mentioned, we find the names Demas and Demetrios (from Demeter), Apollonios (from Apollo), Dion, Diodoros, Diodotos and Diokrates (derivatives of Zeus under his other name Dis/Dios), Heliodoros (from Helios), Menogas and Menas (from Mên), Eutuches (from Tyche), to which might be added Herakleon and Heraklides, names linked with the hero Herakles. Indeed the New Testament letters to Philemon and Colossians contain a number:

Tychicus (from Tyche), Epaphras (from Aphrodite) and Nympha, though doubtless their allegiance to a new God rendered the old links tenuous. What is lacking so far in the remains, is any evidence of a person's name derived from Sarapis or Isis, the Egyptian gods well-represented on Colossae's coins. Nevertheless, in the main concerns of human activity—food, health, pleasure and interest in nature and the cosmos—Colossae was replete with gods that promised to satisfy such needs.

Plate 3.43

Plate 3.43 *A section of the pedestal erected in honour of Korumbos for the repair of the baths at Colossae, listing some of the names of those who provided for the monument. These include Truphon grandson of Diodoros, Menogas who was the fourth in descent of males of the family to hold the name closely followed by Diodoros who held the name for three generations. Diodoros and Menogas are 'theonyms', that is, names that are derived from the names of gods, in this case Zeus and Mên.*

Select Bibliography - Chapter Three: The Gods in City and Country

Athenaeus *Deipnosophists* 6.263c, 8.361d–e, 10.438e, 14.636a.

Aulock, H von, *Münzen und Städte Phrygiens*. Tübingen: Ernst Wasmuth Verlag, 2 vols, 1980, 1987, 2.448–51. 453, 465–68, 470–82.

Ausonius *The Moselle* 23; *The Order of Famous Cities* 30-33.

Cicero *On the Nature of the Gods* 3.24.

Clerc, M, 'Inscriptions de la Vallée du Méandre', in *Bulletin de Correspondance Hellénique* 11 (1987): 353.10; 354.12.

Diodorus Siculus 36.13.

The Greek Anthology 9.418.

The Greek Magical Papyri in Translation. Edited by HD Betz; 2nd edition; Chicago / London: University of Chicago Press, 1992, 4.3165-76.

Greeks and Romans in Imperial Asia: Mixed Language Inscriptions and Linguistic Evidence for Cultural Interaction until the End of AD III [IK 59]. Edited by RA Kearsley; Bonn Habelt, 2001, §§129, 142.

Euripides *The Bacchae*.

Head, BV, *Catalogue of the Greek Coins of Phrygia*. London: British Museum, 1906, §§43-45, 229.

Hesiod *Theogony* 1.360.

http://www.aburbecondita.com

http://www.acsearchinfo.com

http://www.artcoinsroma.it

http://www.asiaminorcoins.com/gallery/

http://www.cngcoins.com

http://www.ma-shops.com/loebbers

http://www.munzeo.com

http://www.vcoins.com/ancient/tomvossen

http://www.wildwinds.com/coins

Inscriptiones graecae ad res romanas pertinentes [IGR]. Edited by R Cagnat *et al*. Vol 3; Paris: E Leroux, 1927, §260.

Inscriptiones Graecae ad res Romanas pertinentes [IGR]. Volume IV, edited by R Cagnat, *et al*; Paris: E Leroux, 1927, §§ 868, 870.

Julian (the Apostate) *Hymn to the Mother of the Gods*.

Description de Medailles Antiques, Grecques et Romaines. Edited by TE Mionnet; Paris: Univerändoter Nachdruck, 1809, §§420, 423, 425.

Monumenta Asiae Minoris Antiqua [MAMA] Vol IV: Monuments and Documents from Eastern Asia and Western Galatia. Edited by WH Buckler, WM Calder and WKC Guthrie; Manchester: Manchester University Press, 1933, §267.

Monumenta Asiae Minoris Antiqua [MAMA] Vol VI: Monuments and Documents from Phrygia and Caria. Edited by W Calder and W Buckler; Manchester: Manchester University Press, 1939, §47.

Pausanias *Travels* 4.31.8.

Pfuhl, E and H Möbius, *Die Ostgriechischen Grabreliefs: Textband & Tafelband* 4 vols; Mainz: von Zabern, 1979, 1.594.

Pliny *Natural History* 2.5.14–16.

Plutarch *On the Fortune of the Romans*.

— *Mar* 17.9–10.

Roman Provincial Coinage. Edited by A Burnett, M Amandry, PR Alegre; 2 vols plus Supplement; British Museum Press, 1992.

Sophocles *Antigone* 1115–16.

Strabo *Geography* 12.5.3.

Virgil *Aeneid* 6.

Weber, G, 'Inschriften aus Sued-Phrygien', in *Athenische Mitteilungen* 18 (1893): 206.3, 4.

Alcock, SE and R Osborne (eds), *Placing the Gods: Sanctuaries and Sacred Space in Ancient Greece*. Oxford: Clarendon Press, 1994.

Alvar, J, *Romanising Oriental Gods: Myth, Salvation, and Ethics in the Cults of Cybele, Isis and Mithras*. Translated and edited by R Gordon; Leiden: Brill, 2008.

Anagnostou-Laoutides, E, *Eros and Ritual in Ancient Literature: Singing of Atalanta, Daphnis and Orpheus*. Piscataway, NJ: Gorgias Press, 2005.

Armstrong, S, 'Roman Phrygia: Cities and their Coinage', unpublished PhD thesis, University College London, 1998.

Arnold, CC, *The Colossian Syncretism: The Interface between Christianity and Folk Belief at Colossae*. Grand Rapids, MN: Baker, 1996.

—'Sceva, Solomon, and Shamanism: The Jewish Roots of the Problem at Colossae' in *Journal of the Evangelical Theological Society* 55 (2012): 7–26.

Arya, DA, 'The Goddess Fortuna in Imperial Rome: Cult, Art, Text', unpublished PhD thesis, University of Texas, Austin, 2002.

Birecikli, Fatma, 'Ana Hatlarıyla Friglerde Din', in *Gazi Academic View* 7 (2010): 215–32.

Burkert, W, *Ancient Mystery Cults*. USA: Harvard University Press, 1987.

Burrell, B, *Neokoroi: Greek Cities and Roman Emperors*. Leiden: Brill, 2004.

Cadwallader, AH, 'Honouring the Repairer of the Baths: A New Inscription from Kolossai', in *Antichthon* 46 (2012): 150–83.

—'Aspiring to the *homonoia* of the gods: tracking religion and identity in the coins of Colossae', unpublished paper SBL Annual Meeting 2012.

Clarke, JR, *Art in the Lives of Ordinary Romans: Visual Representation and Non-elite Viewers in Italy, 100 B.C.–A.D. 315*. Berkeley: University of California Press, 2003.

Clines, R, *Ancient Angels: Conceptualizing Angeloi in the Roman Empire*. Leiden: Brill, 2011.

Colvin, S, 'Names in Hellenistic and Roman Lycia', in *The Greco-Roman East: Politics, Culture, Society*. Edited by S Colvin; Cambridge: Cambridge University Press, 2004, 44-84.

Cook, AB, *Zeus: a Study in Ancient Religion*. 3 vols; Cambridge: Cambridge University, 1940.

Cook, SA, 'A Lydian-Aramaic Bilingual II', in the *Journal of Hellenic Studies* 37 (1917): 219–31.

Drew-Bear, T, C Thomas, and M Yıldızturan. *Phrygian Votive Steles*. Turkey: Museum of Anatolian Civilizations, 1999.

Elsner, J and I Rutherford (eds), *Pilgrimage in Graeco-Roman and Early Christian Antiquity: Seeing the Gods*. Oxford: Oxford University Press, 2005.

Franke, PR and MK Nollé, *Die Homonoia-Münzen Kleinasiens I. Katalog*. Saarbrucken: Saarbrücken Verlag, 1997.

French, D, *Roman, Late Roman and Byzantine Inscriptions of Ankara: A Selection*. Ankara: Turkish Republic Ministry of Culture and Tourism, 2003.

Friesen, SJ, *Twice Neokoros: Ephesus, Asia and the Cult of the Flavian Imperial Family*. Leiden: Brill, 1993.

Harmanşah, O and P Johnson 'Pınarlar Maaralar, ve Hitit Anadolu'sunda Kırsal Peyzaj: Yalburt Yaylası Arkeolojik Yüzey Araştırma Pıhkğin (Ilgın, Konya), 2011 Sezonu, Sonuçları' (Springs, Caves and the Rural Landscape in Hittite Anatolia), in *Araştırma Sonuçları Toplantısı* 30.2 (2013): 73–84.

Heinrichs, A, 'What is a Greek God?' in *The Gods of Ancient Greece: Identities and Transformations* (edited by JN Bremmer and A Erskine; Edinburgh: Edinburgh University Press, 2010), 19–42.

Hooke, J†, 'Health and Medicine in the Lycos Valley: a survey of first century issues and resources that may have impacted on the city of Colossae', unpublished Masters Thesis, Flinders University, 2008.

Horster, M and A Klöckner (eds), *Cities and Priests: Cult Personnel in Asia Minor and the Aegean Islands from the Hellenistic to the Imperial Period*. Berlin/Boston: de Gruyter, 2013.

Howgego, C, V Heichert and A Burnett (eds), *Coinage and Identity in the Roman Provinces*. Oxford: Oxford University Press, 2005.

Huttner, U, *Early Christianity in the Lycus Valley*. Leiden: Brill, 2013.

Johnston, A, *Greek Imperial Denominations ca 200-275: A Study of the Roman Provincial Coinages of Asia Minor*. London: Royal Numismatic Society, 2007.

Katsari, C, 'Money and protonational identities in the Greco-Roman cities of the first and second centuries AD', in *National Identities* 8 (2006): 1–20.

Katsari, C, CS Lightfoot, A Özme, *The Amorium Mint and the Coin Finds: Amorium Reports 4*. Berlin: Akademia Verlag, 2012.

Kerenyi, C, *Dionysos: Archetypal Image of Indestructible Life*. London: ROutledge and Kegan Paul, 1976.

Koester, H, 'The Cult of the Egyptian Deities in Asia Minor', in *Pergamon: Citadel of the Gods*. Edited by H Koester; Harrisburg, PA: Trinity Press International, 1998, 111-33.

Konakçi, E and B Duman, 'Arkeolojik ve Yazılı Kanıtlar Işığında Kolossai (Kolossai with the Light of Archaeological and Historical Evidences)', in *International Symposium on the History and Culture of Denizli and its Surroundings*. Denizli: Pamukkale University, 2007, Vol 2, 57–67.

Labarre, G and M Taşlıalan, 'La devotion au dieu Men: Les reliefs rupestres de la Voie Sacrée', in *Actes du Ier Congres International sur Antioche de Pisidie*. Edited by T Drew-Bear, M Taşlıalan and CM Thomas; Paris: de Boccard, 2002, 251–312.

Lane, E, *Corpus Monumentorum Religionis Dei Menis*. Leiden: Brill, 1976.

Macdonald, DJ, 'The Homonoia of Colossae and Aphrodisias', in *Jahrbuch für Numismatik und Geldgeschichte* 33 (1983): 25–27.

Magie, D, 'Egyptian Deities in Asia Minor in Inscriptions and on Coins' in *American Journal of Archaeology* 57.3 (1953): 163–87.

Maier, HO, *Picturing Paul in Empire: Imperial Image, Text and Persuasion in Colossians, Ephesians and the Pastoral Epistles*. London: T & T Clark, 2013.

Matheson, SB (ed), *An Obsession with Fortune: Tyche in Greek and Roman Art*. New Haven: Yale University Art Gallery, 1994.

Matthews, E (ed), *Old and New Worlds in Greek Onomastics*. Oxford: British Academy, 2007.

Metcalfe, WE, *The Cistophori of Hadrian*. New York: American Numismatic Society, 1980.

Meyboom, PGP, *The Nile Mosaic of Palestrina*. Leiden: Brill, 1995.

Mitchell, S, *Anatolia: Land, Men and Gods in Asia Minor*. 2 vols; Oxford: Clarendon Press, 1995.

—'The Cult of Theos Hypsistos between Pagans, Jews and Christians', in *Pagan Monotheism in Late Antiquity*. Edited by P Athanassiadi and M Frede; Oxford: Clarendon Press, 1999, 81–148.

Pettis, JB (ed.), *Seeing the God: Ways of Envisioning the Divine in Ancient Mediterranean Religion*. Piscataway, NJ: Gorgias Press, 2013.

Quandt, W, *De Baccho ab Alexandri Aetate in Asia Minore Culto*. Halis Saxonum: Max Niemeyer, 1913.

Ramsay, WM, *The Cities and Bishoprics of Phrygia*. 2 vols; Oxford: Clarendon Press, 1895, 1897.

—*The Historical Geography of Asia Minor*. Digitally Printed 2010 ed. Cambridge: Cambridge University Press, 1890.

Riemann, H, 'Jupiter Imperator', in *Mitteilungen des Deutschen Archäologischen Instituts, Römischen Abteilung* 90 (1983): 233–55.

Riley, J, 'Dionysos: Myth, Cult and Influence in Kolossai and on the Letter to the Kolossians' unpublished Hons Thesis, Flinders University, 2006.

Sharankov, N, 'Unknown Governors of Provincia Thracia, Late I-Early II Century AD', in *Zeitschrift für Papyrologie und Epigraphik*, 151 (2005): 235–42.

Spyridakis, S, 'The Italian Cult of Tyche Protogeneia', in *Historia* 18 (1969): 42–48.

Thomas, C, 'The "Mountain Mother": the other Anatolian Goddess at Ephesos', in *Les cultes locaux dans les mondes grec et romain. Actes du colloque de Lyon, 7-8 juin 2001*. Edited by Guy Labarre and Jean-Marc Moret; Paris: de Boccard, 2004, 249–62.

Thompson, LL, 'ISmyrna753: Gods and the One God', in *Reading Religions in the Ancient World: essays presented to Robert McQueen Grant*. Edited by DE Aune and RD Young; Leiden: Brill, 2007, 101–24.

Vermaseren, MJ, *Corpus Cultus Cybelae Attidisque (CCCA): I. Asia Minor*. Leiden: Brill, 1987.

Walters, J, 'Egyptian Religions in Ephesos', in *Ephesos: Metropolis of Asia*. Edited by H Koester; Valley Forge, PA: Trinity Press International, 1995, 281–309.

Plate 4.1 *North-east view across the top of the theatre cavea at Colossae showing remains of the northern wall—called the analemmata—along with other fragments of the structure.*

CHAPTER 4
The Theatre

The ten hectare höyük or mound that rises to over 60 metres above the Lycus Valley plain makes its own distinctive mark on the topography of the area but is inadequately proclaimed as 'the site of Colossae'. It would be better to describe it as the centre of the city of Colossae. The barrenness of architectural remains on the site has often deterred an informed, imaginative appreciation of its contours, yet one part stood out to early visitors—an indentation in the hill that carried all the marks of extensive engineering. With a little help from a few remains that they found, these explorers recognised the *cavea* of a theatre, and it was a large one. The Englishman, William Ainsworth, for example, desired to trace the steps of Cyrus the Persian, the unsuccessful aspirant to the Achaemenid throne (died 401 BCE). This led him to Colossae. He wrote in 1844, there 'is the hollow cavea of a theatre, built on the side of a sloping hill, and of which several seats are still *in situ*; some traces of the wall of the right wing are also visible: a grassy sward covers nearly the whole space.' The concave, hollowed-out section of the Colossae mound is one of the distinctive features of the site.

This is not to suggest that the theatre belonged to the period of the Achaemenid control of the Lycus Valley. Rather it seems that the foundations and shape of the original theatre were carved into the side of the artificial mound sometime in the Hellenistic period when Colossae was part of the Seleucid kingdom. This kingdom was established after the death of Alexander the Great (323 BCE), or perhaps sometime during the period when Colossae came under the sway of the Attalid kingdom (281–133 BCE) with its capital at Pergamon (modern Bergama). Given the size of the mound, there were plenty of options for the theatre site. However, a number of factors were critical in determining the choice.

Choosing a site for a theatre

First, because the front wall of a Greek theatre (the *scaena*), that was built behind the stage, was modest in height and design, care had to be exercised to ensure that the sun did not interfere with the view of the gathered audience. The Roman architect, Vitruvius (c75 BCE to c14 BCE) would later record what had become common practice for the Greeks: that a theatre should not face south, to avoid 'over-heating' and the 'bad smells' thereby produced! The famous republican Roman general, Pompey, is credited with introducing channels into the stairways and seating of theatres to carry cold, running water—an early cooling device. The position of Colossae's theatre, facing East-South-East, carefully ensures that the sun is behind the view of the auditorium in the afternoon, as it tracks the line of the Taurus mountain range until it sinks below the ridges.

Secondly, precisely because the *scaena* in Greek theatres was modest in height, there was an opportunity to evoke some recognition of the gods in their 'natural' environment (most especially Zeus, and the patron of theatre, Dionysos). The natural environment was therefore called in to supplement and provide the awesome setting for the statues, reliefs and characters that would have been part of the viewing for the spectators gathered in the theatre. Honazdağ, known in ancient times as Mount Cadmus, was as ideal for inspiring the Colossians as the ocean was for the residents of the city of Perge (near Aksu) in the south-east or Priene (near Güllübahçe) in the west (before silting distanced the sea from its borders). As Professor Andrew Wilson notes on the positioning of theatres, there was 'often a fine view out across the landscape over the low stage building'. Combine this with the religious factor of the home of the gods and the whole setting—of theatre and nature—could charge performances with a numinous sacred quality.

There may have been a large temple (probably to Colossae's 'patron' god, Zeus) on the artificial acropolis (the second and higher elevation of the höyük) rising above the theatre (which is located to the right of centre in Plate 4.2).

Certainly when the archaeologist from Alsatia in Europe, Georg Weber (famous for his work on the water supply of Ephesos), drew a map of the site in 1891, he included a temple ground-plan at the top of the höyük, though whether he saw remains there, or summised it, is unclear (see Plates 4.5, 6).

There was likely an altar in the Hellenistic theatre for special sacrificial rites that inaugurated a festival performance. Because the theatre gathered a substantial number of the city's people, from the elite to the slaves who accompanied them, this was a key factor in the cohesiveness of Colossian society. It was not just that the gods and their territory were viewed; they were viewed *together* by the populace. The theatre was the critical architectural engine of that social organisation.

Plate 4.2

Plate 4.2 *Aerial photograph of the Colossae höyük highlighting the theatre* cavea *at centre left. The lower level of the primary höyük is tinged green with the upper level in brown and the secondary höyük (the acropolis) rises at centre right. The photograph was taken at 7.30am in mid-summer. The red arrow points North.*

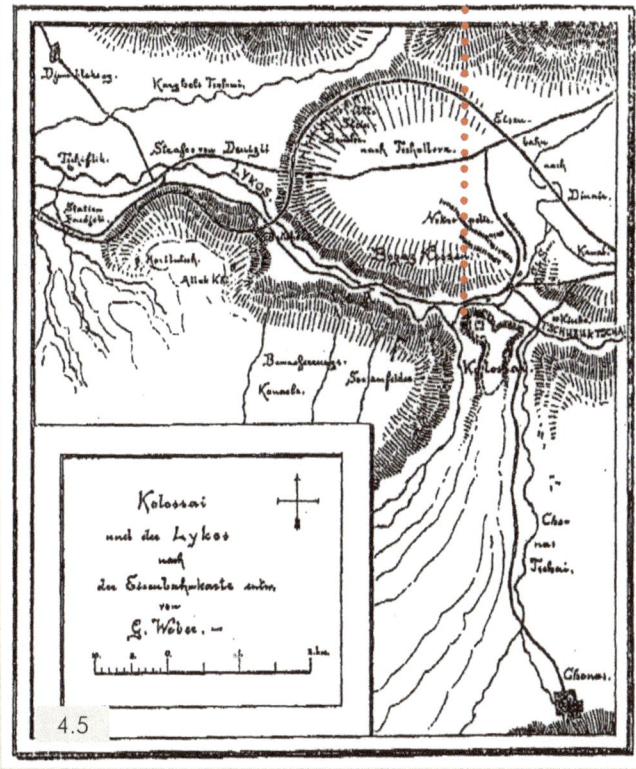

Plate 4.3 The theatre's view of the awesome home of the gods on Mt Cadmus (Honazdağ)

Plate 4.4 The artificial acropolis, the second and higher mound of the Colossae höyük. The theatre cavea is out of view to the right of the photograph.

Plate 4.5, 6 Weber's 1891 map of Colossae, with detail showing the acropolis temple on the höyük and the theatre just above the 'ss' of 'Kolossai'.

CHAPTER 4 - THE THEATRE

The third factor determining site choice was crowd management. The ability to funnel spectators efficiently in and out of the auditorium was crucial. Proximity to main thoroughfares was therefore a prime practical consideration for the positioning of a theatre, quite apart from the city's concern to display its civic credentials. Like the theatre at Ephesos (modern Selçuk), Priene or Aspendos (modern Belkiz) and many others, the theatre at Colossae was served by one of the main roads, passing along its eastern façade. The line of the modern road that cuts into the side of the mound does not follow exactly the path of the 'Theatre Street'. The modern road does however cross the river at a point still housing an ancient bridge. The bridge reflects a typical Roman design such as is found at Caesarea Philippi (modern Banias in Israel). 'Theatre Street' probably crossed at this point.

Indications of the original road are given by two column remains in separate fields just to the east of the new road. They form a line running straight to the ancient bridge (see Plate 4.13). Indeed, lying on the bed of the River Lycus to the western side of the bridge is a column section that at some time in the past has been rolled or has toppled into the water. Its tapered design with locking dowel appears to match a section of a column held in a nearby Honaz café. The length of the two sections indicates a height of 3.5 metres for the columns of a colonnaded way.

Plate 4.7

All this, taken together, suggests a colonnaded way running past the theatre (subject of course to the discoveries that only excavation can provide). How extensive it was can only be conjectured, but the early Italian explorer, Antonio Picenini, reported seeing, in 1705, pieces of columns, inscriptions and other remains 'for the space of a mile'. Even in the mid-nineteenth century, Thomas Lewin

Plate 4.7 *The theatre at Priene was built into the hill-side. It is one of the best-preserved theatres of the Hellenistic period. The altar occupied the central position at the perimeter of the auditorium, flanked by a series of special seats (bemas) for civic leaders, high priests and elite visitors. The altar carries a dedication by a certain Pythotimos the agonothete (performance organiser) and is dated to about 190 BCE. Photograph courtesy of Rosemary Canavan.*

Plate 4.8 *A Roman bridge—extended by a modern concrete support—that still undergirds a modern sealed road along the eastern (theatre) edge of the Colossae höyük.*

Plates 4.9, 10 *Column sections located in fields just to the east of the Colossae höyük, the one topped with extra stones showing part of the mound in the background.*

Plate 4.11 *The column section at the base of a summer-dried Lycus river-bed.*

Plate 4.12 *Upper section of column originally from a place close to the Colossae höyük, now preserved at a local Honaz café.*

could write of 'a theatre and other public buildings, with broken columns strewn over a considerable space'. The proximity in Lewin's admittedly-loose description of theatre and columns seems to confirm the conjectured alignment given here. Colossae's theatre would have been an imposing public feature in a walk along 'Theatre Street'.

This display and access is related to the next reason for the theatre's position. The theatre was a central gathering point for the city's population. This was the site for the reinforcement of civic cohesion through festival plays, the discussion of major issues and the honouring of notables either from within the city or those luminaries who were visiting. Accordingly, the theatre had to be positioned, designed and adorned so as to provide a major display of the city's values. The second century Greek travel writer, Pausanius, declaimed, 'Can one call "city" a place that has neither public buildings nor gymnasium nor theatre nor square nor water to supply a single fountain…?' Clearly Colossae had its theatre and, follow Pausanias, it would have been connected in a larger architectural fabric that included many familiar features. The baths, for example, are probably to be located to the centre-left edge of the modern road in Plate 4.13 (See Chapter Seven, *The Waters and the Baths*).

THE SIZE AND DESIGN OF THE THEATRE

But the theatre was crucial. Colossae's theatre, even with its bare remains, appears to be reasonably large. Its diameter, allowing for the porticus and arcade structures surrounding the seating areas, was approximately 70–75 metres, which makes it larger than the theatre at Priene but smaller than either of the two theatres at neighbouring Laodikeia (about 95 metres for the Hellenistic-style theatre and 110 metres for the Roman theatre) or neighbouring Hierapolis (about 100 metres for the Hellenistic

Plate 4.13 *The possible line of 'Theatre Street' showing the position of the two 'field' column sections in the upper right and the Roman bridge at lower left.*

theatre and 103 metres for the Roman). All of these are dwarfed by the theatre at Ephesos (142 metres). Colossae's structure appears to retain the Greek-style feature of an auditorium that swings beyond the half-circle favoured by Roman design; indeed it follows an arc closer to an oval than a circle.

A comparison could be made with other theatres of similar diameter across the Mediterranean world. The theatre at Pergamon has a diameter of only 80 metres but, due to its architectural design and gradient, its capacity is estimated at 10,000 people. Iguvium in Italy with a theatre diameter of 70 metres had an estimated capacity of 3,900 to 4,800. Spoletum's *cavea* is wider (72 metres) but its capacity was smaller: 2,800 to 3,500. Priene's diameter is only 57 metres in diameter but its capacity is estimated to be 6,500 people.

These comparisons serve as a rough approximation of the capacity at Colossae, that is, probably, between 5,000 and 7,000 people. Even the lower figure points to a sizable city and dependent region that alternately serviced and enjoyed the theatre.

Plate 4.14 *A section of a door jam at the theatre, showing the slot for one inserted wooden bar at the left and the sliding channel to receive a second wooden beam at the right. The size indicates a large doorway.*
Plate 4.15 *Aerial view of the theatre* cavea *on the edge of the Colossian mound. Photograph by Hakan Kurt.*

CHAPTER 4 - THE THEATRE

The importance of a theatre (or two, such as at nearby Laodikeia [modern Goncalı], even three if one adds the smaller meeting or concert space called a bouleterion or odeion) was far more than entertainment. Theatres had a potent religious function, working hand in hand with temples, especially during religious festivals. And, as always in the ancient world where politics was interwoven with religion, political gatherings were staged at the theatre, from regular large meetings to influence the populace to *ad hoc* special events such as the welcome of a dignitary or the address of some crisis. When Luke, the New Testament writer of the *Acts of the Apostles* (19:23–41), or the writer of the ancient novel *Challirhoe*, told a story of a feverish gathering in the city's theatre, all they were doing was providing a well-known example, among many in the ancient world, of exactly the occasion a theatre could be exploited for an event other than entertainment.

THE THEATRE IN ANCIENT SOCIETY

The theatre in a sense was a concentrated distillation of society. Here the hierarchical levels of social order were reinforced in seating, entrances, attendance, statues and inscriptions and the dispensing of honours. This civic engineering of the populace was already incorporated into the Greek-style structure with which Colossae began its theatrical experience. Usually Greek-style theatres had at least two levels of seating—the *ima* (the lower span) and the *summa* (the upper span) of the *cavea*—each divided by steps into segments called *kerkides* in Greek or *cunei* in Latin. Between the two or three levels there was a walkway—called the *diazoma* or *praecinctio*—as much for marking distinctions between classes or ranks of people as required for access.

These social distinctions played out architecturally became more rigidly enforced by the Emperor Augustus under his edict, the

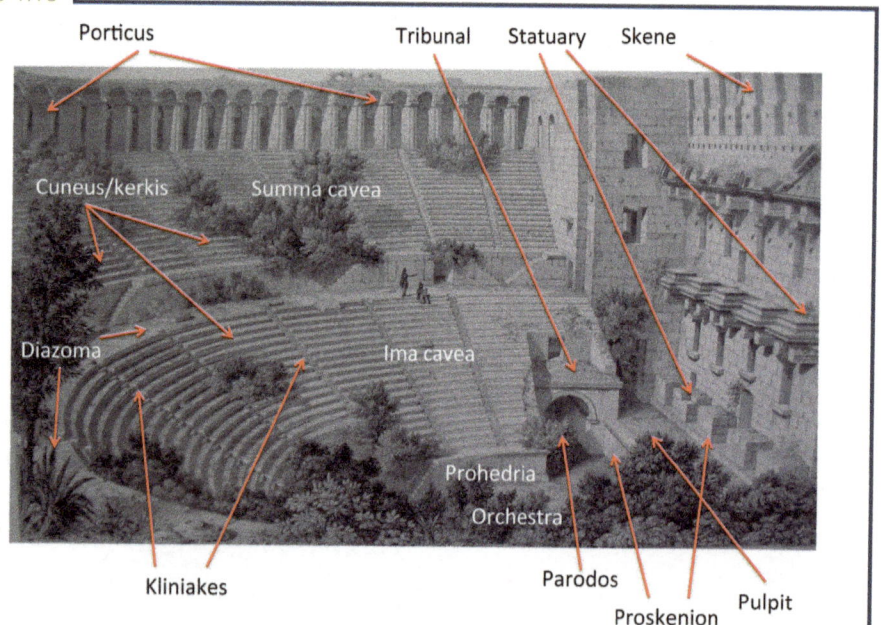

Plate 4.16

Plate 4.16 *The Roman-modified Hellenistic theatre at Aspendos (modern Belkiz), as sketched by the nineteenth century French explorer, Charles Texier. It remains substantially intact today. The different parts of the theatre have been labelled, mainly using Greek terminology.*

Lex Julia Theatralis. Slaves were confined to standing positions at the back of the theatre. Women were separated from men. Special places were set aside for young men in training, for returned veterans, for guilds or 'voluntary associations' such as the one called 'The Friends' that we know had a group in Colossae.

The gradations of society from senators to freed persons were reflected in allocations of seats in the theatre, from those closest to the *orchestra* or stage to those in the back stalls. So, if we were to take one Colossian household we know of from the mid-first century, the household addressed by St Paul in his letter to Philemon in the New Testament, we can plot where each of the four people (three men and a woman) mentioned in the household would sit. Philemon would be somewhere in the middle to the top of the first ten rows in the *ima cavea*. If the reference to Archippos as Paul's 'fellow-soldier' (Philemon 2) is more than just a bare metaphor, Archippos would have sat amongst the veterans in the upper side levels of the *ima*—unless he was called upon to keep order! Apphia would be with other women (though probably not with the prostitutes!) in a designated *cuneus/kerkis* of the *summa cavea*.

> Augustus would not allow women to view even the gladiators except from the upper seats, though it had been the custom for men and women to sit together at such shows.
>
> Suetonius *Augustus*

Plate 4.17

And Onesimos would be standing at the back with other slaves along the front of the *porticus*. The theatre therefore reminded the members of a single household of their respective places in society and in relation to each other. Each knew where the other stood … or sat!

Although cities in Asia Minor were rarely required to follow this Augustan law in its minutiae, the spirit appears to have been observed, right down to the architectural limitations on mixing between the various classes of society within the theatre. This hierarchical placement could even be signalled in the size and type of seats and whether the inscription identifying the seating for a group was written *on* the bench of the seat or, for an individual, along its edge at the front (such as we find at the theatre at Termessos, modern Güllük). Those with larger seating bases, inscribed on the front and located close to the performance, were for the elite members of society; the more cramped places, higher in the theatre, were for the lower levels of society. Perhaps the elite had more corpulence to accommodate!

Plate 4.17 *The association called 'The Friends' (*hoi hetairoi*) honour Gluko in a funerary inscription from Colossae. The inscription is highlighted in red. It includes 'Greetings to the passers-by' in the 'lintel' above the heads of the figures.*

There are fragments from Colossae that indicate that Colossian society was organised no differently in the theatre from elsewhere. There are just enough hints in the aerial pictures of the theatre, allowing that sections of the theatre are at present buried, to indicate two levels divided into cunei. The seats of course are all but gone, or buried. Hüseyin Baysal, the Director of the Denizli Museum, thinks that 12 to 15 rows of seating are hidden beneath the current soil level at the base of the *cavea*.

One can see a section of theatre seating has been moved into place as a boundary marker, in a current agricultural field division between the lower and upper section of the primary höyük. The end of such a row of seats at the stairs (the *gradus*) was often finished with a more elaborate design, such as a lion's paw. The French explorer Charles Texier visited Colossae in 1834 and reported that some sections of steps between each cuneus were still visible. He may have also seen the following at the theatre, a seat at the end of a *cuneus* section bordering those steps, which contains a lion's paw moulding.

The identical design is found on a right angled section of seating from the theatre (now at a Honaz café) which may have come from the *tribunalia* at the sides of the seating or a *loggia* or 'corporate box', specially constructed for eminent citizens or guests.

Plate 4.18 *A section of theatre seat on the höyük at Colossae may contain an inscription on the leading edge but it is so abraded as to defy reconstruction. No inscription is visible on the top of the bench surface.*
Plate 4.19 *The end section of a theatre seat with lion's paw moulding.*

FRAGMENTS OF COLOSSAE

However, there is a stronger indication that the hierarchy of society was reinforced at the theatre. At a café in Honaz, there is a bema seat that comes from the theatre.

Plate 4.20

Although showing considerable signs of weathering, typical of the local limestone often used in Colossian construction, it is remarkably similar to other seats found in various theatres around the Mediterranean. Many of these seats are now not *in situ*. But at Priene five such seats in very good condition still hold pride of position at the theatre. Spectators at the theatre would all have a good idea of their place in society by measuring their proximity to these seats!

Plate 4.20 *A corner seat and edge from the Colossae theatre. It shows a lion's paw moulding.*
Plates 4.21, 22 *A throne or bema from the theatre at Colossae at left, and an early sketch of an elaborate throne (no longer extant) from the second century stadium at Athens.*
Plate 4.23 *One of a series of bema seats prominent in the front row at the theatre at Priene, which were swung on an axis either side of the central altar (see* Plate 4.7).

CHAPTER 4 - THE THEATRE   85

Plate 4.24

These seats at Priene were specially dedicated to the patron god of the theatre, Dionysos, by a series of high-ranking citizens called *agonothetes*. The *agonothete* was the city official with prime responsibility for the organisation of theatre events. And the seats ensured that his position would be recognised, along with high priests of local cults especially involved when a festival connected with a god was staged. Colossae boasts an inscription where the person being honoured is named as having held, amongst a number of offices, the position of *agonothete*. It is likely therefore not only that he organised many of the theatre events but that he was present in a preeminent seat, thereby gaining appropriate returns of recognition for his efforts. Indeed Colossae had such a renowned *agonothete* that he was granted the office for life—one Aurelius Tatianus, the son of a certain Gluko. Occasionally also, those who had brought honour to the city through political, rhetorical or athletic accomplishment would be acknowledged publicly not just through inscriptional dedication but by applause at their entrance into the theatre. He (and more rarely, she) may even have received a special crowning with a wreath, such as is carved on the side of the bema in the nineteenth century sketch above (Plate 4.22). One athlete at Colossae, by the name of Zenon, received such an honour some time in the first half of the third century CE, because of his prowess at local 'New Olympics', as they were called, held at the neighbouring city of Tripolis (near modern Yenicekent). He would have taken a seat just behind the leading officials. This also shows how important was the exchange—and competition—between cities. Theatres were crucial to such inter-city rivalry.

MODIFICATIONS TO THE THEATRE ALONG ROMAN ARCHITECTURAL LINES

The visit of an eminent Roman official would be highlighted by a public, civic welcome at the theatre, as almost certainly happened in June 129 CE when the emperor Hadrian visited the city. To capture such recognition from the emperor on his 'Pan-hellenic Tour', as he swept from Greece through Asia Minor extolling Greek values, meant that the city had to offer the sort of prestige and accomplishments that demonstrated a fidelity to and imitation of Rome and its (modifying) embrace of Greek features and ideas. Colossae apparently qualified, having just been awarded the special status of its own mint a few years previously by Hadrian. The city authorities would have ensured that its prime gathering point, the theatre, measured up to expectations.

This is probably an indication, yet to be conclusively borne out by approved archaeological investigation, that the theatre at Colossae underwent a series of modifications that adapted its Greek style into some identifiable Roman features. Roman theatres were more enclosed structures with full-scale *scaenas* that

Plate 4.24 *Probably the earliest coin-type of the Roman imperial period minted at Colossae, showing the young Caesar, Hadrian.*

closed off the front of the theatre by tighter construction links with the auditorium and had higher tiers that matched the height of the *summa cavea* to some degree. There was also a portico enclosure that ran the arc around the top of the auditorium.

GLADIATORS AT COLOSSAE

There was one further significant change that Roman architecture brought. The orchestra was closed off from the seating at the front by a walled area that enabled something of the atmosphere of an amphitheatre to be experienced even in the theatre. St Paul seemed to know what happened in such a theatre—he could use as a metaphor, "fighting with wild animals" to talk of his time in Ephesos, casting himself as a *venator*, someone pitted in combat against ferocious beasts (1 Corinthians 15:32)! He was not alone in such language. Quintilian, the famous Roman teacher of oratory in the first century CE, regularly used gladiatorial contests as a metaphor for rhetoric. But it did mean that the events for which the Romans were famed could be staged in the theatre and not just in a Colosseum-like structure. Many Greek theatres in Asia Minor underwent such changes, such as at nearby Hierapolis (modern Pamukkale) and Aphrodisias (modern Geyre). They became venues for staged wild-beast hunts and, of course, gladiator contests in addition to their more usual functions. Indeed, a recently discovered epitaph from Stratonikeia (modern Eskihisar) shows that the line between

Plates 4.25, 26 *Fragments from the Colossae theatre, a decorative edge section on the left and a corner section of moulded architrave on the right.*

CHAPTER 4 - THE THEATRE

theatre and gladiatorial fight was fairly thin: one gladiator, appropriately named Achilles, had been a pantomime actor and summoned the skills of his previous thespian stagecraft to dispatch opponents with full-blown histrionics!

One small fragment—now destined for the Denizli Museum—emerged some years ago in the new wall of a local resident of Honaz. It hints at the change that came over the theatre at Colossae. It is a two-tiered section of a frieze of 'theatre sports'. The fragment measures approximately 45 by 40 centimetres and originally would have been part of a longer frieze. It may have contained three tiers, though only two remain, albeit with the right frame edging still visible. Very similar two-tiered reliefs are found in a number of localities, including nearby Hierapolis, Sagalassos (modern Ağlasun) and Manisa. Even in this fragment a number of different gladiator types are visible, in combat with one another, probably as members of different squads (which were called *pali*). Gladiators were armed and armoured in different ways, each with particular advantages and disadvantages, to add spice to the display and the manner of dying.

Plate 4.27

In the top register, the gladiator at the left, from the angled-brim helmet and the heavy armour (especially apparent on his leading leg) is a *provocator*, the one usually charged to initiate the action. The straps across his back that held a breast-plate (the *cardiophylax*) in position can also be seen. His right arm is heavily strapped with a *manica*. The combat appears to have been with a *retiarius* going by the heavily bandaged left arm and the band across his back to hold his shoulder and neck protection (the *galerus*) in place. The *retiarius*' leggings also seem shorter and lighter, exactly what was needed for this quick-moving fighter. Though normally given from a crouched position, his raised right arm (and finger?) may indicate surrender—quite advisable given that he seems to have lost his trident. The object at the left of the *provocator* may be his shield, distinguishable by a faint boss (an *umbo*) in the centre, claimed perhaps by the referee (the *rudis*) whose foot may be all that remains in the fragment at the extreme left. There were rules governing the gladiatorial contests, administered by these referees who wore distinctive clothing (usually a purple-banded white tunic). Needless to say, they maintained a discrete distance from the flurry of the event, exercising their interventions with a suitably lengthy wand. There may also have been some conventional measures of honour between combatants, erratically applied, it seems, if a declamation credited to the rhetorician Quintilian is any indication, where one man stood in as gladiator for a friend and met his death. But of the detail of regulations and customs we know little.

Plate 4.27 *The 'gladiator frieze' from Colossae.*

In the lower register, at the left, there is only one partial gladiator remaining. He is probably a *thraex* type, going by the helmet that retains an indication of a crest bending back at the top (intruding into the moulding) and the hint of a small convex shield (the *parmula*). Whoever he is fighting is lost from the piece. But the next section along retains the stock pair of combatants, both wearing the standard thick belts above their loincloths. In this case, there is another *retiarius*, without helmet, showing the manicle on his left arm topped with a shoulder deflector; he holds up the sword of his beaten opponent. He exalts over a fallen *secutor*, who has honoured his vow—the *sacramentum gladiatorium*—and lies prostrate, still wearing his longer-finned brim helmet, but 'nude', that is, without his weaponry.

The *Sacramentum Gladiatorum*

Uri, vinciri, verberari, ferroque necari patior

I submit to be burned, to be bound, to be beaten and killed by an iron weapon

---

A rare element in this fragment is the herm, towards which the victor turns. The herm was an honorific sculpture, a long stone, squared around its perimeter, containing a head at the top and genitalia protruding at the middle (indicating dignity and virility). Sometimes a herm was dedicated to a patron, more usually to a god. Because gladiatorial games were a development of Roman rule in Asia Minor, the focus might be part of the imperial cult. If the worn head includes a beard along with a florid hairstyle, akin to some of the second-century emperors, it might indicate Zeus himself. Alternately, as Pausanias the second-century travel writer tells us of the stadium at Olympia in Greece, it might be an honouring of one of the favourite gladiator gods, Hermes. If so, he may sport a beard which he began to grow after being characteristically portrayed as a youth in classical times. He was called Hermes Engonios—'of the games'—though that epithet was sometimes applied to Dionysos, Apollo and even Zeus himself. This may be an indication also of the Greek stamp on a ready acceptance of this Roman sport. Gladiators in the East were readily portrayed as heroes, thus drawing on the full array of Greek mythological and sporting history, even if their performances and the terminology involved, remained separate from 'the Games' (the *agônes*). However, the particular god of the gladiatorial contest was Nemesis and there may be a hint of a wheel protruding onto the relief moulding at the right side of the herm pillar to confirm this as the goddess of vengeance.

Following the example of the emperors who sometimes owned large troupes of gladiators, local high-priests often did the same, especially if they were high-priests of the imperial cult. It is possible that some of the high-priests named on Colossian coins in the second century, dignitaries such as Claudius (who may have been a high-priest of the sanctuary of Roma and/or Zeus), may well have kept a troupe that he could use, hire out for festival performances in the theatre and pass on to his successor. Alternately, he may have entered a rent-a-troupe agreement with a *lanista* (the owner of a gladiator school). As happened at Aphrodisias, the tombs of these high-priests were sometimes surrounded by representations of their *familia*—the gladiators who were so much part of the priest's beneficence to society. Or they may simply have been part of the frieze along the podia of the stage structure as at Aizanoi (near modern Çavdarhisar) and Sagalassos. What is clear is that gladiatorial shows were part of the *religious* frame of the Empire.

With the ability to stage such events in the theatre, some of the practices of the hippodrome and amphitheatre crept into the auditorium. The partisan groups designated by colours—the 'Blues', 'Greens', 'Reds' and 'Whites'—cheered on their designated hero(es). This began to extend to the performance of plays as well, with the factions sometimes encouraged to finance an event starring their own favourites. These public performers became remarkably popular, gathering not only advertising hoardings along the agora but also graffiti in toilets and cartoon renditions in the public agora and private homes.

Some early Christian writings made use of the agonistic imagery of the theatre (the First letter to Timothy 4:7–10; 6:11–12; Second letter to Timothy 4:6–8, First letter of Clement 7.1, Shepherd of Hermas *Similitude* 8, 3.6). And St Jerome, the early biblical commentator (347–420 CE), saw in the phrase 'Do not let anyone disqualify you' from the New Testament Letter to the Colossians (2:18), a

Plate 4.28, 29 *This Colossian coin from the time of the Emperor Septimius Severus (193–211 CE) features the emperor on the obverse. On the reverse stands Artemis holding a stag by the antlers. The authorising magistrate, by the name of Menekles, held the office of 'stephanephoros'. He is probably an 'eponymous' official, meaning that dates on documents, for example, would be made by reference to his name and office. Because he was permitted the recognition of wearing a crown at public occasions, he may also have awarded laurel crowns to victorious athletes, though this honour may not have extended to gladiators, who were always much lower on the status scale.*

reference to the *agonothete* or some other magistrate or the referee himself stepping in to stop a contest, perhaps a subtle reference to something witnessed in the theatre at Colossae. In fact, something like the intrusion envisioned in the letter, actually happened at Amisos (modern Samsun) on the Pontus. One tragic epitaph, now in the Cinquantenaire Museum in Brussels, laments the intervention of the chief referee (the *summa rudis* in Latin, here transliterated into Greek), who overturned the apparent result of the bout, forcing the combat to continue, with terminal consequences for the initial victor.

Soon, the theologians and bishops of the Church, following the lead of the Christian apologist Tertullian (c160–c225 CE), began to rehearse earlier, though isolated, pagan protests against the blood-curdling displays; some Christian dignitaries, for the good of someone's soul, even banned gladiators from being baptised. But for three hundred years or so, theatres like Colossae roared their approval for the contests playing out the viciousness of life before their eyes.

Nevertheless, we should not forget that theatres also accommodated the high cultured events of traditional tragedies and comedies and the requisite political assemblies. The ubiquity of theatre masks as adornments on statues, reliefs, painted rooms, mosaics, oil-lamps, figurines and jewelry shows how much the symbolism of the theatre pervaded everyday life. Masks were especially prevalent as reliefs

Plate 4.30, 31 *A 'secutor' scratched into the plaster of a terraced house at Ephesos on the left and a left-handed ('scaevus') gladiator scratched onto a pavement block at the forum in Philippi.*

Plate 4.32 *The late second century metrical epitaph of Diodoros the gladiator from Amisos. The wording reads:*
> *Here I languish: Diodoros the victorious, yet the dejected.*
> *Having destroyed Demetrios my opponent, I did not slay him straightway.*
> *But then deadly Fate and the conniving treachery of the summa rudis dispatched me;*
> *I have farewelled the light and trudged to Hades. Now I lie in the earth of my origins.*
> *In deference to pious duty, an honourable friend has buried me here.*

Plate 4.32

at the theatre, such as we find at the theatre at Myra (modern Kale), Aphrodisias and, recently discovered, at Stratonikeia. And there were a lot of masks from which to choose—the ancient writer Julius Pollux described around 76 known to him, with about 27 for use in tragic plays. These masks communicated across the distance from the stage to the seated spectators specific understandings of character, expressed through appearance and action. One surviving fragment of a hugely expensive sarcophagus found at Colossae has two identical tragic masks framing a Medusa's head (see Chapter Eight, *The Necropolis*). The mask is of a lamenting, grief-stricken woman and is probably representative of the muse, Melpomene, the patron of death and tragedy, but who was also called 'The Singer'. The wide mouth, the loosened hair, the forlorn eyes and furrowed brow all communicate the lament for the departed.

So, even though the theatre at Colossae is now quite bare, we can see, by piecing together the fragments of information that we have and by comparing other theatres in Asia Minor, just how important this institution was in Colossian life.

Plate 4.33, 34 *The tragic mask of the muse Melpomene on a sarcophagus from Colossae now on display at the Denizli Museum. At the right is a fresco of the muse holding her mask from the 'Room of the Muses' in Terraced House 2 at Ephesos.*

FRAGMENTS OF COLOSSAE

Select Bibliography - Chapter Four: The Theatre

Inscriptiones Graecae ad res Romanas pertinentes [*IGR*]. Volume IV, edited by R Cagnat, *et al*; Paris: E Leroux, 1927, §869.

Chariton *Challirhoe* 3.4.17

Julius Pollux *Onomasticon* 4.143–54.

Lucian *Demonax* 57.

Monumenta Asiae Minoris Antiqua [*MAMA*] *Vol VI: Monuments and Documents from Phrygia and Caria*. Edited by W Calder and W Buckler; Manchester: Manchester University Press, 1939, §§40, 49.

Pausanias *Travels* 5.14.9, 10.4.1.

Petronius *Satyricon* 117.

Picenini, A, 'Travel Diary: Asia Minor'. British Library Add Ms 6269.

Plutarch *Moralia* (*Precepts of Statecraft*) 802D–E.

Quintilian *Principles of Oratory* 2.11.2, 2.12.1, 2.17.33, 4.13.54, 10.5.20.

[Ps-]Quintilian *The Gladiator* (Major Declamation 9).

Seneca *Epistles* 71.23; *Controversies* 9.6.2.

Suetonius *Augustus* 44.2.

Tertullian *On Spectacles*.

Vitruvius *On Architecture* 5.3.

Ainsworth, W, *Travels in the Track of the Ten Thousand Greeks; being a Geographical and Descriptive Account of the Expedition of Cyrus and of the Retreat of the Ten Thousand Greeks as related by Xenophon*. London: John W. Parker, 1844.

Ashby, C, 'The Siting of Greek Theatres', in *Theatre Research International* 16 (1991): 181–201.

Bates, GE, *Byzantine Coins*, Archaeological Exploration of Sardis 1; Cambridge, Mass: Harvard University Press, 1971.

Baysal, HH, 'Le antiche città della valle del Lykos/Lykos Vadisindeki antik kentler' in *Ricerche Archeologiche Turche nella Valle del Lykos/Lykos Vadisi Türk Arkeoloji Arastirmalari*. Edited by F d'Andria and F Silvestrelli; Lecce: Congredo Editore, 2000, 19–41.

Bean, GE, *Turkey Beyond the Maeander*. London: John Murray, 1980.

Berve, H and G Gruben, *Greek Temples, Theatres and Shrines*. trans. R. Waterhouse; London: Thames & Hudson, 1963.

Cadwallader, AH, 'Revisiting Calder on Colossae', in *Anatolian Studies* 56 (2006): 103–11.

—'Assessing the Potential of Archaeological Discoveries for the Interpretation of New Testament Texts: The Case of a Gladiator Relief from Colossae and the Letter to the Colossians', in *The First Urban Churches*. Edited by J Harrison and LL Welborn; Atlanta, GA: SBL Press, 2015, 41-66.

Carter, MJ, 'Blown Call? Diodorus and the Treacherous *Summa Rudis*', in *Zeitschrift für Papyrologie und Epigraphik* 177 (2011): 63–69.

Chandler, RH, *Travels in Asia Minor and Greece or An Account of a Tour made at the Expense of the Society of Dilettanti.* London: J Booker, 1775.

Chase, RG, *Ancient Hellenistic and Roman Amphitheatres, Stadiums, and Theatres: The Way They Look Now.* Portsmouth, NH: Peter E Randall, 2002.

Fagan, GG, *The lure of the arena: social psychology and the crowd at the Roman games.* Cambridge: Cambridge University Press, 2011.

De Bernadi Ferrero, D, *Teatri Classici in Asia Minore.* 4 vols; Rome: L'Erma di Bretschneider, 1966–74.

Forni, G, 'L'indagine demografica e gli anfiteatri in Dacia', in *Apulum* 13 (1975): 141–54.

Frederiksen, P, 'The Greek Theatre. A Typical Building in the Urban Centre of the *Polis*?', in *Even More Studies in the Ancient Greek Polis.* Edited by TH Nielsen; Stuttgart: Franz Steiner, 2002, 65–124.

Goette, HR and P Wilson (eds), *The Men Who Built the Theatres: Theatropolai, Theatronai and Architektones.* Oxford: Oxford University Press, 2007.

Golden, M, *Greek Sport and Social Status* Austin TX: University of Texas Press, 2008.

Golvin, J-C, *L'amphithéâtre romain: Essai sur la theorisation de sa forme et de ses fonctions.* Paris: de Boccard, 1988.

Green, JR, *Theatre in Ancient Greek Society* London: Routledge, 1994.

Green, R and E Handley, *Images of the Greek Theatre.* London: British Museum Press, 1995.

Hamilton, WJ, 'Extracts from Notes made on a Journey in Asia Minor in 1836', in *Journal of the Royal Geographic Society of London* (1837): 34–61.

Hornum, MB, *Nemesis, the Roman State and the Games.* Leiden: Brill, 1993.

Hrychuk Kontokosta, AC, 'Gladiatorial Reliefs and élite funerary monuments' in *Aphrodisias Papers IV: New Research on the City and its Monuments.* Edited by C Ratté and RRR Smith; Portsmouth, RI: JRA, 2008, 190–229.

Isler, HP, 'Bemerkungen zu kleinasiatischen Theatern des Hellenismus', in *100 Jahre Österreichische Frisungen in Ephesos. Akten des Symposions.* Edited by H Fiesinger, and F Krinzinger; Wien: 1999, 683–688.

Konakçi, E and B Duman, 'The Silent Witness of the Mound of Colossae: Pottery Remains', in *Colossae in Space and Time.* Edited by AH Cadwallader and M Trainor; Göttingen: Vandenhoeck & Ruprecht, 2011, 247–81.

Lewin, T, *The Life and Epistles of St Paul.* London: Francis and John Rivington, 1851.

Moretti, JCh, 'L'architecture des théâtres en Asie Mineure (1980–1989)', in *ΤΟΠΟΙ* 2 (1992): 9–32.

Özi, Ü, 'Historical Water Schemes in Turkey', in *International Journal of Water Resources Development* 12.3 (1996): 347–84.

Patrich, J, *Studies in the Archaeology and History of Caesarea Maritima.* Leiden: Brill, 2011.

Pflaum, H-G, *Les Carrières Procuratoriennes Équestres sous le Haut-Empire romain.* Paris: P. Geuthner, Vol. 1, 1960.

Rawson, E, 'Discrimina Ordinum: The Lex Julia Theatralis', in *Papers of the British School at Rome* 55 (1987): 83–114.

Ritti, T and S Yilmaz, *Gladiatori e 'venationes' a Hierapolis di Frigia*. Rome: Accademia nazionale dei Lincei, 1998.

Robert, L, *Les gladiateurs dans l'Orient grec*. Limoges: Champion, 1940.

Rose, P, 'Spectators and Spectator Comfort in Roman Entertainment Buildings: A Study in Functional Design', in *Papers of the British School at Rome* 73 (2005): 99–130.

Roueché, C, 'Inscriptions and the Later History of the Empire', in *Aphrodisias Papers 2: The theatre, a sculptor's workshop, philosophers and coin-types*. Edited by RRR Smith and KT Erim; Portsmouth, RI: JRA, 1991), 99–108.

Sear, F, *Roman Theatres: An Architectural Study*. Oxford: Oxford University Press, 2006.

Seesengood, RP, *Competing Identities: The Athlete and the Gladiator*. London: T & T Clark, 2006.

Shadrake, S, *The World of the Gladiator*. Stroud: Tempus, 2005.

Staab, G, 'Zu den neuen Gladiatorenmonumenten aus Stratonikeia in Karien', in *Zeitschrift für Papyrologie und Epigraphik* 161 (2007): 35–46.

Texier, C, *Description de l'Asie mineure*. Paris: L'Institut de France, 1839.

Thonemann, P, 'Households and families in Roman Phrygia', in *Roman Phrygia: Culture and Society*. Edited by P Thonemann; Cambridge: Cambridge University Press, 2013, 124–42.

Ward, RB, 'Women in Roman Baths', in *Harvard Theological Review* 85 (1992): 125–47.

Weber, G, 'Der unterirdische Lauf des Lykos bei Kolossai', in *Athenische Mitteilungen* 16 (1891): 194–99.

Wiedemann, T, *Emperors and Gladiators*. London: Routledge, 1992.

Winter, F, *Studies in Hellenistic Architecture*. Toronto: University of Toronto Press, 2006.

Plate 5.1 *The höyük (artificial mound) of Colossae with the modern town of Honaz in the background at the rise of Honazdağ.*

CHAPTER 5
The Fortress

When some intrepid British soldiers blazed their expeditionary paths into Ottoman territory in southwest Asia Minor at the beginning of the nineteenth century, their knowledge about their travel routes was very limited. Although the area was thoroughly familiar to the local Turkish population, these officers relied instead on a modicum of classical languages and sufficient acquaintance with Roman history to know that ancient cities must be out there somewhere—cities like Colossae. Officers such as retired naval Captains Charles Irby and James Mangles, in their tour of Turkey in 1816 kept passing what they called 'artificial hills'. These were large mounds that often stood out sharply upon the surrounding plains. They surmised that 'it seems likely that they may have been thrown up for fortifications'; for them, the mounds had been fortress sites designed to protect the plains.

No doubt their military training coloured their perspectives; a clear view of plains and sea was, in their understanding, exactly what a military-minded leader would require. At the time, some local people agreed, dubbing the mound an 'unfinished fortress'. Archaeology has since recognised that these *höyüks*, these mounds or tells, are frequently the sites of ancient cities. These were the very things for which these English naval gentlemen were looking, though they hardly had archaeology in mind. They wanted landmarks to enable them to negotiate a country that, increasingly in the nineteenth century, was being eyed as strategically important by Russia and a range of European powers.

The secrets of the Colossae höyük

However, their surmise about an earth fortress is probably close to the truth—at least for the Colossae mound in its origins. Today the höyük is still very large, rising to between 40 and 65 metres and covering nearly ten hectares in its area above the plain. All over the site pottery fragments (called sherds) can be readily seen. What has proved something of a puzzle has been the presence of Bronze Age remains

Plate 5.2 *The sketch of the Colossae 'burrow' as drafted and named by Edmund Davis, 1870.*

along with the expected Greek, Roman and Byzantine evidence. Bronze Age finds were noted from limited surveys conducted by James Mellaart in 1951–54. But the most systematic analysis to date has been conducted by Erim Konakçi and Bahadır Duman of Pamukkale University. In fact, they found evidence of even earlier pottery, dating from the Chalcolithic Period (approximately 4500–3500 BCE) as well as the Bronze Age (approximately 3500–1200 BCE).

Plate 5.4

The importance for our understanding of the höyük is the location of these finds. They were recovered from the lower reaches of the hollow carved out of the eastern side of the höyük, the *cavea* of the ancient theatre.

The theatre was originally a Hellenistic construction that then garnered Roman modifications. The pottery evidence found at the base of the *cavea* suggests that the mound pre-dates the theatre by more than two millennia. In fact, like the theatre at Aphrodisias, the one at Colossae was excavated out of a pre-existing artificial hill.

The original purpose of such a mound is likely to have been defence and this suggests that some sort of wooden protective wall for an ancient settlement was secured around the earth mound. Probably the mound was lower than today but a further question remains. The Colossae höyük is in fact a joined double mound (bi-conical) and this leaves tantalizing questions about the pre-Hittite settlement at Colossae, about which we know little more than that it existed and later attracted a Hittite name that may be the forebear of 'Colossae'.

Plate 5.3 *Examples of pottery from the Chalcolithic and Bronze Ages found in the lower part of the* **cavea** *at Colossae, as identified by Erim Konakçi and Bahadır Duman of Pamukkale University.*
Plate 5.4 *The theatre* cavea *at the höyük.*

FRAGMENTS OF COLOSSAE

From the mound to the mountain—the medieval fortress of Colossae

The fortresses that are readily identifiable in the region today are far less easily climbed. These fortresses are perched, sometimes precariously, in lofty and almost impregnable positions on escarpments of mountain ranges in southern Turkey, including where they edge the sea. These fortresses ranged in functions from military bases to refuge sites and beacon stations. One at Konya is still used, situated atop a massive rocky outcrop, towering over the city and providing a strategic sweep of the surrounding area.

Many of the islands of the Aegean Sea contain such fortresses as well. These fortresses appear to have had a particular concern about protection from maritime attack, though this more likely from pirates than the arabs disturbing the mainland.

These sites were dismissed by some antiquarians and archaeologists, who used the quaint euphemism 'middle ages' to remove them from interest, simply because they were not Greek or Roman. But the fortress high on the slopes of Honazdağ, the ancient Mount Cadmus, did not initially receive this negative judgment. Described as almost inaccessible, it was interpreted by a number of early European travelers to the area as being the central site of ancient Colossae.

Plate 5.5 *The theatre at Aphrodisias is smaller than that of Colossae, but similar, with a* cavea *(auditorium) carved out of a pre-existing hill.*
Plate 5.6 *An example of a hilltop medieval fortress at Pergamon, according to an early postcard in the William Beamont collection, 1854.*

CHAPTER 4 - THE THEATRE

Plate 5.7

It was large, even if no longer in use when nineteenth-century explorers ventured through. It seemed to sweep along a large section of the spur and provided an encompassing view of the Lycus Valley running east to west to the north and held a commanding watch over the steep pass through the mountain range to the south.

The English geographer, JA Cramer, stated in 1832 that the fortress stretched for almost a mile along the ridge, confirming the sketch of Pitton de Tournefort one hundred years previously (see Chapter Two, *Stationing Armies in Colossae*). For some Europeans at that time, its size and tactical advantages compensated for the poverty and lack of any monumental remains on offer in the district—including at one of those höyüks close by. And so, when etchings or sketches were provided in Bible dictionaries or travel journals of the early to mid-nineteenth century, the fortress above Honaz was promoted as the site of ancient Colossae—or at least its acropolis of sorts. William Nicholson's *Bible Explainer* for example hoped to enlighten his early nineteenth-century readers by stating that 'The site of the ancient city is now occupied, partly by a village, and partly with the debris of the former city; the principal ruins of which are some fragments of old walls on the rock upon which the castle stands …'

Plate 5.8

THE ROLE OF THE BYZANTINE FORTRESS

In fact this fortress, like scores of others in mountainous regions of southern Turkey, is a Byzantine foundation. The earliest of such garrisons probably was built sometime in the seventh to eighth century as Arab raiders made

Plate 5.7 *The view from the fortress overlooking the modern town of Honaz.*
Plate 5.8 *View of a section of the fortress ruins high above the Lycus Valley.*

Plate 5.9 *View from the fortress to the eastern end of the Lycus Valley, where the Royal Road led eastwards to Apameia and beyond to Susa.*
Plate 5.10 *Francis Arundell's 1828 sketch which is titled 'Chonas,—anciently Colossæ' showing the castle fortress on the mountain, upper left (compare Plate 1.14). The name 'Chonas' (which Arundell sometimes spelt 'Khonos') is the forerunner of today's 'Honaz'.*
Plate 5.11 *Aerial view of the craggy outcrop that held the fortress. The 'old kilise' was refashioned as a mosque by Sultan Murad II (1404–1451) before the fall of Constantinople. It sits in the lower centre of the photograph and the mountain pass in Arundell's sketch is in the upper sector. The fortress occupied almost the entirety of this area.*

their often brutal plundering incursions into the rich agricultural and trade areas of the plains. By the ninth century, as archaeologists Hugh Barnes and Mark Whittow point out, the 'Byzantine state's network of castles' had become extremely extensive and generally reflected the move of most settlements away from open plains and into side valleys. Land in the plain continued to be worked, but by labourers and land-owners operating under the protection of a more secure base. Sometimes churches continued to operate in confidence. For example, the Church of St Michael, probably located not far from the höyük, continued to hold its massive pilgrim feast each September, a panegyric that attracted hundreds of visitors through to the mid-thirteenth century. But church and festivities were well under the watchful eye of the mountain fortress.

The fortress at Honaz was especially important because of its strategic position in relation to the length and breadth of the Lycus and Maeander Valleys. It became so crucial to the military and administrative structure of the empire under the Byzantine emperors that the eminent Byzantine historian, Clive Foss, thinks that the city at Chonai (Colossae's later name), over which the fortress kept watch, was made the capital of the 'theme' (the province/region) called Thrakesion in the Byzantine Empire, at least for a time. (Ephesos appears to have regained its status as the capital in the thirteenth century.) Laodikeia's vulnerability on the plain meant that it lost its preeminent position, though it retained its ecclesiastical status with the title of 'metropolis', a tag that, in the mid-tenth century CE, came to be applied to

Plates 5.12, 13 *At the left, is a section of protective wall of the Byzantine fortress. At right, is a section of the crag that was quarried out to form an area for a building in the fortress complex.*

Chonai as well. In fact, the great defender of icons, Theodore of Studios, wrote in the early ninth century of an exarch (commander) who had military responsibility for five themes, not just Thrakesion, but who was based at Chonai. And Yacut, the Arab chronicler commissioned by King Roger II of Sicily (1095–1154) to provide a survey of the Byzantium Empire, drew on earlier sources that credited the theme of Thrakesion as having 10,000 troops stationed in it. The bulk of these were doubtless deployed from Chonai, watching over the site that is now popularly called Colossae, and the Lycus Valley plain, ensuring that pilgrimages, churches and agriculture could remain safe. Certainly from the ancient mound of Colossae comes coin and pottery evidence that that part of Colossae/Chonai was still well-patronised. Such patronage is bolstered by a sense of security conveyed by the fortress.

The notice that Chonai receives in Arabic and Greek literary texts gives a clear indication of just how important Chonai was to the Byzantine empire from the eighth to the thirteenth centuries. But from 1070 Chonai moved in and out of Turkish hands as well. Chonai became a much-desired centre for Byzantines and Turks not only in their struggles with each other but also among themselves. Both Pseudo-Alexis (assassinated in 1196) and Theodore Mangaphas (died in captivity c.1205), in their ambitions to be made emperor, prized Chonai as a key place in their strategies—holding the fortress provided a more secure base for their plans. A

Plate 5.14 *An 'anonymous follis' coin found on the höyük of Colossae by Erim Konakçı and Bahadır Duman. It was minted at Constantinople probably during the reign of Michael IV the Paphlagonian (1031–1041 CE) or shortly after under his successor, Constantine IX Monomachus. But instead of bearing the image of the emperor, it has a half-length figure of Jesus Christ on the obverse (at the left). He is recognised by the nimbus halo with a pellet or small boss in each band around his head, the abbreviations for his name, IC-XC, to the left and right of his head and the words XC Emmanouêl around the perimeter. The reverse (at the right) is framed around a central equilinear cross, adorned with pellet-strings. Each quadrant contains part of a phrase (reading from top to bottom) IC-XC-NI-KA which means* Iêsous Christos nika, *'Jesus Christ conquers'.*

key sign of how important the fortress was at this time was the new Emperor Theodore I's willingness in 1206 to sign Chonai over to the Seljuk Sultan Ghiyath al-Din Kay-Khusraw I in return for the promise of support for his reign. Although there was a brief return to direct Byzantine rule in 1257, by 1261 the area was firmly in Turkish hands and by 1429 had become integrated into the Ottoman administrative system. Significantly, it appears from Ottoman records that Honaz remained a hub for 30 or so small villages in the area, indicating that it continued to be regarded as a centre of control and protection.

However, this did not mean an end to the struggles for control of the fortress. Different power groups within Turkish military politics manoevured for the site, including a succession of members of the Bey family in the thirteenth and fourteenth centuries. As late as the eighteenth century, the rebel aga, Soley Bey Ogle was using the fortress as his defiant post, even installing cannons in its battlements. The purported discovery of a coin of Sultan Ahmed III (ruled 1703-30) within the fortress area lends credence to the notion of the continued importance of this strategic base (though single coin finds are notoriously difficult to interpret).

The town of Denizli was established in the thirteenth century (under the leadership of Esedüddin Ayaz), replacing Laodikeia as a population centre. But the fortress of Chonai, now known as Honaz, remained celebrated (sometimes over against Denizli), as in the glowing language in this poem for Murad bin Mehmed, responsible for the establishment of a mosque within the battlements.

Plate 5.15 *Byzantine pottery from the site of the Colossae höyük collected by Erim Konakçi and Bahadır Duman of Pamukkale University.*

Plate 5.16 *A coin of Ahmed III (Sultan 1703-1730), from a private Turkish collection, was reported as found at the fortress above Chonai. The zeri gold coin has the long-standing sultan's 'tughra' symbol on the obverse (front) face and the 'Düribe fi İslâmbol' legend on the reverse, both beautifully crafted in exquisite calligraphic style. 'Düribe fi İslâmbol' simply means 'minted in Istanbul' (İslâmbol being an early Ottoman re-naming of Constantinople).*

FRAGMENTS OF COLOSSAE

> A prized birthplace is the castle of Honaz
>
> Clearly it holds a special place in the principality of Germiyan
>
> The sultan's castles and cities may be plentiful
>
> But this castle is exalted above all the others.

Features of the fortress area

Today the fortress is in ruins but enough of the various buildings remain to indicate its vast size. There are large cisterns, so important to maintain the life of a fortress city, that still retain some of the hydraulic plaster that seals the vaulted room so that precious water can be stored.

Early sketches of the fortress indicate the presence of a mosque within its walls. This almost certainly was a converted church. In 1705, the Italian traveller, Picenini, departed for a brief period from the larger expedition led by the Englishman, Edward Chishull, and recorded that there was a church in the castle on the mountain slope. The building's remains still stand on the steep climb of the mountain, though its clear enclosure by the castle has evaporated with time. The church style is a variety of an octagon.

Its conversion to a mosque—the 'Sultan Murad Cami'—with the final cementing of Turkish control of the site, was accompanied also by the laying out of an area for use as a cemetery. Some eighteenth and nineteenth century grave markers still remain.

Significantly, stone from Byzantine buildings can be seen in parts of the graveyard, a witness to how much the area on and around the höyük of Colossae became a supplier of stone for the new defences. One archaeologist of the early twentieth century, George Lampakis, reported that one stone, then being used as a grave border, contained an ancient Greek inscription, though this is no longer visible.

Plate 5.17 *Remains of the Byzantine fortress buildings above the town of Honaz.*

Many of the materials used to build the castle fortress, just as the remains in the old cemetery indicate, were quarried from across the broad city site of Colossae less than three kilometres to the north. One footing of a wall of a building, for example, is supplied by a long column that is identical in proportions and composition to one found in the river running through the central site of Colossae and similar to two in the eastern fields on the approach from Honaz. Such re-deployment is typical of Byzantine practice, but the comparative barrenness of architectural remains at the central site of Colossae can be explained by the extent of the re-use of materials from the site in other places, such as for the Ak-khan (or caravanserai).

Plate 5.18 *Remains of one cistern at the fortress above Honaz.*
Plate 5.19 *Hydraulic plaster lining in the cistern.*
Plate 5.20 *Arch rib reinforcing the cistern ceiling.*
Plate 5.21 *Remains of the 'old kilise' amid modern graves. A section of the old fortress wall can be seen lower left of centre next to the small tree.*

At the bridge where we passed over the Lycus there is an antient well-built kane, called Accan; it is of white marble, and was doubtless built out of some antient ruin. I saw a head of a statue in the walls, a relief of a Medusa's head and another stone with a relief on it of two dragons.

Richard Pococke 1745

The mountain fortress that surveyed and guarded the eastern and southern entrances into the Lycus Valley, was also one of the beneficiaries of this sort of reassignment, quarrying parts of the old city environment at an earlier period than the khan. The fortress therefore is a long-standing witness to the importance of ancient Colossae, precisely because it is filled with its fragments.

Plate 5.22, 23 *Late Ottoman grave stones near the 'old kilise'.*
Plates 5.24, 25 *Remains of a late antique column section with palmette flutes at the still-used cemetery near the Byzantine church-become-early-Ottoman mosque. At right, a broken section of a clay-fired tile.*

CHAPTER 5 - THE FORTRESS

SELECT BIBLIOGRAPHY - CHAPTER FIVE: THE FORTRESS

Constantinus Porphyrogenitus *On the Themes* 1.3.
Theodore of Studios *Epistle* 2.63.
Yakut VI.864.

Arundell, FVJ, *A Visit to the Seven Churches of Asia Minor with an excursion into Pisidia*. London: John Rodwell, 1828.
Barnes, H and M Whittow, 'The Survey of Medieval Castles of Anatolia (1992–96)', in *Ancient Anatolia*. Edited by R Matthews; London: BIAA, 1998, 347–58.
Baykara, T, *Selçuklular ve Beylikler Çağında: Denizli, 1070–1520*. Istanbul: IQ Kültür Sanat, 2005.
Belke, K and N Mersich, *Tabula Imperii Byzantini Bd 7: Phrygien und Pisidien*. Vienna: Österreichischen Akademie der Wissenschaft, 1990.
Brooks, EW, 'Arabic Lists of the Byzantine Themes', in *Journal of the Hellenic Society* 21 (1901): 67–77.
Cahen, C, 'Notes pour l'Histoire des Turcomans dans l'Asie Mineure au XIIIe Siècle: La premiére Principauté turcomaine de Denizli', in *Journal Asiatique* 239.3 (1951): 335–49.
Chandler, R, *Travels in Asia Minor and Greece or An Account of a Tour made at the Expense of the Society of Dilettanti*. London: J Booker, 1775
Chishull, E, *Travels in Turkey and Back to England*. London: W. Bowyer, 1747.
Cramer, JA, *A Geographical and Historical Description of Asia Minor*. Oxford: OUP, 2 vols, 1832.
Foss, C, *Byzantine fortifications: an introduction*. Pretoria: University of South Africa, 1986.
—*Survey of Medieval Castles of Anatolia I: Kütahya, II: Nicodemia*. London: BIAA, 1985, 1996.
—'Chonai' in *The Oxford Dictionary of Byzantium*. Edited by AP Kazhdan; New York / Oxford: Oxford University Press, 1991, 427.
—'The Survey of Medieval Castles of Anatolia, 1982–1984', in *Ancient Anatolia*. Edited by R Matthews; London: BIAA, 1998, 359–66.
Hacigökmen, MA, 'Türkiye Selçluklulari Zamanında Konya'nın Devlet Merkezi Oluşu', in *Türkiyat Araştırmaları Dergisi* 25 (2011): 231–60.
Irby, Capt C and Capt J Mangles, *Travels in Egypt and Nubia, Syria and Asia Minor during the years 1817 and 1818*. London: T White, 1823.

Konakçi, E and B Duman, 'Arkeolojik ve Yazılı Kanıtlar Işığında Kolossai (Kolossai with the Light of Archaeological and Historical Evidences)', in *International Symposium on the History and Culture of Denizli and its Surroundings*. Denizli: Pamukkale University, 2007, Vol 2, 57–67.

— 'The Silent Witness of the Mound of Colossae: Pottery Remains', in *Colossae in Space and Time: Linking with an Ancient City*. Edited by AH Cadwallader and M Trainor; Göttingen: Vandenhoeck and Ruprecht, 2011, 247–81.

Kutlu, M, 'Seljuk Caravanserais in the Vicinity of Denizli: Han-Abad (Çardakhan) and Akhan', Unpublished Master's Thesis, Bilkent University, Ankara, 2009.

Lampakis, G, *Οἱ ἑπτὰ ἀστέρες τῆς Ἀποκαλύψεως*. Athens: 1909.

Lewis, PE, 'Colossae: The Buried City', in *The Australasian Coin & Banknote Magazine* 16 (2013): 1–4.

Mellaart, J, 'Preliminary Report on a Survey of Pre-Classical Remains in Southern Turkey', in *Anatolian Studies* 4 (1954): 175–240.

Nicholson, W, *Bible Explainer*. New York: Fleming H Revell, 1900.

Niehwöhner, P *et al*, 'Bronze Age höyüks, Iron Age hilltop forts, Roman poleis and Byzantine pilgrimage in Germia and its vicinity. 'Connectivity' and a lack of 'definite places' on the central Anatolian high plateau', in *Anatolian Studies* 63 (2013): 97–113.

Picenini, A, 'Travel Diary, Asia Minor [1750]'; (British Library, Add Ms 6269).

Pococke, R, *Description of the East and Some Other Countries*. 2 vols; London: W Bowyer, 1745.

Sear, DR, *Byzantine Coins and their values*. London: Seaby Press, 2nd Ed, 2000.

Sear, F, *Roman Theatres: An Architectural Study*. Oxford: Oxford University Press, 2006.

Ünal, MA, 'XVI. Yüzyılda Honaz Kazası', in *International Symposium on the History and Culture of Denizli and its Surroundings*. (Denizli: Pamukkale University, 2007), vol 1, pp 103–111.

Uslu, K, MF Bezayit and T Kara *Ottoman Empire Coins 1687–1839*. Istanbul: Sahsi, 2010.

Plate 6.1 *The Colossae höyük viewed from the southern edge of the necropolis with the cloud-capped Taurus mountains behind.*

CHAPTER 6
Weaving Threads: Clothing in Colossae
Rosemary Canavan

Nestled in the Lycus Valley, the ancient city of Colossae, like its neighbouring cities of Laodikeia and Hierapolis (Pamukkale), was built on the banks of the Lycus (today's Çürüksu) River. Flowing by the mountain of Salbakos (Babadağ) in the west and Mount Cadmus (Honazdağ) in the south, the river provided water and its alluvial deposits to a valley subject to seismic activity. The resulting topography of undulating plains and water catchment offered good pasture and settlement conditions. In this place the textile industry of the Lycus Valley developed. There was opportunity for cooperation but also reason for competition. The changing fortunes of Colossae must be considered in part to be due to this competition.

Unfolding the development of this textile industry begins with the context of the valley and its resources that make textile trade viable. Once the context is established the investigation can move to the components of the industry, incorporating all the allied processes from shepherding sheep, to dyeing and weaving in and around Colossae. These are pieced together from the available inscriptional and visual material. There are very few texts related to the ancient city of Colossae. The Letter to the Colossians that appears in the New Testament of the Christian Bible therefore assumes special significance. This letter was written in the first century CE to a community of Christ followers and it exhorted them to clothe themselves with virtues and love.

The context

The record of human remains in this area date to the Chalcolithic Age (4500–3500 BCE) with numerous cultural artefacts belonging to the Bronze Age (3500–1200 BCE). The importance of the locality is attested by the succession of rulers who took control of the area including Hittites, Phrygians, Lydians, Persians, Hellenes, Pergamenes and Romans. Each of these rulers recognised the agricultural potential of this valley and its strategic placement for trade.

At the same time, the art of domestication of animals and weaving and dyeing of cloth developed. Hittite clay tablets from about 1500 BCE record the quality of pasture and well-fed sheep. Blue-purple and red-purple woollen fabrics are noted as a means of payment of tribute in an agreement between Ugarit and Hittite leaders.

Colossae, as one of the oldest cities in the region, is first mentioned by the ancient historian, Herodotos (c484–c425 BCE), when he wrote of the campaign of the Persian King Xerxes against Athens in 480 BCE. Herodotos noted that Xerxes passed through Colossae. Then in 401 BCE Xenophon, while travelling with Cyrus, brother of the Persian King and attempted usurper of the throne, recorded that he stayed seven days in Colossae. Xenophon (c430–c354 BCE) identified Colossae as 'a city, prosperous and large'

Plate 6.2

using, within a few lines, the same language he used for Celaenae, a city (also called Apameia) approximately 100 kilometres further east, where Cyrus had an estate with a forest and wild animals for hunting. Celaenae (modern Dinar) is also situated on a river, the Maeander (Menderes), a further parallel to the Colossian terrain. While in residence in Colossae, Cyrus performed animal sacrifice indicating that domestic animals were available there.

Laodikeia (Goncalı-Eskihisar) was established by Antiochus II (261–246 BCE) on the site of previous settlements successively named Diospolis and Rhoas. Though a smaller city than Colossae at first, fortunes were to change substantially with Laodikeia flourishing as both a Hellenistic and then a Roman centre. The naming of Laodikeia as *conventus juridicus*, seat of Roman judiciary, assisted the rise of Laodikeia as the focal point of trade in the Lycus Valley at the crucial intersection of trade routes. The existence of a communication and trade route, from Miletos via the Maeander Valley to Phrygia, is recorded as early as the sixth century BCE by Hipponax, a poet from Ephesos. In light of both Xerxes and Cyrus passing through Colossae, it appears that this route was established prior to the founding of Laodikeia in 261–253 BCE. Miletos was one of the central art and trade centres of the Hellenistic period and from 133 BCE, under the Romans, the city became a major metropolis of Asia. This route passed through to Celaenae-Apameia and continued east.

The Roman road from Ephesos to Magnesia (modern Tekin), Tralles (Aydin), Antiocheia (near Kuyucak), Laodikeia and Apameia was built in 130 BCE by the Roman consul in the province of Asia, Manius Aquilius. The road from Pergamon (Bergama) to Laodikeia on Lycus is recorded in the third-century (CE) Roman survey register, the Antonine Itinerary and the map known as the Peutinger Table. Clearly, this was an important travel route. The road went via Germe, Thyatira (Akhisar), Sardis (Sart), Philadelphia (Alaşehir), Tripolis (Yenicekent-Buldan), Hierapolis (Pamukkale) and on to Laodikeia. These two roads from Ephesos and Pergamon both came into the Lycus Valley meeting in Laodikeia. Colossae was not mentioned in the Peutinger Table as being on the East-West trade route, but is included by the late nineteenth century archaeologist, William Mitchell Ramsay, as a station on that route. Laodikeia and then Apameia were

Plate 6.2 *The view east towards Colossae, down Syria Street in the heart of Laodikeia*

considered the main intersection points where the north-south roads came together with this trade route. The strategic placement of these cities assisted the prominence of Laodikeia as the centre of trade for the Lycus Valley.

The ancient geographer, philosopher and historian, Strabo (c64 BCE – c24 CE) related the excellence of the black wool from the sheep at Laodikeia and included Colossae as sharing this great resource. Richard Pococke, traveller to the site during his journeys in the East, 1737–41, recalled Strabo's comments concerning the black sheep. Pococke affirmed the truth of this and observed, 'three parts of them being black in all the country from Naslee to this place, and some of them are black and white like the Ethiopian sheep'. In contrast, Richard Chandler, travelling only twenty years later in 1764–65, remarks that of the sheep he saw brought to the Laodikeian ruins by shepherds at night, there were 'only one or two which were very black and glossy'.

The 'glossy black' wool of Laodikeia and the 'glossy violet-dark' wool of Colossae was attributed to selection and cross-breeding of the sheep. Marcus Vitruvius Pollio (c80/70 BCE – c15 BCE) was an author, architect and engineer. In his writings on architecture, he suggested that the secret of the colour of the wool lay in the sheep being taken daily in breeding time to drink the water. Vitruvius is not complimentary about this water but, rather, described it as 'foul smelling'. The Lycus Valley is still sheep country today but the black sheep are no longer in evidence in any number beyond the few dark sheep that have been sighted in the high country above Colossae.

Plate 6.3, 4 *White sheep on Honazdağ and, at right, white sheep in the Hierapolis ruins. Photographs by the late Julie Hooke.*

Hierapolis (Pamukkale), whose white travertine terraces are visible from Laodikeia, was a key centre for washing and dyeing due to its excellent hot springs. As Strabo explained, 'The water at Hierapolis is remarkably adapted also to the dyeing of wool, so that wool dyed with the roots rival those dyed with the coccus or with the marine purple.' The mineral salts of the waters of Hierapolis (Pamukkale) supply a mordant that is able to set vegetable dyes to an extent that competed with the dye extracted from the murex mollusc (known not just from Tyre but also from the coastal districts of Caria in south-west Turkey).

An inscription from the business district in Laodikeia uncovered in recent excavations has identified a place of the dyers and a small dyeing workshop. It is dated to the fifth century CE. Almost certainly, Colossae boasted its own local industry as well. But Hierapolis (Pamukkale) because of its hot springs gushing forth in the urban centre became a prime location over a long period for textile production in the Lycus Valley.

The general picture therefore is of a group of cities with a valuable resource in their high quality wool and the allied industries of textile manufactures and dyeing. It is to the textile industry that I now turn.

Plate 6.5, 6 *Hierapolis (Pamukkale) travertine cliffs where the calciferous waters, flowing out of springs, cool and crystalise into white cascades.*

THE TEXTILE INDUSTRY: SHEEP AND SHEPHERDS

Vital to this industry was the tending and pasturing of the sheep. Since antiquity there has been evidence of shepherds on the north Phrygian highlands. In fact, Herodotos noted that the Phrygians were 'most well-endowed with sheep'. Eight hundred years later, the Roman poet, Claudian, noted the region of Phrygia as 'blessed with flocks'. In the second century CE shepherds are immortalised in rough-hewn depictions at a rural sanctuary at Amorion (Hisarköy) and elsewhere. Sheep have been a constant farming activity in the region for millennia.

An inscription at Laodikeia refers to an association of graziers and resembles a similar guild at Hierapolis (Pamukkale). The farmers in this region were most likely grazing sheep and goats. Their livelihood relied on good pasture and there was competition for the best lands in and around the valley, not only between similar agricultural pursuits but also between diverse interests in the land. One second or third century inscription from Dionysopolis, about 28 kilometres to the north of Colossae, records a judgment in favour of viticulturists against those allowing their animals to graze on vineyard land, to the cost of the vines. No doubt this was far from an isolated conflict.

Plate 6.7, 8 *At the left are examples of the murex mollusc from which is extracted a rich purple dye, crucial to the aristocratic colour used in fine textile products in the ancient world. Hittite as well as Tyrian trade in this dye came to be rivalled by the dye extracted from the madder root, at right, once it had been fastened by the highly mineralised waters at Hierapolis. The Lycus River contained similar mineral content and this fostered the quality of wool, natural and dyed, that came from Colossae.*

Animal husbandry is attested on a stele from Colossae currently in the garden of the Denizli Archaeological Museum where three pigs, increasing in size, are depicted along the base of a funerary monument. The livelihood and business of the deceased was invested with these animals, with which he is remembered in his death. Underneath the funerary couch above the pigs is a dog, farmhand to the pig farmer. The celebration in death inscribed in marble indicates a prosperous business.

Just how important the industry was, is attested on another epitaph from Laodikeia which has a pig's head as one of the delicacies on the funerary banquet table.

There are quite a number like this from the general region. At the foot of the usual funerary table carved into another large marble stele in the Denizli Museum depot, are two sheep, not the usual family dog. The funerary stele was raised to Munatius by his children. The specific provenance is unknown but it does come from somewhere in the Denizli area and is dated to the second or third century CE, providing clear evidence of the area's sheep farming. The Italian epigrapher, Professor Tullio Ritti, added two similar epitaphs to this in his collection from Denizli Museum, both previously unpublished. One, from the same period, is a pedimentary stele honouring Alexandros son of Stephanos and his wife Tatas and has inscribed figures in an arch in the pediment (that is the triangular shape at the top of the stone) of a calf on either side and a sheep in the middle, indicating that this family raised cattle and sheep. Its exact provenance is also unknown but it does come from the Lycus Valley region. A further fragment

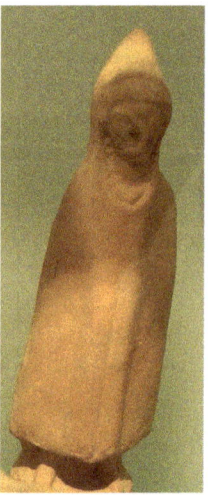

Plate 6.9

Plate 6.10

Plate 6.9, 10 *Above is a rare terracotta figurine of a hooded cloaked shepherd, at Amphipolis Museum. This garb is found on many stone reliefs, often epitaphs, from Phrygia. Below is a modern shepherd with his sheep at Colossae.*

116   FRAGMENTS OF COLOSSAE

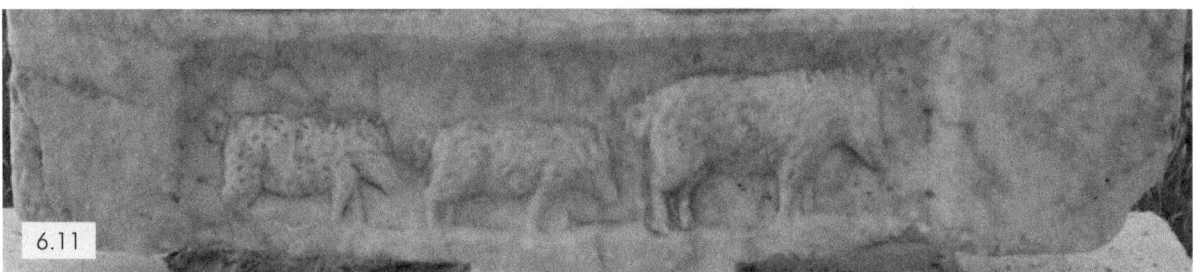

of a stele has an illegible inscription, other than *in memoria*, and depicts the deceased with grapes on either side of his head and in the corner, between the arch and frame of the pediment, a goat. These previously unpublished steles add significantly more information about the agricultural mix of the region and provide strong evidence for the textile industry. The importance of sheep husbandry is so great that at times sheep have replaced the usual presence of the family dog on these funeral reliefs.

Plate 6.11 *Detail of the pigs at the base of a stele from Colossae commemorating the pig farmer. For the full funerary relief of the pig dealer, see chapter 8* The Necropolis.

Plate 6.12 *The fragmentary funerary epitaph of Adrastos, Ailiane and Diokles. The reclining couple with cups of wine in hand are flanked by a seated woman who supplies the pig's head and a seated man who provides the grapes to go with the bread.*
Plate 6.13 *This small, probably fragmentary epitaph (without inscription) comes from the Phrygian highlands and is now located in the grounds of the Roman baths at Ankara. It is noteworthy for the 'elevated' place of sheep in the couple's lives.*

Shepherds were always on the move, seeking out the best seasonal grazing options around the Lycus valley; they probably extended their wanderings to Aphrodisias (modern Geyre), Trapezopolis (near Bolu), Tripolis, Hydriale (Sigma Kasabası) and Carura (Tekkeköy). The significance of sheep-raising in this region is exemplified through the repetition of a depiction of a local manifestation of Zeus: *Zeus Ktesis Patrios*, which means something like Zeus the protector of the property of one's inheritance. Significantly perhaps, the honouring of this form of Zeus was to be done with a vessel that had its handles covered with white wool, at least according to the fourth century (BCE) expert on ritual, Autokleides. At Herakleia Salbake (near modern Vakıf), not far from Colossae, were found three images of the god (now in the Denizli Archaeological Museum): a stone relief showing the god grazing his sheep; a small square altar revealing the god on the front in carved woollen clothing, and on one side a dog and on the other a bolt of lightning; and a funerary relief with Zeus holding an eagle-topped crook in the left hand and a second eagle in the other and wearing woollen clothing. On this funerary relief the distinct texturing of the clothing indicates a heavier cloth of rough wool weave or perhaps felt that might have functioned as both cloak and blanket.

Plate 6.14

Plate 6.15

Also at the Denizli Archaeological Museum is a stele, given a Laodikeian provenance, which celebrates a certain Papias Klexos, as shepherd. William Ramsay suggested he was in charge of large flocks and other shepherds. Alternative readings of this stele identify Papias as bishop and shepherd of the people. Whichever is the true reading, this stele further confirms that the imagery of the shepherd was notable in this region.

The textile industry: trade

Already noted previously is the strategic positioning of Laodikeia at the intersection of trade routes, linking the Lycus Valley through Sardis (Sart) to Smyrna (İzmir), through Apamea to Pisidian Antioch (near Yalvaç) and beyond, as well as south to Attaleia (today's Antalya). Without the trade flow, the wool and garments would have likely remained local produce.

Plate 6.14 *Altar of Zeus Ktesis Patrios with a leaping dog on the side.*
Plate 6.15 *Funerary relief with Zeus Ktesis Patrios and a small figure of youthful Hermes, himself a famous controller of animals, at his right.*

Inscribed on a mausoleum among the ruins at Hierapolis (possibly dated before 260 CE) is the name of one merchant trader who certainly facilitated the trade flow. Titus Flavius Zeuxis sailed to Italy seventy-two times. Celal Şimşek surmises that Zeuxis transported the woven products manufactured in Hierapolis to the port of Ephesos and then by ship to Mediterranean countries. While the inscription does not give that detail, it does indicate that there were merchants like him operating the trade lines of Asia Minor and across to Italy, and if they even approach the distance Zeuxis covered (some 16,000 kilometres in all) then these were much-frequented, busy routes.

In contrast, a stele from Apollonia Salbake (near Tavas), depicts a man, Menas of Kibyra (Gölhisar), leading his mule. The mule has a saddle or blanket over his back. The illustration on the stele suggests he is a merchant or perhaps a muleteer carrying mail. He probably did not travel as far as Zeuxis even though he would have fulfilled just as important a trade function.

A recent discovery in 2005 of a pedestal lodged in the riverbed at Colossae yielded an inscription for Markos son of Markos, chief interpreter. This single find, dated late first to early second century, reveals the diversity of languages in this region, reflecting the various ethnicities of traders. As chief interpreter, Markos was the head of a team of interpreters in the civic administration. Located at Colossae it is possible that Markos and his team provided services to the Lycus Valley, especially those coming from the East, thereby adding to the contribution Colossae made to the region's trade.

Plate 6.16 *The stele is carved from marble rather than the local limestone; this adds to the honour and status accorded Papias Klexos. The stele is inscribed with a wreath, crowning him in death. There is a rosette on the top pediment. The inscription reads 'Papias Klexos, shepherd and worthy hero. Greetings to the passers-by.'*

Plate 6.17 *The first century (CE) tomb of Titus Flavius Zeuxis, a much-travelled merchant of Hierapolis. The inscription on the mausoleum reads, 'Flavius Zeuxis having sailed to Malea in Italy by ship seventy-two times, raised a memorial for himself and for the children Flavius Theodorus and Flavius Theudas and for any others for whom they make room.'*

CHAPTER 6 - WEAVING THREADS: CLOTHING IN COLOSSAE

The textile industry: the workers

In the first century, Gaius Plinius Secundus (23–79 CE), a Roman author, naturalist and natural philosopher, was acclaimed for his writing of *Naturalis Historia*. While Pliny the Elder, as he is known, did not focus on the textile or tanning trades, his work provides the best history of these crafts. Pliny records that trade in raw materials, such as unprocessed or semi-processed wool, is as important as the textile trade itself. This textile trade is not confined to wool or woolen garments but includes linen and silk, yarns, garments, cloths and rugs plus the essential support industry of dyeing. It was general practice to dye the wool rather than the garment. The water of Hierapolis ensured strong colours from vegetable dyes such as the madder root. What emerges is a landscape that offered opportunity for cooperation and competition between neighbouring cities, cooperative home-based trades and associations of weavers, dyers and other textile workers.

Plate 6.18

A large heroon dated to the second or third century CE currently rests near the bath complex and before the Arches of Domitian, the triple portal of the Frontinus Gate at the northern end of the main street of Hierapolis. This heroon bears the inscription of honour by the association of the dye workers.

Hierapolis (Pamukkale) has a significant number of inscriptions naming the association of dyers and purple dyers. An honorary inscription for an unknown procurator, a high-ranking Imperial official, is offered by the revered association of purple dyers (*porphurabathōn*) in the first to second century CE. Another tomb honours the council of presidents of the purple dyers. It certainly appears that working in purple, even of the madder root, had gained significant patronage and prestige. According to a full inscription from the late second to early third century CE, Marcus Aurelius Diodorus Corescus bequeathed 3000 *denarii* to this council of the association of purple-dyers for the provision of poppies to be burnt on the tomb on the customary day of remembrance of the deceased. Should this be neglected the remainder of the capital was to go to the association of shepherds, thus indicating the proximity of industry and status between these two groups of workers.

In nearby Laodikeia, fullers (*aplougoi*), who both finished newly woven garments and also cleaned soiled ones, are attested in inscriptions. And, again in Hierapolis (Pamukkale), an association of water-mill workers is thought to have been primarily engaged in providing water for fullers of that city.

Plate 6.18 *The pedestal honouring 'Markos son of Markos, chief interpreter and translator of the Colossians', was discovered in 2005 in the bed of the Lycus River near the traditional site of the church of St Michael.*

There is evidence of similar guilds, associations or *collegia* throughout Asia Minor. These include linen weavers (*linuphoi*) in Tralles (Aydin), linen weavers working flax in Thyatira (Akhisar) as well as spinners and weavers (*linourgoi*) and carders/woolworkers (*lanarioi*), and wool workers (*eriougoi*) in Philadelphia. In Miletos (near Balat) we also find linen weavers (*linourgoi*) recorded and in Ephesos (Selçuk) towel weavers (*lentiuphantai*) as well as carders/woolworkers (*lanarioi*). There are other wool processors who are organized in associations: carders, combers, dyers (*bapheis*), felters and fullers (*grapheis*). One can see that there

Plate 6.19

was quite a range of specialised work in the textile industry, each esteemed to such an extent that those involved felt completely at home to have their group displayed publically in inscriptions and monuments.

Plate 6.20

Plate 6.19, 20 *The 'heroon' set up by the association of dye workers at Hierapolis. A 'heroon' is a funeral monument that in its structure is little different from other large tombs but may not contain the remains of the deceased; rather they are honoured as 'heroes' (hence the name 'heroon'). The term 'hero' had become quite democratised in the late republican and early imperial period, no longer restricted to those who emulated the feats of a Herakles or Achilles. Here it implies that the members of the dye-workers' association are so remembered. The inscription in the detailed photograph section reads: 'The association of dye workers honours this heroon'.*

CHAPTER 6 - WEAVING THREADS: CLOTHING IN COLOSSAE

Comparisons of associations in Sattai (İçikler) and Thyatira in Lydia with those in Hierapolis (Pamukkale) show that there were local differences in how these associations displayed their worth. The inscriptions on funerary monuments in Hierapolis are on sarcophagi or on buildings with funerary beds, while in Sattai they are commonly stylized on stelai and in Thyatira they are mostly found on statue bases. And in Hierapolis we can discern a particular hierarchy in the nomenclature of associations, which gave an elevated status to purple dyers, no doubt because purple gained a particular clientele amongst the upper levels of society.

An association of leather workers is well attested in Sattai (Içikler). A *bomos* in the necropolis at Colossae bears the inscription to Dion, son of Appas, as leather worker. First published by William Calder in 1939, the *bomos* is testament to Colossae's history of textile and allied trades. The hides of domesticated grazing animals provided the raw material for leatherwork. This trade is a significant part of the textile industry, with leather used in footwear, belts and fastenings. A community of Jewish leather workers is also attested in Chonae (re-established city of Colossae) in the mid-twelfth century CE showing a continuation of the Jewish presence known by the names of members of associations at Hierapolis (Pamukkale) in earlier centuries.

The evidence from texts and images suggests that a high proportion of females were involved in wool processes such as carding, spinning and weaving but there is a distinct lack of inscriptional evidence of associations for or including these women, even though there is a recent discovery of a tantalising list of women's names from Laodikeia that may indicate an association of some kind (or a table of priestesses). The suggestion is that women were

Plate 6.21 *In and around the northern necropolis, the northern baths and the shops that line the street connected to the agora at Hierapolis, is a network of water channels that carried water throughout the urban landscape fulfilling many different purposes. These water channels are virtually identical in design and construction to those found at Colossae and almost certainly were used for identical purposes of work, domestic needs, and the provision of civic facilities. These conduits would have been covered with tiles or stones to protect water quality and minimise evaporation.*

engaged in these activities at home, operating a cottage industry, even if this industry contributed to public markets and trade. In Greek mythology, it was the goddess Athena (the Roman equivalent is Minerva) who gifted women with the capacity for weaving. Weaving and spinning were considered sacred duties and were associated symbolically with spinning the thread of life. Clotho, the youngest of the Greek Fates, had the responsibility for spinning, in particular the spinning of the thread of human existance. The Roman historian Titus Livius Patavinus (59 BCE–17 CE), known as Livy, wrote a comprehensive *History of Rome*. In this epic that is dominated by male protagonists, Livy related the story of Lucretia who, alone of the wives of a group of Roman aristocrats, is found at home sitting among her slave women 'employed at her wool'. Livy acclaimed Lucretia as the model of a virtuous wife. Four centuries later, the Latin poet Ausonius, extolled his mother whose chastity and wifely virtue were demonstrated by her 'hands busy spinning wool'. One inscription from the Republican period, found in Rome, shows how widely held such attitudes were. It offered a eulogy for the deceased woman and described her wifely duty, noting that 'She kept house, she made wool'. The classicist, Robert Sallares, considers that the tasks of spinning, carding and weaving were so labour-intensive that they reinforced the confinement of women and restricted the time available for public movement.

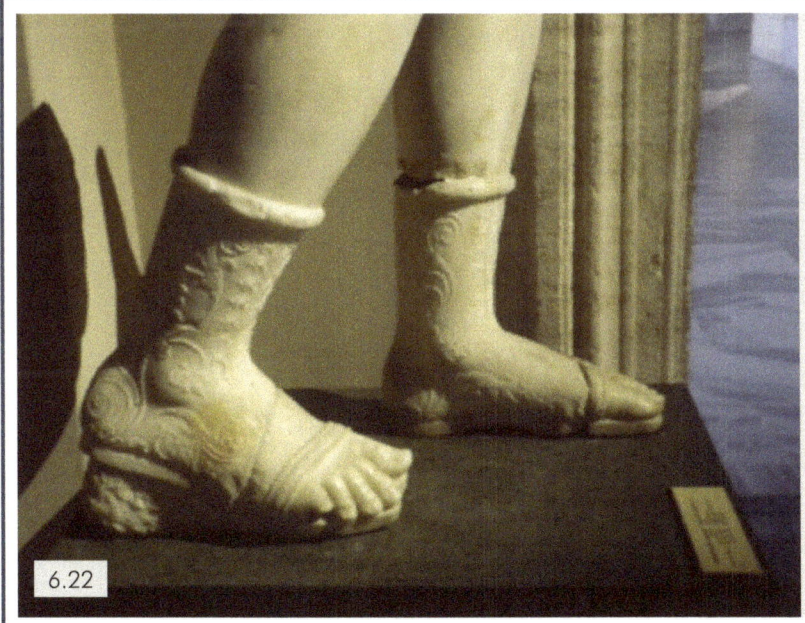
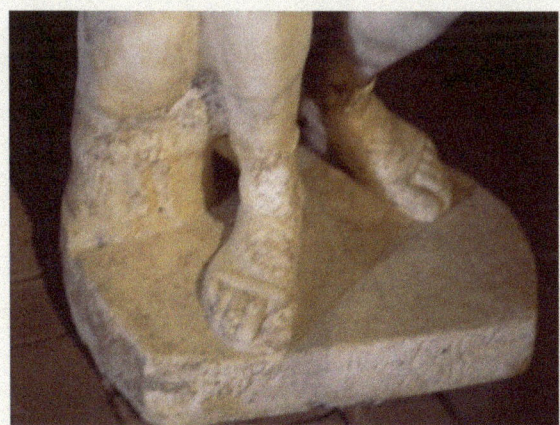

Plates 6.22, 23 *Examples of leather footwear featured on statues. At the left, the statue (in the Archaeological Museum in Istanbul) is from Cyme (modern Namurt Limani) on the coast near Lydia and is dated to the third century* BCE. *At the right is an example from a statue in the Denizli Museum at Hierapolis dated to the second century* CE.

Plate 6.24

Women are frequently remembered on stelai surrounded by symbols of wool baskets and spindles. A number are found in the Denizli Museum, that come from from the Lycus Valley region. One stele from the second century CE is raised to the memory of Tatia, daughter of Apollonios. She wears a distinctive ruffled dress suggestive of woolen clothing; significantly, to her right there stands a wool basket. In another stele, seen in Plate 6.24, the distaff (or spindle) is positioned at her right arm and, just to confirm her virtues, images of a mirror and comb are added.

This interconnected value system for women and for textiles is to be found everywhere across the Roman Mediterranean world.

Men who engaged in spinning and weaving were considered effeminate, for doing 'women's' work. First century Roman writers like Petronius, Martial and Suetonius refer to weavers with disdain and loathing, demeaning their speech as coarse.

> Here the weaver assails you; there the fuller and the cobbler who
> has just been kissing leather. Here the owner of a filthy beard, and a
> one-eyed gentleman; there one with bleared eyes, and fellows whose
> mouths are defiled with all manner of abominations.
>
> Martial *Epigram*

Graffiti at Pompeii, south of Rome, have been found that mention weavers. The scribblings were in Greek characters and many of the names of weavers and their women were Greek or Latin slave

Plate 6.24 *The funeral stele of Ammas surrounded by all the symbols of feminine virtue. She is proclaimed a 'heroine' in the inscription, thereby constructing a connection between her virtuous living, her conventional productivity in textiles and the esteem in which she was held.*

names. There were Jewish slaves among these weavers too, further attesting to the low status of the weavers. The tractate (book or section) *Kiddushin* in the collection of Jewish rabbinical teachings called the Babylonian Talmud, held that male carders and wool dressers were very lowly members of society; moreover, they were deemed morally unsound, probably because of their close contact with women.

But as we have seen already, low esteem was not the case for all involved in the textile industry. Another wealthy citizen of Hierapolis, Marcus Aurelius Alexander Moschianos had his designation as 'decurion [councillor] and purple seller' inscribed on his tomb. The elevated social position of the association of purple dyers in Hierapolis is indicated by an inscription dated to the early third century CE informing all who saw it that this association donated substantial funds to decorate the first and second storeys of the theatre, and this refinement was executed with the prized and expensive Dokimeion marble. Not only the association of purple-dyers but also that of wool-washers raised very similar inscriptions honouring a significant citizen, Tiberius Claudius Zotikos, son of Boas. The woolwashers of Hierapolis were also recorded as being given 100 denarii for the periodic decoration of the tomb of Eutuches Pompeios. So it is clear, that in the textile-rich Lycus Valley, those involved

Plate 6.25

Plate 6.26

Plate 6.25, 26 *A sarcophagus in the garden of the Istanbul Archaeological Museum displays items symbolic of the life and work of a married couple. Note, at the left (and see the detail), the basket with spindles among the symbols of the woman's fitting occupation.*

CHAPTER 6 - WEAVING THREADS: CLOTHING IN COLOSSAE

Plate 6.27

in the industry in various ways, could hold prominent positions in the community, and be honoured for the work they engaged. It may indicate that in the Lycus Valley, with such a long history of wealth-generation through textile manufacture, that higher levels of esteem were given to textile workers and businesses compared to elsewhere in the empire, such as at Rome itself.

In Roman Imperial times, there were prosperous guilds of wool-dealers (*epiopoloi*) and cloak dealers (*eimatiopolai*) in Ephesos. These indicate a ready market for woolen products from the nearby Lycus Valley transported down or along the Maeander River. A further indication of the ongoing trade is the continuance of the legal regulation called the *scriptura*. This originated as a grazing or pasture tax, but under the Romans was included in the customs law of Ephesos. It began life during the Attalid dynasty (282-129 BCE) whose capital was the city of Pergamom. But the law covered all the coastal ports of Asia Minor, regulating their operations as well as the collection of import and export duties. It appears that all goods imported and exported from the province of Asia were subject to this law, including those non-coastal cities not mentioned in the *scriptura* list, such as those of the Lycus Valley. Cities such as Colossae would have been liable for payments under this law based on the goods that were sent for export as well as those items from abroad that were not manufactured at home. Under Roman administration, some cities gained a much-sought-after-exemption from payment. Colossae's southern neighbor, Aphrodisias, was exempted from this tax in 39 BCE thereby demonstrating that this tax operated through the region.

The mix of textile-related employment known through the attested associations in the Lycus Valley, along with the hints at the regulation of trade and work indicate a measure of interdependence amongst the cities. The trades not frequently attested are likely gathered in family and domestic settings throughout the valley and these may have produced specialties in design that reflect local traditions. All these contribute to the regional textile industry, even though the products may be known abroad by a famous city of the region. We know, for example, of a number of items that carried 'Laodikeian' as a trademark, from as far afield as Gaul. But Colossae and its industries were well established in the valley and occasionally gather specific notice. More broadly, they contributed to the production of traded textile goods within and beyond the region.

Plate 6.27 *The tomb of Eutuches Pompeios in the northern necropolis of Hierapolis, is dated to the second or third century* CE. *The inscription records that he left 100 denarii to the association of woolwashers for periodic decoration of his tomb.*

The textile industry: the clothing

Cloth and clothing from the East were sought after for their colour and ornamentation. The Phrygians were renowned as the inventors of embroidered dress such as enhanced the trade of Hierapolis. Alexander the Great (356–323 BCE) with his love of luxurious clothing, imported dyed cloths from the Greek cities of Asia Minor for himself and his officers.

Wool could be woven directly into garments such as dalmatics (a tunic with wide sleeves, fashionable for Romans in the second century CE), *paragaudae* with purple borders, short cloaks, *chlamydes* and seamless overcoats, *paenulae* (such as seem to gain mention in the New Testament writing, 2 Timothy 4:13). The *paenulae* finally developed into the overgarment called the 'chasuble', a vestment used by Christian priests in their Divine Liturgy.

Plate 6.28

Laodikeia was known at one time by the name of 'Trimitaria', a title likely derived from *trimitos*. 'Trimitos' means having three threads in a warp or sackcloth or a garment made from such a specially-woven cloth. On the stele from Colossae honoring a man named Gluko, the weave of the cloth is quite distinctive for its mottled appearance, likely made by weaving two finer threads with a thicker one and producing a 'crinkled appearance'. This is probably an example of *trimitos* cloth used as a cloak or outer garment, and is clearly in use at Colossae rather than necessarily indicating the tunic famous from Laodikeia.

Famous clothes of one seamless piece known as *Laodicena* are reported in the *Expositio totius mundi*, a fifth century text originally written in Greek that covers, amongst many subjects, the trading habits of peoples across the known world. There is also a textile merchant, Julius Vericundus, who is attested in his epitaph as *negotiator Laodicenarius*, specializing in *Laodicena* or in textiles from Laodikeia. A *negotiator* often bought and sold staple goods in bulk or traded in wholesale quantities of goods. The *negotiator* was distinct from the *mercator* who was usually a freedman or plebian who ran a stall in the market or set up along the roadside. The inscription of Julius Vericundus signals he was a wholesaler. This gives some indication of the size of trade in the specialized *Laodicena* garments from the Lycus Valley as well as textiles such as wool and dyed cloth.

Plate 6.28 *A marble funerary stele from Colossae raised by the 'association of friends' for Gluko. The outer garments featured on the figures of the relief are likely to be of the trimitos weave.*

In 301 CE, the Roman Emperor Diocletian (245–311 CE) issued an *Edict on Maximum Prices*. The Edict was introduced and sent Empire-wide in an effort to curb inflation by controlling prices. As well as asserting particular coins as the stable economic currency and setting wages, the Edict introduced a maximum price for over a thousand goods. These included wool and clothing. The list gives evidence of the trade of identifiable wool and garments from Laodikeia and the Lycus Valley at the end of the third century and is a probably good indication of earlier woolen goods as well.

Wool, from Laodikeia, washed	*1 pound, denarii 150*
Hooded cloak, Laodikeian	*denarii 4500*
Hooded cloak, Laodikeian, resembling one from Nervii	*denarii 10,000*
Dalmatic, unmarked, Laodikeian, twilled	*denarii 2000*
Bordered tunic, Laodikeian, to be sold at a price in which the value of the purple has been included	
Hooded cape, Laodikeian, best quality	*denarii 5000*

The Edict proved to be counterproductive to trade and caused hardship for those whose wages were frozen at a period of a devalued currency. Not surprisingly the Edict was quickly ignored. While the system may not have been successful, the record of the goods traded at that time supplies valuable information of the wool and garment trade of the Lycus Valley. When one compares the daily wages of a stone-mason (50 denarii) or a farm labourer (25 denarii), it is possible to get an idea of the refined quality—and hence the expense—of many of the woolen products listed above.

Plate 6.29 *A Greek section of the Diocletian Price Edict at Stratonikeia. The Edict was displayed prominently in Latin and Greek on the wall of the Odeion, a major civic meeting space.*

The trade in high-quality wool and garments catered to the needs of the rich élite. The great weaving cities were located where there was an abundance of high quality raw material. Hierapolis was one of these, located in the Lycus Valley, renowned for its black wool and hot mineral springs ideal for dyeing. Similar was Colossae. While the garments bore the name of Laodikeia, this category appears to be the trademark or series of styles developed in the Valley as a whole.

Naturally it is to be expected that there would be varying qualities of wool and garments produced at Colossae, Laodikeia and Hierapolis. Beyond the 'top-end' wool and garment trade, clients such as the Roman soldiers had more basic needs. The army required medium grade quality materials. A number of discoveries have revealed examples of their purchases. In 128 CE, a receipt for 19 tunics and 5 cloaks for the Judean army by the wool weavers of the village Socnupaci Neos was recorded; in 138 CE, payment in advance was noted to the weavers of a village near Philadelphia for one *chiton* and four cloaks for the army of Cappadocia and one blanket for the military hospital in Sebaste (modern Selçikler).

One second-century CE inscription from Colossae names a number of offices related to trade, all held by one esteemed citizen (unknown because of damage to the inscription, but elsewhere dubbed 'Zosimos'). He was the overseer of the agora/marketplace (*agoranomos*), the municipal clerk (*grammateus*), the city treasurer (*argurotameias*), the warden regulating surrounding villages (*paraphulakes*), the public advocate (*ekdikos*), even the commissary for buying and distributing corn (*sitones*). These offices indicate that Colossae was an important city for the administration of

Plate 6.30

Plate 6.30 *A Hellenistic black slip-ware base which could readily have been re-used as a weaver's loom weight (a practice known elsewhere, such as in the Jordan Valley). It may come from a lekythos, (a slender, single-handled jug often used for storing oil) or even a type of krater (a double-handled bowl frequently used for mixing wine and water). Photograph courtesy of the late Julie Hooke.*

trade. Laodikeia may have been larger and more influential in the first and second centuries CE but Colossae retained its own independence and exercised its own authority over villages and pasturelands in its orbit.

The letter to the Colossians

The people of the Lycus Valley were immersed in an industry that wrapped them in clothes that not only fulfilled the functions of warmth and protection. Clothes also gave them an identity in the regional landscape. The community at Colossae and indeed in Laodikeia and Hierapolis were very likely involved in many of the layers of the textile industry—sheep-raising, shearing, spinning, weaving, dyeing and making garments as well as trading the goods and being enrolled as members of the associations. For many, the textile industry and its associated trades such as leather-manufacturing, provided their livelihood and brought prosperity to the region. It is fitting therefore that when a letter is written to the Christian community at Colossae—which, according to its own directions, was also required to be read in Laodikeia and Hierapolis—it refers to clothing as *the* metaphor for the identity of the community.

The letter written to the Christian community at Colossae around 68 CE is attributed to Paul the Apostle. This letter employs clothing as a metaphor for constructing identity: an identity focused on Christ. The Christian community are urged to strip off the old self (3:9) and clothe themselves with the new (3:9), clothing themselves with compassion, kindness, humility, gentleness, patience (3:12) and love (3:14).

In sum then, we can affirm that the ancient city of Colossae was a key part of the wool, cloth and clothing industry of the Lycus Valley, an industry that sponsored social and commercial associations and even metaphors for thinking about other ideas. Sheep still roam the ancient ruins witnessing to an earlier age of prosperity. Hierapolis specialised in the dyeing processes and Colossae contributed pasture, sheep, shepherds and wool-workers and those who worked in related industries, such as the manufacture of leather-goods. Colossae produced cloth and clothing that came to take the generic name of the neighbouring city of Laodikeia. There is still much that is unknown about the collaboration and competition between these cities. The future excavation of Colossae may well bring new information such as has come to light at Hierapolis and Laodikeia.

Select Bibliography - Chapter Six: Weaving Threads: Clothing in Colossae
by Rosemary Canavan

Associations in the Greco-Roman World: A Sourcebook. Edited by RS Ascough, PA Harland and JS Kloppenborg; Waco: Baylor University Press, 2012, §§156, 157.

Athenaeus *Deipnosophists* 11.473b–c.

Ausonius *Parentalia* 2.

Claudian *Against Eutropius* 2.272.

Corpus Inscriptionum Latinarum. Edited by T Mommsen *et al*; 1863–, 13.2003.

Denizli-Hierapolis Arkeoloji Müzesi Yunanca ve Latince Yazili Eserlerin Kataloğu. Edited by T Ritti Napoli: Liguori Editore, 2008, §§75, 76, 77, 95, 107.

Die Inschriften von Ephesos [IK 11–17]. Edited by H Engelmann *et al*; 8 vols; Bonn: Habelt, 1979–1984, 3.63.

Die Inschriften von Laodikeia am Lykos (IK49). Edited by T Corsten; Bonn: Habelt, 1997, §§51, 112.

Discoveries at Ephesus by JT Wood; London: Longmans, Green & Co, 1857, 24.

Herodotus *Histories* 5.49, 7.30.

Hipponax *fragment* 36.

Hitit Çağı'nda Anadolu. Edited by S Alp; Ankara: Tübítak, 2000, §§73-81, 90-92.

Inscriptiones Graecae ad res Romanas pertinentes [IGR], Volume IV. Edited by R Cagnat, *et al*; Paris: E Leroux, 1927, §§841, 863, 870, 1226, 1252, 1632.

Livy *History of Rome* 1.57.

Martial *Epigrams* 12.59.6.

Monumenta Asiae Minoris Antiqua Vol IV: Monuments and Documents from Eastern Asia and Western Galatia. Edited by WH Buckler, WM Calder and WKC Guthrie; Manchester: Manchester University Press, 1933, §297.

Monumenta Asiae Minoris Antiqua Vol V: Monuments from Dorylaeum and Nacolea. Edited by CWM Cox and A Cameron; Manchester: Manchester University Press, 1937, §175.

Monumenta Asiae Minoris Antiqua Vol VI: Monuments and Documents from Phrygia and Caria. Edited by W Calder and W Buckler; Manchester: Manchester University Press, 1939, §§11, 21, 47, 50, 87, 227.

Petronius *Satyricon* 132.

Pliny *Natural History* 7.190-93.

Rayet, O, 'Inscriptions inédites trouvées a Milet, Didymes et Héraclée du Latmos', in *Revue Archéologique* 28 (1874): 112–13.

Sterrett, JRS, 'Inscriptions of Tralleis', in *Athenische Mitteilungen* 8 (1883): 319–20.3.

Strabo *Geography* 12.8.16, 13.4.14.

Suetonius *On Grammarians* 23.

Supplementum Epigraphicum Graecum. Edited by H Pleket *et al*; Amsterdam: Gieben, 1984– , 4.541; 29.1183; 35.1369.

Vitruvius *On Architecture* 8.3.14.

Xenophon *Anabasis* 1.2.6.

Arnaoutoglou, Ilias. "Hierapolis, Sattai, Thyateira and their Craftsmen Associations: A Comparative Analysis." (2011), https://www.academia.edu/4678817/Hierapolis_Saittai_Thyateira_and_their_craftsmen_associations._A_comparative_analysis.

Ascough, RS, PA Harland and JS Kloppenborg. *Associations in the Greco-Roman World: A Sourcebook*. Waco: Baylor University Press, 2012.

Cadwallader, AH, and M Trainor, (eds), *Colossae in Space and Time: Linking to an Ancient City*. Göttingen: Vandenhoeck & Ruprecht, 2011.

Cadwallader, AH, 'Two New Inscriptions, a Correction and a Confirmed Sighting from Colossae', in *Epigraphica Anatolica* 40 (2007): 109–18.

Canavan, R, *Clothing the Body of Christ at Colossae: A Visual Construction of Identity*. Tübingen: Mohr Siebeck, 2012.

Chandler, R, *Travels in Asia Minor 1764–1765*. Edited by E Clay; London: The Trustees of the British Museum, 1971.

Drew-Bear, T, C Thomas, and M Yıldızturan. *Phrygian Votive Steles*. Turkey: Museum of Anatolian Civilizations, 1999.

Erdemir, H, 'Woollen Textiles: An International Trade Good in the Lycus Valley in Antiquity.' In *Colossae in Space and Time: Linking to an Ancient City*. Edited by Alan H. Cadwallader and Michael Trainor; Göttingen: Vandenhoeck & Ruprecht, 2011, 104–29.

Faber, GA, 'Dyeing and Tanning in Classical Antiquity', in *Ciba* (1938), www.elizabethancostume.net/cibas/ciba9.html.

Fischer, PM, 'Textile Production at Tell 'Abū al-Kharāz, Jordan Valley', in *A Timeless Vale: Archaeological and related essays on the Jordan Valley in honour of Gerrit van der Kooij*. Edited by E Kaptijn and LP Petit; Leiden: Leiden University Press, 2009, 109–17.

Haspels, CHE, *The Highlands of Phrygia: Sites and Monuments*. 2 Vols; Princeton, NJ: Princeton University Press, 1971.

Johnson, S, 'Laodicea and its Neighbours', in *Biblical Archaeologist* 13 no. 1 (1950): 1–18.

Jones, AHM, 'The Cloth Industry under the Roman Empire', in *The Economic History Review* 13 no. 2 (1960): 183–92.

Judeich, W. 'Inschriften', in *Altertümer von Hierapolis*. Edited by C. Humann; Berlin, 1898, pp. 67–180.

Kleiner, D, and S Matheson, eds. *I Claudia: Women in Ancient Rome*. New Haven: Yale University Art Gallery, 1996.

Magie, D, *Roman Rule in Asia Minor to the End of the Third Century*. 2 vols; Princeton: Princeton University Press, 1950.

Meijer, F, and O van Nijf, *Trade, Transport and Society in the Ancient World: A Sourcebook*. London: Routledge, 1992.

Miranda, E, 'La comunità giudaica di Hierapolis di Frigia', in *Epigraphica Anatolica* 31 (1999): 109–56.

Moeller, W, 'Male Weavers at Pompeii', in *Technology and Culture* 10 no. 4 (1969): 561–66.

Ormerod, HA, 'A Note on the Eastern Trade Route in Asia Minor', in *The Classical Review* 26 no. 3 (1912): 76–77.

Pococke, R, 'In the East', in *General Collection of the Best and the Most Interesting Voyages and Travels in all Parts of the World*. Edited by J Pinkerton; London: Longman, Hurst, Rees and Orme, 1811.

Ramsay, WM, 'Antiquities of Southern Phrygia and the Border Lands I', in *The American Journal of Archaeology and of the History of the Fine Arts* 3 no. 3/4 (1887): 344–68.

— *The Cities and Bishoprics of Phrygia*. 2 vols; Oxford: Clarendon Press, 1895, 1897.

— *The Historical Geography of Asia Minor*. Digitally Printed 2010 ed. Cambridge: Cambridge University Press, 1890.

— *The Letters to the Seven Churches*. Edited by Mark Wilson; updated ed. Peabody, Mass: Hendrickson Publishers, 1994.

Ritti, T, 'Nuovo dati su una nota epigrafe sepolcrale con stefantico da Hierapolis di Frigia', in *Scienza dell'Antichita* 6–7 (1992–3): 41–68.

Ritti, T, (ed.), *Denizli-Hierapolis Arkeoloji Müzesi Yunanca ve Latince Yazili Eserlerin Kataloğu*. Napoli: Liguori Editore, 2008.

Sallares, R, *The Ecology of the Ancient Greek World*. Ithaca, NY: Cornell University Press, 1991.

Simşek, C, 'Denizli Textile and Apparel Exporter's Union'. Republic of Turkey, Prime Ministry Undersecretariat of Foreign Trade, Denizli Textile and Apparel Exporters' Union General Secretariat, 1997.

— *Laodikeia (Laodikeia ad Lycum)*. Istanbul: Ege Yayinlari, 2007.

Skeel, CAJ, *Travel in the First Century after Christ with Special Reference to Asia Minor*. Cambridge: Cambridge University Press, 1901.

Thonemann, P, *The Maeander Valley: A Historical Geography From Antiquity to Byzantium*. Cambridge: Cambridge University Press, 2011.

Treggiari, S, 'Women in Roman Society', in *I Claudia: Women in Ancient Rome*. Edited by D Kleiner and S Matheson; New Haven: Yale University Art Gallery, 1996, 116–24.

Vearncombe, E, 'The Merchant of Hierapolis: Implications for the Study of Travel and Early Christianity'. Paper presented at the Travel and Religion in Antiquity Seminar, Montreal, Canada, 2006.

West, L, 'Phases of Commercial Life in Roman Egypt', in *The Journal of Roman Studies* 7 (1917): 45–58.

Plate 7.1 *The head of Tissaphernes on a Persian coin. After his capture at the baths of Colossae, on a charge of treason, his head was placed elsewhere!*

CHAPTER 7
The Waters and the Baths

THE PERSIAN PRESENCE AT COLOSSAE

There are very few references in ancient texts to the city of Colossae, apart from the New Testament letters to the Colossians and Philemon and the Byzantine stories of St Michael of Chonai (see Chapter Nine, *The Mighty Archangel*). But one reference stands out for its intrigue—the assassination of a Persian satrap by order of the Persian King Artaxerxes. The story fascinated Greek and Roman authors, who puzzled over the reasons for removing a successful promoter of Persian interests. The period is the Achaemenid period (550–330 BCE), a name drawn from the ruling dynasty amongst the Persians. The Persians were the greatest empire in history, prior to the Greeks under Alexander and then the Romans. No wonder then that a story of empire interested later successors. The story was told and retold over a number of centuries. Colossae provides the backdrop to the story, and, in particular, its baths.

Tissaphernes was the satrap (regional governor) of Lydia and Caria. These administrative regions, at the western end of the Persian empire, controlled cities that frequently had originally been Greek foundations in the classical period. There were ongoing tensions between mainland Greeks (Spartans and Athenians) and the Persians over these cities. Issues of identity and loyalties were key in this part of the empire. Tissaphernes had long laid claim to the most insightful connections with the Greeks.

Plate 7.2

Plate 7.3

Plate 7.2, 3 *Tissaphernes in satrapal tiara on the front of the coin (a siglos?) with, on the reverse, the musical instrument called a cithara that represents the god Apollo. The letters surrounding the cithara read* ΒΑΣΙΛ *meaning* βασιλεύς, *'king'. Apollo was also the god who inspired oracles, so the subtle communication to the Greeks with whom Tissaphernes had a close relationship, may have been designed to express his regal aspirations. The usual representation of the Persian king is given on the coin, a 'daric', at the right. The iconography was the same on silver coins.*

It's what had made him such a valuable general to Artaxerxes. Inevitably, he was involved in diplomatic and commercial wranglings and the occasional military stand-off. But what compounded Tissaphernes' often-complicated life was the deep suspicion that existed between him and a fellow satrap, Pharnabazus. Even though Tissaphernes had demonstrated his own loyalty to King Artaxerxes by informing him of the usurping pretensions of Artaxerxes' brother, Cyrus the Younger, in 401 BCE, he became subject himself to the same, targeted innuendo a few years later—at the instigation of Pharnabazus.

The suggestion of sedition may have been well-founded, given that the designation 'king' on coins Tissaphernes minted to pay some Greek mercenaries, was ambiguous. It was unclear who was meant as this 'king'—was it the actual Persian king, Artaxerxes, or the satrap whose head in folded tiara (as distinct from Artaxerxes' raised head-piece) was stamped on the coin's face? Tissaphernes' standing had already been dealt a serious blow when he lost a battle against the Spartans at Pactolus River (modern: Sart Çayı) near Sardis, a loss that cut back his own satrapal estate holdings in the area. In any case, Cyrus' mother, Parysatis, still nursed a festering grief over Cyrus' death and she retained enough access to her older son, Artaxerxes, at the Persian imperial court to work to the detriment of Tissaphernes' interests.

The plot against Tissaphernes was hatched with brilliant subterfuge. In 395 BCE, Artaxerxes sent two letters to a Persian commander, Tithraustes, who was based at Celaenae (Apameia, modern-day Dinar), the capital of the satrapy, the Persian province of Phrygia. This Tithraustes was to engage another high-ranking member of the Persian nobility, one Ariaios, who was still carrying damage to his position because of his close friendship with Cyrus the Younger, even though six years had passed since Cyrus' death. Here was the opportunity to re-establish himself favourably with the Persian court. His task was simple: to capture Tissaphernes at Ariaios' estate at Colossae and deliver him to Tithraustes. To ensure that Tissaphernes was lulled into a sense of security, Tithraustes had a second letter—to be delivered to Tissaphernes himself, informing him that King Artaxerxes had entrusted the conduct of the campaign against the Spartans to his charge. The struggles between the Persians and Greeks had been long-standing and complicated especially in western Asia Minor. The letter to Tissaphernes had all the appearance of a confirmation of his position above his opponent Pharnabazus. The invitation from Ariaios to join him at his Colossian estate for discussion of preparations for that campaign must be seen in this light, as Tissaphernes arrived in Colossae with only 30 companions, a clear sign that his guard was down and he suspected nothing.

The story then takes an interesting turn and it is well to remember that Greek historians control the telling of the tale. For them, the need to argue for Greek superiority was critical and so they advanced a familiar deprecating contempt (even if it meant that Greek colonies in Asia Minor would suffer a little at the comparison). Asia was a place, they suggested, that induced softness—in attitudes, in military capability, in perception. In the classical typology this equated to femaleness: soft lands produced soft men.

> It is reasonable that this land is nearest to the spring in terms of its nature and the moderation of its seasons. Manly courage, endurance, labor and high-spiritedness could not be produced in such an environment, neither in a native nor in a foreigner. But it is necessary for pleasure to rule there.
>
> From the text called *Hippocratic Airs*, 5th century BCE

No matter that the gardens of the Persian court were famous for their display of water; no matter that royal Persian authorities encouraged some replication of Persian architecture and lavish horticulture in the provinces of the empire (see Chapter Two, *Stationing Armies at Colossae*). This counted for naught. The telling point in the narrative that some ancient Greek authors latch onto, is that Tissaphernes laid aside his *akinakes*, a double-edged short sword that, in part, was a mark of an officer's authority and manliness. It was as if he had resigned his commission; at the very least it showed to gloating Greek historians he had succumbed to feminine lack of awareness. To drive the point home, he was then carried to Tithraustes at Celaenae, the next major city east on the Royal Road in an enclosed chariot. Plutarch, the Roman writer who picked up the Greek story, tells us that this was a style of transport 'normally reserved for women'. Tissaphernes' character was, by that small phrase, destroyed. He was as much emasculated as he was soon beheaded. The severed trophy was then despatched down the road to the Persian imperial court. As a postscript to the story, Tithraustes was promoted to satrap of Lydia, and Ariaios to the satrapy of Caria. Both were well-rewarded for their scheming execution of the plan.

There is a further element which may explain a little of Colossae's importance to the Achaemenid regime—its fecundity. The Persians had long connected the basic elements of earth and water with their own authority and control. The Greek historian, Herodotos, claimed that the Persians named 'earth' and 'water' as the symbols of submission to Persian sovereignty. They may even have been used in small token offerings as indications of surrender by those who were defeated by the Persian armies. Colossae was (and is) richly watered

Plate 7.4

Plate 7.4 *The fertile plain of the Lycus Valley still extends out from the Colossae höyük today.*

CHAPTER 7 - THE WATERS AND THE BATHS 137

Plate 7.5

and richly fertile, an ideal place for noble estates and the display of Persian power. For Persian thinking, not only was Colossae richly endowed with those elements that symbolised Achaemenid power; these elements were controlled by those who promoted themselves as rightful rulers of all the earth and the waters that made the earth fruitful.

Little wonder that Greek writers attempted to put a positive spin on Greek failure to wrest Asia from Persian control until the Macedonian, Alexander 'the Great', finally managed it. They argued that these very qualities—rich soil, rich supplies of water—made the inhabitants 'soft'. It was a way of compensating bruised egos. But for the Persian satrap, Tissaphernes, Colossae symbolised all that Persia represented in Asia—the control of earth and water. His blind-spot was that he failed to recognise that he had become a threat to that standing in the assessment of the Persian court in the East. Colossae was the loyal expression of Persian dominance, and became, in that sense, the Persian sentence on those who failed to live up to the king's expectations. Decapitation was the usual Persian mode of execution in cases of high treason. Tissaphernes had been adjudged a traitor.

COLOSSAE AND ITS NETWORK OF RIVERS

Colossae's water-supply was fed by three rivers which, though narrow, could, at different times of the year, flow with remarkable ferocity. The nineteenth century geographer, William Ainsworth, said that one river was called 'Lycus'—from the word for 'wolf': *lykos*—because of 'its sudden risings and impetuosity.' And this was used as a symbol on one minting of Colossian coins where the wolf replaced the traditional relaxed and reclining river god.

The value of a powerful flowing river is that mills can be driven to service a number of industries that are important for urban life. Mills seem to have become a regular feature of Roman cities from about the second century (CE), and there is evidence from Hierapolis that they were used, not only for the production of flour but also for the cutting of stone. Such river-based buildings were in operation when European travellers explored along the river in the eighteenth and nineteenth centuries but whether these were successors to constructions in late antiquity is not known.

Plate 7.5 *The 'wolf' of Colossae, the river Lykos, on a coin from the magistracy of Philopappos issued during the reign of the emperor Antoninus Pius (138–161 CE).*

The calcifying effects of the river meant that, at least in the modern era, these mills regularly had to shift their position, just as water channels and conduit pipes in Greek and Roman times needed regular maintenance to thwart the accretions that built up in the water lines. Nevertheless, the ancient architectural writer, Vitruvius, thought that it was precisely these water qualities that fostered the fine quality of black wool that the area produced (see Chapter Six, *Weaving Threads: Clothing at Colossae*).

About three kilometres to the east of the höyük there is a series of natural springs that ensure the Lycus—the Çürüksu of today—runs all year round (see Plate 7.9), though modern efforts to regulate water for agriculture have diverted a considerable flow from the river into an irrigation channel. Even so, during spring or after heavy rains, there can be a spectacular waterfall tumbling into the Lycus ravine to the west of the höyük. This stream, called the Cadmus (the Ak Su) by the ancient geographer Strabo, is one of two tributary streams feeding into the Lycus in the vicinity of Colossae.

The Greek historian, Herodotos, loved one mysterious story about the river Lycus. The waters were said to disappear beneath the ground for a length of about half a mile, before bursting out in full exuberance. Such strange happenings are known elsewhere in Turkey (such as the Tcharshamba River near Konya which reportedly 'disappeared' into the side of a mountain; it is now substantially engulfed

Plate 7.6 *The remains of an Ottoman mill calcified into the escarpment at the Çinaraltı Restaurant near the site of Colossae.*
Plate 7.7 *Grinding wheels at a Honaz café, taken from the site of Colossae.*

Plate 7.8 *An early photograph (1909) of the raging Lycus River, taken by the Greek archaeologist, George Lampakis.*
Plate 7.9 *The regular winter waterfall feeding into the Lycus River.*
Plate 7.10 *The limestone fissures that create the illusion of the Lycus River emerging from underground—during a period of reduced summer flow.*
Plate 7.11 *The travertine overhangs along the Lycus River to the west of the Colossae höyük.*

by the Apa reservoir); the limestone rock with its strata of honey-comb labyrinths certainly allows these marvels to happen.

Herodotos probably never visited the place to check. Many early European explorers were foiled in attempts to identify the ancient site because they relied on the presumed geo-scientific accuracy of Herodotos' fanciful story. William Hamilton even tried to 'save' Herodotos' reputation by pointing to the travertine cliff formations as having once covered the Lycus ravine, only later to be disturbed by an earthquake. William Ramsay, and Clive Foss a century later, were right, however, in lamenting the too-ready use of 'earthquake' to explain a baffling puzzle. Much as the nineteenth-century explorers hated to give up on their reliance on ancient authors, nevertheless they had to accept that Herodotos had it wrong.

The river seems to have been incorporated within the boundaries of the city (as happened at other cities such as Aezani [modern Örencik Ovasi] and Pergamom [modern Bergama]). The remains of a wall to the north of the river (those parts remaining after many large blocks were 'quarried' for farm pens!) appear to serve as a boundary for the necropolis basin, suggesting that a stretch of the river was included in the formal city bounds and added to the beauty of civic arrangement.

COLOSSAE AND THE HARNESSING OF WATER

Even given its calcifying capacity, the water has a 'soft' feel and may well have been an attractive resource for purification in religious rites. Nevertheless the water from the various natural sources, even when supplemented by cisterns and collection pools, had to be turned to the various uses required in a city.

Plate 7.12

Plate 7.12 *Part of the remaining northern wall of the formal city of Colossae, showing two periods of construction and repair.*

CHAPTER 7 - THE WATERS AND THE BATHS   141

Plate 7.13

This is where a feature noticed by early travellers still stands out in the area of the city around the höyük especially just to the north of the river. The Reverend Edmund Davis, for example, reported in 1874 that he 'passed several petrified water-courses like those at Hierapolis'. What he probably meant were the carefully constructed channels, some of them at considerable height that still interlace parts of the city area, which are in appearance virtually identical to those found at Hierapolis. Like those at Hierapolis, they would not originally have been exposed but covered to contain the flow and minimise evaporation and contamination—probably with angled terracotta tiles or paving stones. Some channels at Colossae are quite raised in height, carefully to convey the flow of water across uneven ground.

An indication of the engineering skill applied to the management of water is found close to the necropolis. A series of chutes fan out from an expanded delivery point on the eastern side of the southern extremity of the necropolis basin, not far from the modern road. A similar three-part fan is to be seen on the western side of the basin as well and there are the remains of a series of connecting channels running across the southern edge of the basin that seem to connect the two sets of chutes.

The engineering techniques of hydraulic carriage and movement over uneven surfaces were perfected by the Romans though known and used in part by the Greeks. The exact purpose for this elaborate web of channels and chutes has not been determined but their proximity to the necropolis is suggestive. There may be indications of a nymphaeum or purificatory pool connected with one set of chutes at the western side and probably a set of mills on the eastern side. Certainly, according to the Roman architectural expert, Vitruvius, nymphaea and then baths held priority for the allocation of water, only then followed by domestic use.

Plate 7.14

Plates 7.13, 14 *Stone elbow-joint for protecting the angled flow through terracotta water-pipes that presumably fed water into a larger receptacle or channel. The join moulding is still visible around the perimeter of the hole. At bottom right is a stone water-pipe sleeve, lying at the western base of the höyük. It was designed to secure the place of terracotta pipes used for the efficient control and transfer of water.*

Plates 7.15, 16 *A wall supports a water conduit, with a close-up showing the calcified build-up.*
Plates 7.17, 18 *Water channel at Colossae (left) compared with one from neighbouring Hierapolis (right).*

CHAPTER 7 - THE WATERS AND THE BATHS

Plate 7.19 *The necropolis basin with sets of three chutes at each edge: above at centre and centre left are two groups of three delivery points that fan out from a single channel at the southern end of the eastern side of the basin escarpment of the Colossian necropolis. At below centre right, further chutes are visible with remains of a substantial building.*
Plate 7.20 *Two of the divided channels fanning out from the delivery point above the chutes.*

Plate 7.21 *Aerial view of the eastern chute complex near the necropolis.*
Plate 7.22 *The modern water channel at the western side of the necropolis is in the foreground. Behind it, at centre left, lie the remains of part of the ancient network of water channels that supplied the various civic, industrial and domestic needs of the city of Colossae, including the public latrines.*
Plate 7.23 *One of the set of chutes at the eastern side of the necropolis that probably were part of the engineering for the operations of mills.*

THE ROMAN BATHS AT COLOSSAE

One expert on Roman baths, Garrett Fagan, reminds us that the successful operation of baths does not depend on the erection of aqueducts. Various engineering constructions can work perfectly well to supply the necessary water for the different facets of the baths establishments. Whether part of the network of water channels was involved in the provision of water for one or more of the bath complexes at Colossae is unknown. However, one inscription, dated to the end of the first century CE or beginning of the second century, records not only the repair of the baths at Colossae but also the provision of a (new) hydraulic infrastructure and this probably involved similar engineering constructions as here.

Plate 7.24

The extant remains of the damaged inscription do not provide the reason why the baths needed to be repaired, but we do know of an earthquake that hit the Lycus Valley around 61 CE and caused huge damage to the neighbouring city of Laodikeia. This may well have had a detrimental impact on parts of Colossae's civic and domestic infrastructure.

Baths were an essential mark of a Greek and Roman city's life—a key display of the refinements of civilisation that urban life brought and, for those with the enormous resources required for the task, a sure means of heightening one's standing in civic life. Little wonder that throughout Asia Minor, the evidence from inscriptions indicates that baths were a favourite target for 'euergetism'—the munificent provision of structures, goods and services for the benefit of the city populace. And little wonder that Korumbos is called 'patriot', a lover of his country, for his lavish donation (see Plate 3.33).

The need for the repair of such integral civic structures sometimes afforded the opportunity to make significant changes to the cityscape and to specific buildings. The

Plate 7.24 *The 1.5 metre white marble bomos would have held a statue or bust at the top. It listed the names of thirty Colossian citizens recording their dedication of honours to the benefactor Korumbos, who had provided considerable money for the repair of the baths and the improvement of the water supply. It is dated to the late first or early second century CE.*

Roman senatorial province of Asia (established in 129 BCE) ushered in a long, unfolding period where the Greek cities, once they came under Roman rule, became eager to demonstrate that they were loyal imitators of Roman values—even if they retained a healthy dose of their Greek heritage. Indeed the Greekness of Phrygian cities like Colossae became more earnestly displayed as city officials recognised that Roman authorities were portraying themselves as the rightful inheritors of the Greek heritage. Those who carried the status of 'polis', that is, an autonomous city, into Roman sway, eagerly sought to retain as much of that autonomy as loyalty could sustain and 'being Greek'—Hellenising—was an acceptable way of achieving this. Baths were a crucial identity-marker of the Greek polis but when Rome began to adapt the baths architecture and structure, just as they did the theatre, most cities followed suit.

It is likely therefore that at some stage there was a shift in the structure and meanings associated with the baths at Colossae. The Greek style of bath was largely factored around individual tubs, even when they were combined in an enclosed venue such as we find at Thessalonike and Pella in Greece.

The Hellenistic period seems to have introduced a larger bath for cooling off after exercise in the gymnasium and from this development there was an easy transition to the combination of gymnasium and baths that is characteristic of cities in Asia Minor in the first century CE. Traces of this Greek inheritance survive in inscriptions in the early Roman imperial period. The baths are called *balaneion* in the Korumbos inscription rather than the term preferred in Latin for grand structures, *thermae*, though too much should not be made of this distinction, as not even Roman authors were strict in their usage. The second century inscription honouring

Plate 7.25

Plate 7.25 *Example of Greek-style baths adjoining the agora at Thessalonike.*

an unknown multiple office-holder in the governance of Colossae, (whom, elsewhere, we have dubbed 'Zosimos'), shows that he held the specialist positions of *elaiones* (superintendent of oil supply) and *ephebarch* (principal of the training school for young men). These were crucial offices involved in the running of public baths in the Roman period in Asia. And, in the list of names honoring Korumbos the repairer of the baths at Colossae, we may even have a list of previous graduates (the ephebes). Certainly, the dedicants are very concerned to display their paternal line—some display a genealogy going back five generations!

Local farming knowledge has indicated that remains of Roman-style baths were to be found on the northeast side of 'Theatre Street' near the river. Although agricultural pursuits have covered most of these remembered ruins, there are two pieces of evidence that suggest there is substance in the information. The first is a sudden drop in the height of a section of the land in the identified area, compatible with the presence of a major walled structure.

The second piece of evidence is the amount of careful walling of the Lycus river bank at this point of the river. The Roman baths that serviced an army barracks at Vindolanda (sometimes called Chesters) at Hadrian's Wall in England demonstrate that a river can readily be incorporated into the baths complex with the application of the ingenuity of Roman-style engineering. The presence of other remains along the river bank, such as column bases, moulded footings and the like, suggests that this area was a key part of the city. At this stage, however, there is no knowledge of the layout of the baths and the various rooms and types of bathing that the baths at Colossae housed.

The photographs following over provide examples of remains seen in the river near the baths site.

Plate 7.26

Plate 7.26 *An example of the Roman style bath structure of the hypocaust at Ankara. Heat generated from a massive consumption of local timber sent warm air through the carefully laid-out system to warm the floors of the baths complex, laid over the brick pillars seen here.*

Plate 7.27 *View across the acropolis to the possible location of the baths in the non-treed light-green area at the top left of the photograph.*

Plate 7.28 *Wall foundations in the Lycus River adjoining the mooted site of Roman baths (photograph taken in summer 2010).*

Plate 7.29 *A single-piece pedestal or small column base.*
Plate 7.30 *A shield boss and pedestal fascia fragment.*
Plate 7.31 *Carved footing mount for bench or table.*
Plate 7.32 *Seat fragment.*

When the emperor Hadrian visited the Lycus Valley in 129 CE, he was drawn to places where the god Zeus was a major figure, like Laodikeia and Colossae. But these cities also had to have demonstrated loyalty to the Roman imperium in other ways, so as to warrant an imperial *adventus* (as the visit was called). One of the means of displaying fidelity to Rome and its values was through building programs that imitated in some measure those marks of civic architectural identity that reflected Rome. And the baths were one of those key indicators. Hadrian himself had made substantial contributions towards the building or repair of baths in a number of cities of the empire.

> *Hadrian*: What is man?
> *Epictetus*: Man is like a bath-building. The first room is the warm-water room for anointing oneself; the newborn child is anointed. The second room, the sweating-room, is childhood. The third room, the dry sauna, is youth. The fourth room, the cold-water room is old age. So the saying is true at all stages.
> *A late Latin imaginative summation of the symbolic importance of baths,*
> *using the emperor and a philosopher as the characters.*

In the first half of the fourth century, a Phrygian neighbor of Colossae on the Anatolian plateau, petitioned to become a 'city'. Orcistus (modern Alikel Yaila) listed as its key claim on the imperial behest, water and its derivative institutions, baths and mills. Even in the early days of the Christian empire under Constantine, the baths were recognized as a critical indicator in the assessment of a city's, indeed, a person's worth.

So strongly were the baths intertwined with Roman identity that prior to Constantine's accepting Christianity as the official imperial religion, Christians at various times and places were banned from the baths. Such bans effectively proclaimed that Christians were not Roman, were not civilised; they had no part in the defining mark of being Roman. Of course, this did not prevent Christian baptism—the rivers were as readily used; but we also know that Christians made use of the public baths for baptism if that could be arranged.

Even when Christians had free access to the baths, however, there remained a reserve about their use that goes back to the strictures that some austere Roman writers placed upon them. As much as baths might be connected with hygiene and Roman identity, adorned with statues of the 'health-gods' Asclepios and Hygeia and provided a main venue for the display of Roman and civic edicts, there was little doubt that the sheer pleasure—physical and social—that the baths provided, was a magnet for their use.

This potential hedonistic edge attracted the scathing glare of some Stoic philosophers like Seneca and the satirical barbs of Horace, Martial and Lucian. Christian scruples about the appearance of moral rectitude also expressed itself. A Synod of about 28 bishops met at neighbouring Laodikeia in about 365 CE, and passed one canon which ruled that 'No-one in the priesthood, nor lower-ranked clergy nor ascetics nor any Christian or laymen shall wash in the baths with women; for this is the greatest reproach among the heathen'. What this suggests is that the baths, at least in Laodikeia and in the cities under its archiepiscopal control, like Colossae, regularly entertained mixed bathing, even though elsewhere in the empire this was not always the case. Perhaps there is something in the ancient Jewish rabbi's lament, that 'the baths of Phrygia and its wines separated the ten tribes from their brethren'.

Plate 7.33

Plate 7.33, 34 *Coin reverse showing the gods Asclepios and Hygeia 'of the Colossians', dated to the time of Commodus. The two healing gods on the front of a small altar at the Museum of Ancient Civilisation, Ankara.*
Plate 7.35 *The shady, refreshing bounty of the Lycus River today.*

Select Bibliography - Chapter Seven: The Waters and the Baths

Babylonian Talmud *Shabbat* 147b.

Corpus Inscriptionum Latinarum [=CIL] edited by T Mommsen *et al*; Berlin: Berlin-Brandenburg Academy of Sciences and Humanities,1863– [http://cil.bbaw.de/cil_en/index_en.html], 3.352.

Eusebius *Ecclesiastical History* 5.1.5, 5.4.2.

Hellenica Oxyrhynchia 11.2–13.3.

Herodotos *Histories* 4.126–27, 5.18, 6.48–49, 7.32, 8.98, 9.122.

Hippocratic Airs 12.

Inscriptiones Graecae ad res Romanas pertinentes [IGR], Volume IV. Edited by R Cagnat, *et al*; Paris: E Leroux, 1927, §870.

Justin *Epitome* 6.1.2–7.

Libanius *Orations* 2.305.

Lucian *Hippias*

Martial *Epigrams* 3.44; 6.81, 9.33

Nepos *Conon* 2.2; 3.1–2; 4.1.

Pausanias *Travels* 3.9.7.

Plutarch *Ages* 1.35, 10.1–5, *Artaxerxes* 3.2–3, 4.2, 6.4, 18.1, 20.3, 23.1, *Alcibiades* 24.5, *Lysiander* 4.2.

Polyaenus *Strategems of War* 7.16.

Strabo *Geography* 12.8.16.

Seneca *Epistle* 56.

Synod of Laodicea *Canon* 30.

Thucydides 8.50–54, 87

Vitruvius *On Architecture* 8.3.14, 8.6.1-2.

Xenophon *Anabasis* 1.2.6; 1.5.5; *Hellenica* 3.4.21–25

Ainsworth, WF, *Travels in the Track of the Ten Thousand Greeks; being a Geographical and Descriptive Account of the Expedition of Cyrus and of the Retreat of the Ten Thousand Greeks as related by Xenophon*. London: JW Parker, 1844.

Bethe, JAE (ed), *Pollucis Onomasticon*. Stuttgart: Teubner, 1967.

Cadwallader, AH, 'Refuting an Axiom of Scholarship on Colossae: fresh insights from new and old inscriptions', in *Colossae in Space and Time*. Edited by AH Cadwallader and M Trainor; Göttingen: Vandenhoeck and Ruprecht, 2011, 151–79.

—'Honouring the Repairer of the Baths: A New Inscription from Kolossai', in *Antichthon* 46 (2012): 150–83.

Dandamaev, MA, *A Political History of the Achaemenid Empire*. Leiden: Brill, 1989.

Dusinberre, ERM, *Empire, Authority and Autonomy in Achaemenid Anatolia*. Cambridge: Cambridge University Press, 2013.

Fagan, GG, *Bathing in Public in the Roman World*. Ann Arbor: University of Michigan Press, 1999.

Farrington, A, 'Imperial Bath Buildings in South-West Asia Minor', in *Roman Architecture in the Greek World*. Edited by S. Macready and FH Thompson; London: 1987, 50–59.

Hyland, JO, 'Tissaphernes and the Achaemenid Empire in Thucydides and Xenophon' PhD Uni Chicago 2005.

Koloski-Ostrow, AO (ed), *Water Use and Hydraulics in the Roman City*. Dubuque, Iowa: Kendall/Hunt, 2001.

Kosso, C and A Scott (eds), *The Nature and Function of Water, Baths, Bathing and Hygiene from Antiquity*. Leiden: Brill, 2009.

Lampakis, G. *Οἱ ἑπτὰ ἀστέρες τῆς Ἀποκαλύψεως*. Athens: 1909.

Laurence, R, S Esmonde Cleary and G Sears, *The City in the Roman West c. 250BC – c. AD 250*. Cambridge: Cambridge University Press, 2011.

Levick, B, 'In the Phrygian mode: a region seen from without'. In *Roman Phrygia: Culture and Society*. Edited by P Thonemann; Cambridge: Cambridge University Press, 2013, 41–54.

Magie, D, *Roman Rule in Asia Minor*. 2 vols; Princeton, NJ: Princeton University Press, 1950.

Munn, M, 'Earth and Water: The Foundations of Sovereignty in Ancient Thought', in *The Nature and Function of Water, Baths, Bathing*. Edited by C. Kosso and A Scott; Leiden / New York: Brill, 2009, 191–210.

Schwabacher, W, 'Satrapenbildnisse. Zum neuen Munzportrat des Tissaphernes', in *Charites: Studien zur Altertumswissenschaft (Festschrift Ernst Langlotz)*. Edited by K Schauenburg; Bonn: Athenäum-Vrelag, 1957), 27–32.

Trundle, M, *Greek Mercenaries from the Late Archaic Period to Alexander*. London: Routledge, 2004.

Robert, L, 'Inscriptions', in J des Gagniers *et al*, *Laodicée du Lycos: le Nymphée, Campagnes 1961–1963*. Quebec: L'Université Laval, 1969, 247–389.

—'Documents d'Asie Mineure XXIII–XXVIII', in *Bulletin de correspondence hellénique* 107 (1983) : 497–599

Rosen, RM and I Sluiter (eds), *Andreia: Studies in Manliness and Courage in Classical Antiquity*. Leiden: Brill, 2003.

Sekunda, N, 'Changing Patterns of Land-holding in the South-Western Border Lands of Greater Phrygia in the Achaemenid and Hellenistic Periods', in *Colossae in Space and Time: Linking with an Ancient City*. Edited by AH Cadwallader and M Trainor; Göttingen: Vandenhoeck and Ruprecht, 2011, 48–76.

Şimşek, C, 'Kolossai', in *Arkeoloji ve Sanat* 107 (2002): 3–17.

Stierlin, BH, *Persian Art and Architecture*. London: Thames and Hudson, 2012.

Thomas, E, *Monumentality and the Roman Empire: Architecture in the Antonine Age*. Oxford: Oxford University Press, 2007.

Wakefield, HD, 'The Decline and Fall of Tissaphernes', in *Historia* 30 (1981): 257–79.

Yegül, F, *Baths and Bathing in Classical Antiquity*. New York: Architectural History Foundation, 1992.

Zuiderhoek, A, *The Politics of Munificence in the Roman Empire: Citizens, Elites and Benefactors in Asia Minor*. Cambridge: Cambridge University Press, 2009.

Plate 8.1 *The northern necropolis basin looking to the south-west, showing the escarpment within which many 'cliff-tombs' were carved. Fragments of gravestones and monuments remain in the basin in spite of agricultural activity. At the centre-left of the photograph, the remains of water channels can be seen, which carried water away from the mills at the south-eastern corner of the necropolis basin.*

CHAPTER 8
The Necropolis

The in-ground tombs

When the Scottish Reverend, Alexander Somerville, ventured to the höyük of Colossae in 1885, he noted in his diary, 'On the north of the river there is an extraordinary circular flat depression, which seems paved with stone'. He explained the feature by the petrifying waters of the Lycus making everything smooth, like an Edinburgh sidewalk. He wasn't the first to be confused. The English explorer William Hamilton first set foot upon the necropolis at Colossae fifty years earlier in 1836 and thought he had discovered the city of Colossae itself because he seemed to be walking on pavement. Certainly the two hectares or so of the basin, if covered with 'paving stone', might have misled him.

He soon realized that there was another explanation. 'As in many other places in Lesser Asia, the sarcophagi are cut in solid ground, and so close to each other, that when the covers were laid on, they resembled a pavement formed of gigantic blocks', was the way William Ainsworth summed up Hamilton's discovery. Today there are remains of those heavy covers, but many have been removed, the graves robbed and the 'in-ground sarcophagi' (called 'chamosorion' graves) left exposed, especially along the upper rim fanning out from the basin to the north and west.

Plate 8.2

Plate 8.2 *View of the mound of Colossae and to the north, below the red-roofed farm-house, the necropolis basin.*

Plate 8.3 *Closely cut chamosoria with one cover, at the upper left still (almost)* in situ, *lie at the upper north-eastern lip of the necropolis basin. This particular aggregation of chamosaria may have been owned and controlled by some group at Colossae, perhaps a voluntary association. The bomos of Dion the leatherworker, mentioned below, lies nearby on its side.*

Plate 8.4 *Other 'in-ground sarcophagi' are to be seen on the upper north-western edge of the necropolis basin, including one small one, apparently intended for one child or more. The grave measured approximately 750 centimetres long and 45 centimetres wide.*

Plate 8.5 *A section of the grave lid that sealed a tomb, still in place at the necropolis.*
Plate 8.6 *The sketch of a Colossian epitaph as seen through the eyes of the clergyman, Edmund Davis.*
Plate 8.7 *An early photograph of a Colossian funerary bomos, which had been moved to the railway stationmaster's house then at nearby Appa. Photograph by Gertrude Bell (in April 1907), by courtesy of the University of Newcastle-on-Tyne.*

THE BOMOI

These covers for graves, heavy as they are, were further kept in place by heavy blocks of stone that were carved in such a distinctive fashion that early European explorers struggled to appreciate them. Ainsworth reported them as 'rude grotesque-shaped pedestals, resembling elongated truncated pyramids, which had been placed upon the sepulchres as cippi', by which he meant a grave marker. The French biblical scholar and explorer, Ernst Renan, called them 'bizarre'; his compatriot, Alexandre Laborde had been kinder: he called them 'singular', adding that he hadn't seen the likes of them elsewhere, though we now know that they were used across the region (such as at Eumeneia, near modern Çivril). But they confounded the descriptive and artistic powers of European visitors. When the English reverend gentleman, Edmund Davis, tried to capture their design in a sketch, he could not avoid shaping them like the familiar gravestones that filled cemeteries in his homeland.

These 'cippi' as Ainsworth described them, are better labelled as a particular form of *bomos*, a term that originally meant 'altar'. The *bomos* at a necropolis retained something of this sacred sense and was the focal point of attention (through adornment with oil, wine and wreaths) by way of remembrance. In fact, the predominant term used in funerary inscriptions on these *bomoi*, is *mnêmeion*, a word that accents the importance of memory. Remembering the dead was seen as critical for the city's well-being and continuity. As the scholar of ancient history, Sarah Pomeroy, comments, 'Care in death is consistent with care in life'.

Plate 8.8

The standard design of a *bomos* featured a large plinth base, a shaft, and a pediment with a central boss and acroteria (palm-shaped edgings, often ornate) at the outer corners of the triangular top at front and back of the *bomos* pediment. Generally, it was carved from a single block of limestone. The plinth was set onto the large stone cover sealing the grave. The *bomoi* at Colossae seem to have come in two heights: the shorter about 1.3 metres high, the longer, as in the photographs (Plates 8.7–10), 1.65 metres high (when completely intact). Many of these *bomoi* still dot the landscape of the necropolis at Colossae, though most have been moved, for agricultural purposes, into field boundary lines or rock piles.

Plate 8.8 *Funerary bomos with (rare) relief on the shaft, now also removed from the necropolis.*

They appear, like most of the surviving grave materials, to have been carved from local limestone. Francis Arundell in writing of his 1826 travels mentioned an ancient quarry which he linked, by proximity, with Colossae. The modern quarry at nearby Karateke does not qualify as it shows no evidence of an ancient ancestor. Arundell's indifferent reference was finally pinned down by Professor Celal Şimşek, Director of the Archaeology Department at Pamukkale University. To the south east of the town of Kaklık (approximately 12 kilometres to the east of Colossae, off the modern Denizli-Afyon roadway) on the lower reaches of the mountain range was found the quarry that seems to have supplied much of the material for Colossae's building projects. The recent discovery (following unseasonal rains) of a complete unused (?) sarcophagus in a building at Kaklık may indicate that some value-adding occurred on-site. The stone from that quarry is represented everywhere in the *bomoi* and slabs of the necropolis. Like most ancient towns, short distances from quarry to city were preferred. Only the wealthy and civic authorities, wanting ostentatious display, called for the varieties of marble found elsewhere. Such stone was far more expensive because of rarity, difficulty in cutting and transport.

Plate 8.9 *Bomoi forming a field boundary at the necropolis.*
Plate 8.10 *Upper section of a bomos (now in the Denizli Museum), bearing an inscription naming Markos and his son Dionyseios, indicating that more than one person could be buried in the grave over which it stood.*

This style of burial architecture seems to have developed in the late Roman republican period and continued for some centuries. The local stone was relatively easily worked when freshly cut, and going on the fines recorded for damage to the tombs (around 500 denarii in the second century CE) was much more affordable than some of the more elaborate funerary arrangements discussed below. This cheaper limestone could be smoothed and polished so that, when first completed, it gleamed almost like marble. It could also be painted in whole or in part and could receive a well-executed inscription (depending on the skill of the stone-cutter), allowing the deceased of modest means to find a measure of immortality by the continued public witness to his or her life.

Sometimes, instead of a *bomos*, a flat section of stone was carved with a relief and inscription and often with a top section shaped to present a pediment with a leafy shaped protrusion at each end—the *acroterion*—and a circular boss or rosette in the middle. Occasionally the vertical borders of the stone were carved with pilasters or columns as if holding up the pediment roof. Again the temple allusion is clear; again the sense of something sacred about the dead is being asserted. The stele, as the upright slab is called, was set by a central base-protruding tongue slotted into a groove in a heavy stone footing. One of the most famous from Colossae has a rare motif beneath the ubiquitous funerary banquet scene. The early surface archaeologist and epigrapher, William Calder, called it in his notebook, 'one hog with two hoglings'. These stelai, in the main, seem to have more elaborate reliefs than those on the *bomoi* and, as in the case of the hogling stele, might even use expensive marble rather than local limestone.

Plates 8.11, 12 *The broken stele (from Colossae, now at the Denizli Museum), featuring a traditional funeral banquet scene, showing the reinforcement of gender roles with the male reclining and woman (with infant) seated. It also probably indicates the occupation of the deceased male—pig farmer. At the right is an example of an early Hellenistic stele of different style which—a rare occurrence—has its base preserved (in Kavala Museum, Greece). Note that both reliefs contain a dog, a familiar feature in Hellenistic funerary scenes.*

THE NECROPOLIS IN RELATION TO CITY LIFE

The location and appearance of a necropolis help us to appreciate the identity and values of a people. The necropolis itself is vast, covering not only the large basin but following the line of the escarpment to the north and west into further fields of the 'city of the dead'. Once the many toppled *bomoi* in the necropolis are restored to an upright position in the imagination, and placed among the many other grave types in the necropolis, we realise that, just like Hierapolis to the west, the dead played an important part in the cultural and social life of Colossians and adjoined the major points of access to the city. One third-century (CE) inscription from Colossae actually records that a woman named Ammiane deposited a sum of money with the municipal authority (called a *boulē*) so that a public annual remembrance of her deceased son, Herakleon, could occur. He is called a 'hero' in the inscription—a term which had by then become a common expression for someone who had died young—and a laurel crown was to be placed (presumably on a statue or bust attached to the pedestal) each year. Although not an epitaph as such, it probably gives an indication of what might be done by families, friends and colleagues gathered at a graveside.

Plate 8.13, 14 *A Phrygian-style tomb entrance carved into a cliff face near the Colossae höyük. It evokes a temple-like structure in its façade. (Photograph courtesy of Robert J. Wagner.) At the right is a drawing by the nineteenth century French explorer Charles Texier of a rock tomb façade at Aizanoi which evokes the more finished style of rock tombs such as would have been seen at Colossae.*

THE CLIFF TOMBS

The *bomoi* mentioned above contain the evocative acroteria at their four upper corners, similar to those often adorning the edges of temple pediments. These also recall the 'altar-horns' sometimes added to altars. Whether through the symbolism of temple or altar, sacredness is attached to the dead. The suggestion of a temple is apparent in some different funerary constructions. These are tombs cut into the vertical escarpment that rims the basin of the necropolis and, further to the west, the northern cliff that encroaches on the bank of the River Lycus. These graves are often called 'Phrygian tombs' as they seem to be modeled after the magnificent tomb façade popularly credited to King Midas, which is found between Eskişehir and Afyon (at a village called Yazılıkaya); other similar examples are known in Thrace, Paphlagonia and elsewhere. Even though the remaining cave tombs at Colossae are quite weathered and have been robbed of their sealed doors, enough remains to recognize the immense attraction of the symbolic design for local imitators, though they would necessarily have been wealthy members of the local elite.

This was not the only style of cliff-cut rock tombs. Rock-tombs of a different style are also found at Cappadocia, Termessos modern Güllük), Tlos (near Kalkan) and Pamphylia to name a few. So also at

Plate 8.15, 16 *A simple cliff tomb carved into an outcrop of the escarpment on the eastern side of the necropolis basin. The bed for the remains of the deceased is little more than 1.2 metres long and 0.70 metres wide.*

CHAPTER 8 - THE NECROPOLIS

Colossae, there are cliff tombs that are not so elaborately carved or extensive in their interior spread. These were more simple affairs, with just a single 'bed' area for laying out the deceased before enclosure. So, even among the cliff tombs, some variety is to be found.

One issue that remains to be determined is whether these graves date back to the Phrygian ascendancy across the region in the seventh century BCE or are an indication of a revival of the style by the Romans that began in the late Republican period in the province of Asia. Sometimes also, Roman aristocrats decided to re-use previously existing Phrygian-style graves, so the matter is complicated. A triclinium arrangement inside the tomb—that is with three benches in a u-shape around an open area—is often associated with Hellenistic and Roman arrangements, but it too may reach back to the earliest development of this Phrygian style. It is significant that the presence of the Romans had little effect on the styles of tomb used at Colossae. Rather, there seems to have been considerable Roman appropriation or emulation of local expressions. Indeed, at this point in our knowledge of Colossae, no evidence has been found of the Roman practice of cremation (so pronounced elsewhere in the late Republican and early Imperial period). The evidence observed thus far indicates that inhumation was the general practice even though the manner of inhumation can vary.

Plate 8.17, 18, 19 *A carved rock tomb at the Colossae necropolis, showing the entrance, the squared, flat roof burial chamber and view to the doorway.*

Plate 8.20

Two further styles of dealing with the dead are evident at Colossae, separated however by a period of three to four hundred years. These are the tumulus and the sarcophagus.

The tumuli

The *tumulus* (plural: *tumuli*), is a form of burial where the deceased are placed in a sepulchre chamber (sometimes called a *hypogea*) which is completely covered by earth. This elaborate and expensive means of burying and remembering the dead (and gaining appropriate recognition for doing so in such a manner) is also known from Phrygian times (and earlier). But perhaps some of the best known examples are from the Macedonian period—the immense complex of temple-style buildings covered by an artificially constructed hill, such as excavated at Aigai and the recently discovered 'Kasta Tumulus' at Amphipolis (in western and eastern Macedonia respectively).

One can understand the desire to imitate this grandiose style, with all its gilt-edged remembrance of the period of Alexander the Great being evoked by local dignitaries. We know, for example, that 'Alexander' remained a popular name for the Colossian citizenry even at the end of the first century CE, so the desire to imitate or connect was present in large measure or small.

A number of tumuli are found at Hierapolis, only 25 kilometres away. Colossae also has at least three examples. These were surveyed and excavated in 1997 by Haşim Yıldız, Nesrin Karabay and Celal Şimşek. (The last-named, from Pamukkale University, is now the Director of the excavations at Laodikeia.) All the tumuli had been constructed on the upper level of ground that lies 3 to 5 metres above the basin—the more visible to those passing down roadways along the edge of the necropolis to and from the city proper. In fact, some extant smaller epitaphs from the necropolis deliberately set

Plate 8.20 *The massive tumulus at Aigai (Vergina) in Macedonia that covers the tomb temples of Philip II (father of Alexander the Great), one of his seven wives (perhaps Nicesipolis) and his grandson Alexander IV.*

CHAPTER 8 - THE NECROPOLIS

themselves to address those who wander past, recording in stone 'greetings to the passers-by'. Whether any tumulus at Colossae had such a greeting is not known, however, but it is unlikely—the large scale was enough to grab the attention of wayfarers, even more if some crowning sculpture or marker (whether a cippus, phallus, mushroom, or stele) protruded from the peak of the tumulus. These could not help but draw the gaze to the grandeur of the grave and, by extension, the grandeur of the city being approached by the (usually) main road surrounded by these displays of the dead.

What is known is the considerable size and amount of material that these forms of burial required. The three tumuli that have been excavated reveal a similar internal structure, containing a passage-way (a *dromos*, which may contain steps), an ante-chamber and, in the centre of the mound, the sepulchre itself. The largest tumulus, located to the NNW of the plateau above the basin, retains a considerable amount of earth covering and has a radius of 25 metres. A smaller one, closer to the edge of the basin on the NNE side, has had its interior chamber exposed by erosion of the earth covering. It shows the elaborate and massive blocks that were cut to form the sides of a small house structure—not unlike the tomb constructions found, many with plastered and painted interiors still extant, at Paestum, the ancient centre of Magna Graeca in southern Italy. This gives us some help with dating—these tumuli

Plate 8.21 *The* bomos *tombstone of Karpos and Euthenia and their son Artemidoros in the necropolis at Colossae; it conveys 'greetings to those who pass by', here highlighted in red. Red was often used in the ancient world to paint the letters of an inscription on a white painted stone.*
Plate 8.22 *A tumulus in the northern necropolis at Hierapolis with its retaining walls (the 'revetment') and carved stone at the top, which was usually set on top of the internal roof structure of the central chamber roof before the conical earth mound was supplied.*

Plate 8.23 *The view from one tumulus at the Colossae northern necropolis to the höyük, in the haze approximately one kilometre to the south. The road from Laodikeia passed nearby.*

Plate 8.24, 25 *The antechamber, inner chambers and passageway of tumuli at the Colossae necropolis.*

Plate 8.26, 27 *The exposed inner chamber of a tumulus showing the slab construction.*

Plate 8.28 *An example of a triclinium arrangement for the laying out of the dead in the central chamber of a tumulus tomb at the Colossae necropolis. The walls would have been plastered and either white-washed or more elaborately decorated.*

belong to the third to second century BCE, and are designed to contain up to four corpses, probably laid out full-length. Unfortunately, all the tumuli known at the Colossae necropolis have at some stage been broken into and robbed. However, regional archaeologist, Haşim Yıldız, reported that some artefacts were found in each, the most common being pottery sherds. These confirmed a Hellenistic dating. Also found were a section of a perfume bottle and parts of a small marble alabaster vessel, both of which were probably types of *unguentarium*, the container of perfumed oil linked with respectful preparation and honorific accompaniment of the dead body. This suggests that, as in other parts of the Hellenistic world, certain household items and also valuable goods were buried with the deceased.

A SARCOPHAGUS

A further funerary item is marked out as belonging to a member of the Colossian elite, though from several centuries later. Like the recipients of the lavish tumulus burials, the names of the deceased have not survived. William Calder could not resist adding to his collection of inscriptions from Colossae, two fragments of a broken, marble sarcophagus—a detached stone coffin. Sixty years later, Bay Ali Ceylan, recognised the conjunction of a middle section of the front side of the sarcophagus lying in the Denizli Museum depot with these two pieces. The result is a complete side of an elaborate garland

Plate 8.29 *The re-assembled pieces of one side of a sarcophagus from Colossae. It displays a double presentation of the mask of the tragic muse Melpomene either side of a central Medusa head. Figures of Eros, supporting garlands along with ribbons gently flowing down from their wings, are stationed between the faces with winged, lightly garbed Nikes (or Victories) supporting the garlands at the corners. The two outer garlands hold central rosettes, below which are pairs of birds. Below the Erotes are the remains of hippochamps, horse-headed creatures with curling, serpentine tails, often harnessed to haul the ocean god Poseidon's chariot. The effect of this conglomerate of symbols is to combine a continued affirmation of life with elements of the protection of the final resting place of the deceased.*

sarcophagus, made from Dokimeion marble, which is now on display at the Denizli Museum. This particular style of garland sarcophagus ornamentation is very elaborate, what is sometimes called 'the Asiatic style'. Earlier sarcophagi were more simple box affairs with little design additions on their exterior, but these gave way to increasingly florid designs. The Asiatic-style sarcophagus is usually dated to around 140–160 CE.

The sequence of pairs (masks, animals, minor gods, rosette garlands) compels a focus on the central face of Medusa. She is a frequent figure on grave structures. The image draws on a complex inversion of ideas where the one who petrifies others can herself be set in stone to protect the grave and its inhabitants against attack. The muse, Melpomene, the patron of death and tragedy, is duplicated on either side above a garland that contains a rosette.

These rosettes, which we have noted already on other types of grave monuments, seem to have functioned as a mark of the deceased. A more exact meaning has eluded scholars, whose suggestions have run from a 'symbol of apotropaic power' (ie, again, protection) to a 'sign of life' or a 'symbolic derivation of a funerary offering'. However, in a recently published inscription that contains a list of the names of thirty individual citizens of the city of Colossae, one single name is preceded by just such

Plate 8.30

Plate 8.30 *The garland bearing Eros in a fresco at Terrace House 2 at Ephesos. The colours give an indication of how grave stelae and sarcophagi might be painted. The necropolis was designed to be seen, and colours as well as elaboration could grab the attention of visitors. Indeed, benches were placed at various points in ancient cemeteries just for the purpose of viewing.*

a 'rosette'. Although the pedestal is itself honorific of a public munificence and not funereal, this small addition before one of those honouring the benefactor almost certainly indicates that the person died before the stone-cutter commenced his work.

The elaborate sarcophagus design became very popular in Rome and seems to have generated a substantial export trade from Phrygia. This alone provides an indication that the deceased (who presumably purchased the sarcophagus before his death) was intent on making a substantial statement about his (and his family's) importance in Colossian society. Robert Smith, who has examined more than 460 sarcophagi (whole or in fragmentary form) at nearby Aphrodisias (modern Geyre) states that these particular sarcophagi were fashionable among the wealthiest of Asia Minor's leaders. Careful planning and a substantial outlay of resources were needed in preparation. But also considerable forethought was needed if such an embellished grave was to have its public impact. The garlands convey a link with civic festal celebration, abundance and the associated high status accruing from these, especially in combination with the success implied by the 'Victories' and the fertility and enjoyment conveyed by the figures of the young, naked Erotes. There was a sense also, argues Smith, that such a display of elaborate stone craft was participating in and endorsing the monumental statements made by Rome. Very few sarcophagi are known before the first century CE; the rise in frequency can be interpreted very much as a Roman-inspired phenomenon. Accordingly, these sarcophagi were not intended to be hidden away. They were designed for public view and may have been re-used by other members of the family at various times, probably in conjunction with a mausoleum and garden plot in a prime position in the necropolis. Over time, a certain competition in 'stylistics' developed as

Plate 8.31

Plate 8.31 *Section of the inscription honouring Korumbos for the repair of the baths. The list of names includes Menas son of Ktesas, whose name is preceded by a (highlighted) five-petalled rosette at mid-left.*

sarcophagi (and osteoteks—stone boxes to hold the bones of the deceased) became more elaborate. Professor Christine Thomas, a specialist in the archaeology of Ephesos, calls these developments, 'style-wars'.

Of course, the living were the ones who inherited the benefits of the honour claimed by and accorded to the ones who had died, the more especially if part of the funeral honours took place in the theatre. In the early second century, the governor of Bithynia in northern Asia Minor, Pliny the Younger, noted that images of forebears at home relieve mourning, but the greater comfort is derived by public honour and glory. Sometimes, however, the city populace was more than passive in viewing of the funeral arrangements. Asia Minor attests a number of cases where the locals became agitators, Sometimes they demanded such formal civic distinctions that the traditional walled separation between city and necropolis was breached (as for example at Stratonikeia where the 'heroon', the 'hero's tomb' of an unidentified leader of the city, stands in the main street).

> The Forum, which I think of as a temple of Peace, in which the laws are put into operation, because of which they are in force— shall we occupy it with tombs, pollute it with sinister ashes?
>
> Ps-Quintilian *Minor Declamation*

Sometimes, the family itself might be pressured to extend lavish outlays for the benefit of the populace, as the Roman author Suetonius admitted. There was even one riotous attempt at Aphrodisias to snatch and hold the body of a certain Tatia Attalis from the funerary procession apparently to force a council decision in favour of her burial within the city walls. While we have no evidence of such exceptions to Roman law or such irregular happenings at Colossae, they conceivably may have occurred.

Funerary inscriptions

Sarcophagi were frequently carved on all four sides, or at least the three viewable sides if space allocated for the standing sarcophagus was more enclosed. The lid for this Colossian sarcophagus probably contained the inscribed details of the deceased but it is no longer extant. We must turn to other, less salubrious gravestones to gather further information on Colossae. Most of these come from the *bomoi* and stelai of the second and third centuries CE.

One of the most intriguing is the inscription on a *bomos* that first appears to gain notice in 1891. Georg Weber noted there were numerous inscriptions in the necropolis at Colossae but only offered a couple in his report. However he added a sketch of another, which contained his attempts to record the inscription.

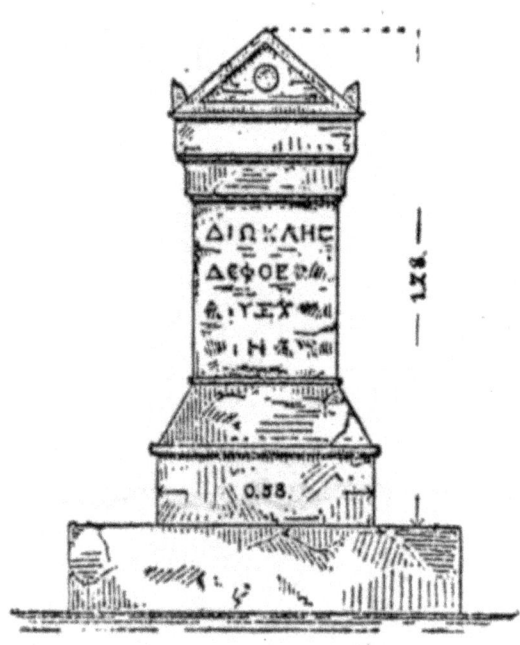

It was up to William Calder to publish the inscription, which is quite simple though deeply cut: 'Dion, son of Appas, a leatherworker. Greetings'. The *bomos* survives, albeit now in damaged form, in the necropolis. From it a considerable amount of information can be learned. Firstly, even though the stone has been incised quite deeply (which explains the survival of the inscription), the spelling is unusual, possibly indicating that there was a form of speaking Greek in Colossae that was quite different from the more polished tones of someone raised in Athens.

Secondly, his name reflects the Colossian habit (at least in early Roman imperial times) of using names that come from Greek gods or heroes. The technical name is a 'theonym'; in this case, Dion is a name built on one of the forms of Zeus, that is, Dis or Dios. Dios is a name that itself is found for a mortal in another epitaph, not yet published.

Thirdly, genealogical succession is important. In all, thirteen known epitaphs are credited to Colossae. (It should be noted that some epitaphs which have turned up in houses in the region have entered the list for Laodikeia, on the basis that Laodikeia was the larger city; some of these may have come from Colossae.) Of these, only two are without any genealogy (which may be an indication of the disruption and increased mobility [forced and voluntary] that occurred under the early Roman empire). In the case of those without genealogy, and possibly also with that of Dion given that there is no mention of wife or son, the arrangements for a proper burial would likely have fallen to a group or society of which the deceased was a member. For Dion, it was probably a voluntary association of 'leather-workers', such as we know existed at Kibyra (near modern-day Gölhisar) and Termessos (Güllük, near Antalya) to the south. We do know of one association at Colossae, called simply 'the hetairoi—the friends', although this was a technical inclusive term in Greek law for voluntary associations. Such groups in many ways provided the sort of social support and execution of responsibilities that substituted for an absent family and allowed an artisan to join the ranks of those who memorialized their own lives and death. This was a particular growing phenomenon of the Roman period.

Plate 8.32 *Georg Weber's sketch which included some dimensions of the bomos (1.28m high above the base; 0.58m across the plinth). The four lines of the inscription accord with that taken by William Calder in May, 1933.*

Fourthly, the epitaph has only four lines, which was the length for an epitaph recommended by the Greek philosopher Plato who seemed to want to discourage prolix funerary inscriptions. Probably this advice was unknown to Dion and his stone-worker; it certainly was rarely observed (sometimes glaringly so) by most epitaphs! And finally, 'he' greets whoever may be passing. In a strange way, if that bystander was one of the literate minority, she or he would have given voice to the inscription (since, in the ancient world, almost all reading was aloud); thereby a moment of immortality was granted to the deceased.

Carved reliefs on epitaphs

Sometimes the *bomoi* and stelai have a relief carved at their centre. These add weight to the genealogy that is inscribed by presenting the stability of family and/or working life that was observed by the deceased. Under the influence of regulations that the Roman emperor Augustus had introduced into the empire, stability of family life was accented (almost as compensation or obfuscation for the instability that Roman imperial presence had brought).

Plate 8.33

One relief on a stele for Tatianos son of Bartas depicts a typical family banqueting scene, with wife, children, a full table and, of course, a dog beneath. But the inscription belies the portrait. There is no mention of wife or children; only that his kinsfolk arranged the burial. It seems that even without an immediate family, Tatianos wanted to convey that he was observant of the dominant ethos of conventional society, as promoted by the Romans and doubtless reinforced by those in authority at Colossae. They would have known only too well the value placed on proper familial relationships in Augustan iconography, such as in the 'Altar of Peace', and in the Acts of Augustus (the *Res Gestae*), copies of which seem to have dotted the Roman province of Asia.

Subsequent emperors, regardless of their personal practice, reinforced these conventions. It may cast some light on the emergence of what is called 'the household code' in the letter to the Colossians (3:18–4:1) and other Christian writings (Ephesians 5:21–6:9; 1 Timothy 2:9–15, 6:1–2; 1 Peter 2:11–20). The pressure on early Christian groups beginning to be noticed by wider civic society was to present themselves as like that wider society, at least

Plate 8.33 *The funerary stele for Tatianos, erected by his distant relatives. The inscription is highlighted in red, as it may have appeared originally, just as the figures would have been fully painted as well.*

CHAPTER 8 - THE NECROPOLIS 171

as far as the exemplary value system was concerned. Christians might reinterpret the rationale behind such household structures but, for the Romans, visible conformity was paramount.

Protecting the graves

We have already seen hints of the concern about the sanctity of the grave and its occupants suggested by the presence of apotropaic symbols (like the Medusa) to ward off intruders. Some gravestones went further and expressly mentioned disturbance of the grave, prohibiting everything from damage to depositing an unrelated corpse in the grave (an act that sometimes the poor were driven to in their desire for a 'decent' burial). One epitaph memorialising a certain Karpon and his wife Tatas proscribed anyone from burying an unauthorized person in the grave; should this happen, the offender was to pay 500 denarii to the local city treasury, called the *tameion*. The second century inscription honouring Markos and his son Dionyseios, mentioned above, contains a similar warning against disturbing the grave, but this time the fine was to be paid to the Roman treasury, the *fiskus*. Perhaps the deceased thought that the oversight of Rome might confer greater protection! At other cities, such a penalty might be prescribed to be paid to a local association or even a synagogue. Sometimes three different authorities were invoked, with a reward to the accuser thrown in for good measure. The figure here at Colossae may be a relatively low amount though similar amounts are 'charged' at nearby Eumeneia and elsewhere, apparently fitting the second century CE quite well—when inflation was still modest.

Plate 8.34

Roman law (as gathered into the large collection of 'Justinian's Digest' in the sixth century CE) regarded grave desecration as an attack upon the divine and so the *fiskus* frequently was invoked as the formal regulatory agency. Though no Christian epitaphs have yet been found at Colossae, those from nearby cities indicate that Christians shared the same

Plate 8.34 *A section of the family-filled procession on one side of the Ara Pacis in Rome following the Emperor Augustus (out of picture) in the offering of sacrifice. Husbands, wives (duly advised to be silent), children and slaves all join in pious order under the guidance of the emperor.*

concerns about the sanctity of the dead as their neighbours. Christian forms of curses, in addition to monetary penalties, warned against committing such a sacrilege: the offender 'will face God'. But the infraction of the sacred ought not obscure the fact that tombs and their fabric (such as the *bomoi*) were property, enforceable and recordable in legal terms. There was as much a funeral industry in ancient Colossae as there is in most places today!

> *Our ancestors always considered it the next thing to sacrilege even to move a stone from cemeteries or to disturb the earth or to tear up the sod. But some men even take away from the tombs ornaments for their dining rooms or porticoes. We consider the interests of such criminals first, that they may not fall into sin by defiling the sanctity of tombs, and we prohibit such deeds, restraining them by the penalty which avenges the spirits of the dead.*
>
> The Edict of the Emperor Julian Against Tomb Desecration

THE FUNERAL INDUSTRY

Certainly the sheer volume of *bomoi*, chamosoria, rock tombs and tumuli at the necropolis, though not matching the number surviving at Hierapolis, still speak of the stone-polishers, stonemasons and their rock-hewing labourers that were part of the necessary personnel of the Colossian social economy, even if the number of actual funerary inscriptions only be small.

Plate 8.35

It may be that the channels and chutes that plummeted water down the escarpment at the southern end of the necropolis (on both eastern and western sides) were designed to power stone-cutting mills. Though not invented by the Romans, water-driven mills had become a refinement of Roman engineering (as we find, spanning four centuries, in the writings of the architect Vitruvius, the naturalist Pliny, the geographer Strabo, the agriculturist Palladius and even the philosopher Lucretius). But mostly, mills were conceived in connection with agriculture, for the crushing of grain and production of flour. At nearby Hierapolis, however, on the sarcophagus of Marcus Aurelius Ammianus, there is a design of a stone-cutting mill, which

Plate 8.35 *A stonemason at work, as depicted on a second century sarcophagus relief from Ephesos, now in the Archeological Museum, İstanbul.*

Ammianus claimed to have invented or constructed. It is highly likely that such an efficient piece of engineering would quickly spread through the region. Certainly by the mid-fourth century stone-saw mills were well-known in the western Roman empire on the rivulet Erubris in Bourdeaux, though whether they adopted Ammianus' design is unknown. The fourth century Latin poet, Ausonius, wrote of the falling water that 'spins his mill-stones in rapid revolutions and hauls the screaming saws through smooth blocks of marble'. If so, the supply of crafted stones for use in the necropolis was close at hand at Colossae, even if accompanied by considerable noise!

The Emperor Diocletian's Price Edict of 301 CE (much of which still stands in the odeion at Stratonikeia), lists the award for stone masons as 50 denarii per day plus food and maintenance, which is the same as for bakers, blacksmiths and a worker in tessellated floors. For comparison, farm labourers were to receive 25 denarii whereas figure painters in houses were to receive 150 denarii.

Specific letter-cutters are not mentioned in the list. Some apparently earned enough (whether or not the Edict was observed) to be memorialised by inscription in some cities as benefactors. But if they could not be benefactors, there was always a chance to turn their skill to other sorts of memorialisation. Such graffiti is in every city, and it will have been in Colossae even if not yet discovered.

Plate 8.36, 37 *The water chutes formed from two groups of three delivery points that fan out from a single channel at the southern end of the eastern side of the basin escarpment of the Colossian necropolis. The water course continued on from one bank of chutes across the necropolis basin to the western side where a further fall in the land allowed another section of chutes for mills or perhaps a nymphaeum to be constructed.*

The necropolis was an integral part of Colossian civic life and its still-quite-visible presence, up close or scanned from the top of the höyük, testifies to its vibrancy over the course of 500 years, perhaps even a millennium. In this sense, the dead continued to make a contribution to the living through the massive attention that the living paid to proper dealing with the deceased. Such attention was integral to the affirmation of the status and the wealth of those who survived them. In addition, the variety and profusion of funerary depositions and epitaphs suggests that there must have been a vigorous stone-masonry trade for the business of death in Colossae, with an associated population to support it. The landscape in the basin to the north of the höyük, now marked by agriculture, was quite

different two thousand years ago. The cemetery testified to a different mark on the landscape, filled with water facilities, mills, pathways and buildings. Here was a mirror, an extension, of the pulsating city of Colossae—the necropolis, the city of the dead.

Plate 8.38 *A section of the Latin version of Diocletian's Price Edict at Stratonikeia that carries the usual abbreviation for a 'denarius': ✕. Parts of the Price Edict have been found at Mylasa (=Milas), Aphrodisias (near Geyre), Aizanoi (=Çavdarhisar), and Synnada (=Şuhut) in Turkey (just to mention a few) and in numerous other places throughout the Mediterranean. There is little doubt that Colossae would have sported a copy of this ubiquitous and ultimately unsuccessful effort to check inflation.*
Plate 8.39 *The stone-cutter Trophimos, asked for the Lord to help him, and left his prayer cut on the less-visible side of a column in Basilica Church at Hierapolis.*

CHAPTER 8 - THE NECROPOLIS   175

Select Bibliography - Chapter Eight: The Necropolis

Ausonius *Moselle* 354.

Die Inschriften von Smyrna [*IK*] Volume 23. Edited by G Petzl; Bonn: Rudolf Habelt, 1982, §440.

Digest of Justinian 47.12.

Inscriptiones Graecae ad res Romanas pertinentes [*IGR*]. Volume IV, edited by R Cagnat, *et al*; Paris: E Leroux, 1927, §871.

Lucretius *On the Nature of Things* 5.515–16.

Monumenta Asiae Minoris Antiqua [*MAMA*] *Vol VI: Monuments and Documents from Phrygia and Caria*. Edited by W Calder and W Buckler; Manchester: Manchester University Press, 1939, §§42, 43, 44, 45, 46, 47, 48, 53.

Palladius *On Agriculture* 1.41.

Plato *The Laws* 12.

Pliny *Natural History* 18.23.

Pliny the Younger *Epistle* 2.7.7.

Ps-Quintilian *Minor Declamation* 274.9.

Regional Epigraphic Catalogues of Asia Minor [*RECAM*] Volume III. Edited by NP Milner; Oxford: British Institute of Archaeology at Ankara, 1998, §4.11.

Strabo *Geography* 12.3.30.

Suetonius *Tiberius* 37.3.

Theodosian Code 9.17.5.

Vitruvius *On Architecture* 10.5.1–2.

Ainsworth, WF, *Travels in the Track of the Ten Thousand Greeks; being a Geographical and Descriptive Account of the Expedition of Cyrus and of the Retreat of the Ten Thousand Greeks as related by Xenophon*. London: JW Parker, 1844.

Arundell, FVJ, *A Visit to the Seven Churches of Asia Minor with an excursion into Pisidia*. London: John Rodwell, 1828.

Bell, G, 'Gertrude Bell Archives' University of Newcastle-on-Tyne.

Cadwallader, AH, 'Revisiting Calder on Colossae', in *Anatolian Studies* 56 (2006): 103–11.

— 'A New Inscription, a Correction and a Confirmed Sighting from Colossae', in *Epigraphica Anatolica* 40 (2007): 109–18.

—'Refuting an Axiom of Scholarship on Colossae: fresh insights from new and old inscriptions', in *Colossae in Space and Time*. Edited by AH Cadwallader and M Trainor; Göttingen: Vandenhoeck and Ruprecht, 2011, 151–79.

— 'Honoring the Repairer of the Baths: a New Inscription from Kolossai', in *Antichthon* 46 (2012): 150-83.

— 'The Struggle for Paul in the Context of Empire: Mark as a Deutero-Pauline Text', in *Paul and Mark in Comparison: Authors at the Beginning of Christianity*. Edited by DC Sim and O Wischmeyer; Tübingen: de Gruyter, 2014.

Calder, WM, 'Early Christian Epitaphs from Phrygia', in *Anatolian Studies* 5 (1955): 25–38.

Cormack, S, 'Funerary Monuments and Mortuary Practice in Roman Asia Minor', in *The Early Roman Empire in the East*. Edited by SE Alcock; Oxford: Oxbow, 1997.

—*The Space of Death in Roman Asia Minor*. Wien: Phoibos, 2004.

Grewe, K, 'Die Reliefdarstellung einer antiken Steinsägemaschine aus Hierapolis in Phrygien und ihre Bedeutung für die Technikgeschichte', in *Bautechnik im Antiken und Vorantiken Kleinasien*. Edited by M Bachmann; Istanbul: Ege Yayınları, 2009, 429–54.

Haspels, CHE, *The Highlands of Phrygia: Sites and Monuments*. Princeton, NJ: Princeton University Press, 1971.

Hopkins, K, *Death and Renewal*. Cambridge: Cambridge University Press, 1983.

Işık, F, 'Zu Produktionsbeginn und Ende der kleinasiatischen Girlandensarkophage der Hauptgruppe', in *Akten des Symposiums >>125 Jahre Sarkophag-Corpus<< Marburg, 4.–7. Oktober 1995*. Edited by R Amedick, D Bielefeld, D Grassinger and C Wölfel; Mainz: von Zabern, 1998, 278–94.

—*Die Girlanden-Sarkophage aus Aphrodisias*. Mainz: von Zabern, 2007.

Jones, CP, 'Interrupted Funerals', in *Proceedings of the American Philosophical Society* 143 (1999): 597–600.

Koch, G and H Sichtermann, *Römische Sarkophage*. München: Beck, 1982.

Koch, G and H Wight, *Roman Funerary Sculpture: Catalogue of the Collections [in the J Paul Getty Museum]*. Malibu, CA: J Paul Getty Museum, 1988.

Kubińska, J, *Les Monuments funéraire dans les Inscriptions grecques de l'Asie Mineure*. Warsaw: PWN, 1968.

Laborde, ALJ de, *Voyage de l'Asie Mineure*. Paris: Firmin Didot, 1838.

Malay, H, 'New Inscriptions from Phrygia', in *Arkeoloi Dergisi* 2 (1994): 173–83.

Mayer, E, *The Ancient Middle Classes: Urban Life and Aesthetics in the Roman Empire, 100BCE – 250 CE*. Cambridge, Mass: Harvard University Press, 2012.

Oliver, GJ, 'An Introduction to the Epigraphy of Death: Funerary Inscriptions as Evidence', in *The Epigraphy of Death: Studies in the History and Society of Greece and Rome*. Edited by GJ Oliver; Liverpool: Liverpool University Press, 2000, 1–23.

Pearce, J, M Millett and M Struck (eds), *Burial, Society and Context in the Roman World*. Oxford: Oxbow, 2000.

Pomeroy, S, *Families in Classical and Hellenistic Greece: Representations and Realities*. Oxford/NY: OUP, 1997.

Pfuhl, E and H Möbius, *Die Ostgriechischen Grabreliefs: Textband & Tafelband* 4 vols; Mainz: von Zabern, 1979.

Reynolds, TS, *Stronger than a Hundred Men: A History of the Vertical Water Wheel*. Baltimore: Johns Hopkins University Press, 1983.

Roueché, C, 'The Funeral of Tatia Attalis at Aphrodisias', in *Ktéma* 17 (1992): 153–60.

Şimşek, C, 'Kolossai', in *Arkeoloji ve Sanat* 107 (2002): 3–17.

—*Laodikeia (Laodikeia ad Lycum)*. Istanbul: Ege Yayınları, 2007.

Sivas, H, 'Rock Cut Necropoleis of Western Phrygia (From Phrygian Period to Roman Imperial Period)', in *SOMA 2005: Proceedings of the IX Symposium on Mediterranean Archeology, Chieta (Italy) 24–26 February 2005*. Edited by O Menozzi, ML di Marzio and D Fossataro. Oxford: Archaeopress, 2008, 161–69.

Smith RRR, 'Sarcophagi and Roman citizenship', in *Aphrodisias Papers IV: New Research on the City and its Monuments*. Edited by C Ratté and RRR Smith; Portsmouth, RI: Journal of Roman Archaeology, 2008, 347–94.

Somerville, WF, *The Churches in Asia: Extracts from the Home Letters of Rev AN Somerville DD from the Region of the Seven Churches*. Paisley: J & R Parlane, 1885.

Spanu, M, 'Burial in Asia Minor during the Imperial Period, with a particular reference to Cilicia and Cappadocia' in *Burial, Society and Context in the Roman World*. Edited by J Pearce, M Millett and M Struck; Oxford: Oxbow, 2001, 169–77.

Strelan, R, 'The Languages of the Lycus Valley', in *Colossae in Space and Time*. Edited by AH Cadwallader and M Trainor; Göttingen: Vandenhoeck & Ruprecht, 2011, 77–103.

Strocka, VM, 'Daitierungkriterien kleinasiatischer Girlandensarkophage', in *Archäologischer Anzeiger* 3 (1996): 455–73.

Strubbe, J, *ARAI EPITUMBIOI Imprecations against Desecrators of the Grave in the Greek Epitaphs of Asia Minor. A Catalogue* [=*IK* 52] Bonn: Habelt, 1997.

Thomas, C, 'Placing the Dead: Funerary Practice and Social Stratification in the Early Roman Period at Corinth and Ephesos', in *Urban Religion in Roman Corinth: Interdisciplinary Approaches*. Edited by DN Schowalter and SJ Friesen; Cambridge, Mass: Harvard University Press, 2005, 281–304.

Thonemann, P (ed), *Roman Phrygia*. Cambridge: Cambridge University Press, 2013.

Vassileva, M, 'The Rock-cut Monuments of Phrygia, Paphlagonia and Thrace: A Comparative Overview', in *The Black Sea, Paphlagonia, Pontus and Phrygia in Antiquity: Aspects of archaeology and ancient history*. Edited by GR Tsetskhladze. BAR International Series 2432; Oxford: Archaeopress, 2012, 243–52.

Thonemann, P, 'A Copy of Augustus' *Res Gestae* at Sardis', in *Historia* 61 (2012): 282–88.

Weber, G, 'Der unterirdische Lauf des Lykos bei Kolossai', in *Athenische Mitteilungen* 16 (1891): 194–99.

Wiegartz, H, *Kleinasiatische Säulensarkophage: Untersuchungen zum Sarkophagtypus und zu den figürlichen Darstellungen*. Istanbuler Forschungen 26; Berlin: Gebr. Mann, 1965.

Wujeski, T, *Anatolian Sepulchral Stelae in Roman Times*. Pozna'n: UAM, 1991.

Yıldız, H, 'Denizli Müzesi Müdürlüğü Lycos Vadisi Çalışmaları', in *Müze Kurtarma Kazıları Semineri* 9 (1999): 247–62.

Yıldız, H and C Şimşek, 'Sarcofagi a Ghirlande dalla Necropoli di Laodicea al Lykos / Laodikeia ana Küme Girlandlı Lahidleri (A ve B)' in *Ricerche Archeologiche Turche nella Valle del Lykos/Lykos Vadisi Türk Arkeoloji Arastirmalari*. Edited by F d'Andria and F Silvestrelli; Lecce: Congredo Editore, 2000, 99–165.

Zanker, P, *The Power of Images in the Age of Augustus*. Translated by A Shapiro; Ann Arbor, Mich: University of Michigan Press, 1990.

Plate 9.1 *A section of a fresco from Decani monastery in Kosovo showing the archangel Michael controlling the waters.*

CHAPTER 9
The Mighty Archangel

THE SACREDNESS OF WATER

Water is the lifeblood of any human settlement. When it is combined with an awesome, imposing landscape or the shrouded remembrance of some uncanny natural phenomenon or some mysterious origin or happening, it becomes charged with religious significance. Frontinus, a first century CE water commissioner in Rome, recognised what everyone knew: 'Esteem for springs still continues, and is observed with veneration. They are believed to bring healing to the sick.' As he also knew at first hand, water then becomes surrounded by regulations, architectural control and even contested claims.

Centuries earlier, the Persians had operated from the same assumptions, claiming tokens of earth and water as signs of submission to their rule, even asserting that control of water was the particular power and authority of their goddess Anahita. The assertion of her power in Anatolia, however, was no coincidence. She took on many of the characteristics of the old Phrygian goddess, Kybebe, more familiarly known under her Greek name of Cybele or simply the 'great mother'.

Thereby, the Persians sought to demonstrate through the power of religious symbolism that one of their deities was already present and known in the land they had conquered. Honouring her was made as much part of the acceptance of Persian rule as it had been a religious obligation under the previous authority.

This is a familiar tactic of invaders whether military or religious or both. They invest their own symbolic figureheads with elements of pre-existing powers to whom the conquered peoples have been

Plate 9.2 *The richly watered Lycus-Maeander Valley with the towering peak of Mt Honaz (ancient Mt Cadmus) at the right and the white steps of Hierapolis to the left of centre. A nineteenth-century sketch by CG Danford.*

Plate 9.3 *A grave stone from Halicarnassus (=Bodrum) that features Cybele, flanked by her usual companions, two lions, and holding a patera, often used to dispense purifying waters.*

Plates 9.4–7 *Winged beings from four different periods: the Mesopotamian goddess Ishtar, an Assyrian guardian spirit, the Phrygian god Attis and the Roman winged Victory.*

devoted. So the gods of the victors do not merely conquer; they absorb. This ensures that a sense of continuity and a measure of acceptance can be harnessed from those who find themselves under new governmental control. And of course, such general ways of operating have quite specific dividends, not least in attracting imaginative and practical harnessing of water.

The presence of angels through history

The same dynamics are played out with angels. Winged beings reach back into the early history of the region and pass on various characteristics through the ages, though often with considerable imprecision about their gender.

Plate 9.8 *Zeus represented as both eagle and thunderbolt in a relief now located at Manisa Museum.*

Arching over all this variety, however, was influence of the most common symbol of Zeus: the eagle, majestically riding the air of the heavens high above mere mortals. But at Colossae, as in many places of mountainous Turkey, the almost equally favoured symbol of Zeus—the thunderbolt—is to be found. The storms that gathered around Mt Cadmus (Honazdağ), the rumblings of the earth through seismic activity, all contributed to a sense of Zeus as loud, flashy, powerful and as timeless as the towering landscape itself.

It is likely that Zeus was the patron god of Colossae in the Hellenistic and early Roman periods. Colossae's coins from the Greek and Roman periods provide the evidence. All bar one of the extant Hellenistic coins from Colossae is ablaze with Zeus' thunderbolt and portrait. When the license to mint its own coins was restored to Colossae early in Hadrian's reign (ruled, 117–138 CE), Zeus was the god chosen to launch the new coinage, albeit not the thunderbolt-Zeus but Zeus Aetophoros, that is, Zeus the bearer-of-the-eagle. This iconography fitted well to express a combination of Zeus' special place in Colossian religious life, Hadrian's own desire to accent Hellenism (a behaving-as-Greek) in his own rule and Colossae's (sometimes grudging) acceptance of Laodikeia's loyalty to Rome expressed through the same image. (See Chapter Three, *The Gods in City and Country*.) In fact, Zeus Aetophoros is sometimes called Zeus Laodikensis (the Laodikeian Zeus)—and this marked Colossae's return to minting. Zeus (whom the Romans called Jove or Jupiter) was not merely the chief of the gods. He was the chief god of the Colossians.

In the first three hundred or so years of the Common Era (CE), Christians did not have a mortgage on angels, most especially because winged supernatural beings increasingly became identified as gods, not simply as messengers of the gods. One oracle from the shrine of Apollo at Klaros (=Ahmetbeyli), but found on an inscription at Oinoanda (=İncealiler), was delivered in response to the question 'Are you god? Or is someone else?' One might have expected an oracle centre to have extolled the god of oracles, Apollo. But the answer was surprising. The oracle proclaimed 'all-seeing Ether' was God; all the Olympian deities (including, presumably Zeus) were 'angels', parts of this all-seeing One. Indeed, angels could even be described as god's eyes.

Christians inherited considerable exposure to angels from their Jewish heritage which itself had been influenced by traditions of winged beings in surrounding religions. But those Christians who had no Jewish background also had a ready store of stories of angels or winged beings in religions that they had come from or with which they were familiar. One book of the New Testament is filled with angels and has its geographical focus as Asia Minor (the book of Revelation). Amongst the many references to angels, one stands out: the archangel Michael (see Revelation 12:7). As we will see, this archangel Michael became such a powerful figure for Christian Colossae that he inherited many of the features of the previous powerful figure of Colossae: Zeus.

The archangel Michael in Asia Minor

Given the rich presence of angels amongst many religious groups in the region, it is no surprise to find Michael emerging quite early as a prominent focus of Christian devotion in various places. John Arnold from the State University of New York, has dubbed Michael, 'an ecumenical archangel'. One famous St Michael pilgrimage site was located at Germia (also called Myriangeloi, 'myriads of angels'; near modern Günyüzü) in Galatia. And a church or sanctuary of St Michael the archangel seems to have been established perhaps as early as the fourth century in Stratonikeia (near modern Eskihisar), though the formal boundary stone for the property of a sanctuary recently discovered there probably dates to a slightly later time. A similar boundary stone from the fifth century comes from Parsa, a small town between Sardis (=Sart) and Smyrna (=İzmir).

But devotion to St Michael was not restricted to church foundations. The village of Ennaton, not far from Philadelphia (=Alaşehir) set up a stone with a lengthy exorcism formula calling on Michael and four other angels to protect the place from storms ... and the bad behavior of the inhabitants! At

Plates 9.9, 10 *The Colossian coin (c200 BCE) of Zeus and his thunderbolt and one of the earliest mintings of a Colossian coin in the Roman imperial period, of Hadrian and Zeus Aetophoros.*

Aphrodisias (=Geyre), a large fresco of St Michael the archangel has been found in a room of the theatre *scaena*, that is, in a chamber where actors and set operators would prepare for performances. It is dated to the sixth century CE, at a time when the theatre was still functioning, so it appears likely that it was a private dedication.

THE STORY OF ST MICHAEL OF CHONAI

But there is one story that predates all these in its witness to devotion to Michael the archangel. This is the story of St Michael of Chonai, one of the key narratives associated with Colossae. There are only four main texts connected with Colossae that we know about. The first two are the most well-known today: St Paul's letter to Philemon and the letter to Colossians in the New Testament. A third is barely known—an encomium, or speech of praise in funerary honour of a late Byzantine Metropolitan bishop of Colossae named Nicetas, written by another archbishop (of Athens) who had grown up in the same area and who was named after it, Michael Choniates (c1138–1222 CE). His 'second name', as we will see, takes on a particular ring, because of the name that the city of Colossae came to be known by: Chonai.

Plate 9.11

Plate 9.12

The fourth text, the story of St Michael of Chonai, virtually spans the period between the New Testament and the last phase of Byzantine control of the area. In brief, the story begins with the Apostle John—famous from Ephesos connections—and the Apostle Philip, long associated with Hierapolis (=Pamukkale). St Paul, so often connected with Colossae, is completely absent. John and Philip combine to rid Hierapolis of the threatening hold of three goddesses who seem rolled into one: Artemis, Echidna and Cybele the 'great mother'.

In the aftermath of this Christian victory against idolatry, the apostles predict that a miraculous healing spring is to be found at a 'place of favour' (sometimes called Chairetopa, as this phrase is found in Greek, or Keretapa in Turkish, a relatively common place-name). It is to be the providential gift of the archangel Michael. Sure enough, the spring is discovered but this only seems to be the beginning of intense conflict over the site. The conflict is

Plate 9.11 *The Director of the Archaeological Excavations at Stratonikeia, Professor Bilal Sögüt, with the inscribed boundary stone for the sanctuary (*asuliasion*) of St Michael.*
Plate 9.12 *A fresco depicting Archbishop Michael Choniates from St Peter's Church in Kalyvia Kuvara near Athens.*

orchestrated from Colossae's neighbor, Laodikeia. In the story, Laodikeia is construed as unremittingly pagan, a last bastion of idolatry. The later, more polished versions of the story couldn't cope with such a portrait of Laodikeia—after all it was early noted as a Christian centre mentioned in the New Testament letter to the Colossians (2:1, 4:13), and in the book of Revelation, albeit severely criticized (3:14–22). These refining writers of the tenth and eleventh century respectively, one a Patriarch of Constantinople (Sisinnius), the other a high-ranking Byzantine bureaucrat (Simeon, called 'Metaphrastes'), changed the story either removing the name Laodikeia altogether or claiming it was a different Laodikeia—in Lycia—rather than Colossae's neighbor. But in the popular early version of the story, Laodikeia is described no longer as its name suggests—'people of righteousness'—but as 'people of unrighteousness', a lawless mob.

The story unfolds with an antagonist from Laodikeia who has a daughter, dumb from birth. The archangel Michael visits him in a dream and instructs him to take his daughter to the sacred waters if he would see his child healed. When he ventures to the *hagiasma* (the healing spring) he discovers that both pagan Greeks and Christians are benefiting from the healing site but the controlling power is the Christian god and the archangel Michael. The daughter is healed, heralding the power of Father, Son and Holy Spirit and the greatness of the archangel Michael. The father bequeaths a building for the site and leaves with his healed daughter, notably without mention of a return to Laodikeia. A keeper for the site named Archippos arrives nearly a century later, coming at the young age of ten, and assiduously serves for a remaining seventy years as prayerful and ascetic custodian.

The shrine and its keeper occasion an increase in popularity with many being attracted to make the pilgrimage to the site, being healed and converted. This seems to enrage other pagans who gather at Laodikeia to mount a succession of assaults on the site and its guardian. They are said to be motivated by the desire to restore the power of the gods, even though behind this avowal, according to the story, stands the Devil, who is described in multiple layers of dark intent. At first they simply molest Archippos;

Plate 9.13

Plate 9.13 *The Martyrion of St Philip at the right and the still-being-excavated Church of St Philip where his remains were venerated. These substantial structures at Hierapolis overlook the theatre and city, and indicate how closely the apostle was associated with the city in ancient legend. This connection launches the story of St Michael of Chonai and Hierapolis also is the city from which hails the first custodian of the St Michael healing spring. His name is Archippos.*

then they try to destroy the sanctity of the site by attacking the architectural fabric. The archangel appears and confronts the malicious enemies with a giant fireball and restrains their hands. The opponents then turn against the spring itself hoping that by channeling ordinary waters into the spring it would lose its sanctity and power. (Ancient understandings of pollution and desecration, known from regulations governing sacred waters at sanctuaries, such as that of Artemis at Ephesos, lie in the background here.) But the power of the holy water is so great that the mundane river waters are turned back upon themselves into new paths in the landscape.

Finally, the most pronounced and massive offensive is planned. The forces of dark intent construct a huge dam high in the mountain so that waters might accumulate to such a huge volume that, when released, the whole area would be swept away. (The use of flooding as a weapon of war is known from the campaigns of the Assyrian king Sennacherib against the city of Babylon in 703 BCE.) Again the mighty archangel steps in, splitting a monolith that had stood intact from the beginning of time, opening a ravine into which the deluge could be funneled and turning the gawking pagans to stone. Then, with Archippos at his side, Michael blesses the healing spring for all time. The word 'funnel' gave the city its popular name, Chonai (Turkish: *huni*), the name by which Colossae came to be celebrated.

Plate 9.14

One can understand how the story became enormously popular, an exciting narrative to tell when on pilgrimage to the site and at church festivals that grew up to celebrate the providence of the mighty archangel. But worked into the story are far more potent, political considerations than a 'ripping yarn'. The conflicts in the story betray actual conflicts at various times in the history of the site.

THE GEOGRAPHY AND HISTORY BEHIND THE STORY

The first level of conflict is really the battle over ownership of the site. Scholars have long suspected that this story, as with many across the Mediterranean world, originates in a pre-Christian foundation. The site was already sacred long before the Christians became the dominant religious interpreter of such places. The dream-like vision of the archangel that vindicates the healing powers of the site under the Christian god and Michael the archangel has the typical form of a coming 'foundation story' with the corroborative authority of an epiphany. A person is confronted by a god, usually in a dream, and

Plate 9.14 *The opponents of the shrine and its custodian are not always included in church iconography of the dramatic rescue by the archangel Michael, but in this fifteenth-century representation, they even carry the picks used to cut the rocks to dam the waters.*

told of a providential marvel that he must honour especially by dedicating a building that marks out and protects the place where the miracle is given. It is no coincidence that Michael takes on many of the features of this pre-Christian god. His heaven to earth shaft of brilliant, light-filled appearing, his thunderous voice, his ability to manipulate nature, all carry the marks of Zeus. Indeed, in the popular story (deleted in the later re-writes), Michael even calls for a form of address that is most frequently associated with Zeus: 'mark my name'—give honour to it, swear by it. The Christian turn of the story comes when Michael, for all his Zeus-like qualities, proclaims that he is as nothing before the might of the Christian God. So orthodoxy is preserved but so is continuity with the past. For ordinary people, whether coming as pagans or converts, the familiar elements were preserved—of divine protection and provision, especially of the health and well-being associated with the mysterious and sacred spring. The transition from pagan to Christian story is, at this level, relatively innocuous; the story even admits that pagans, or 'Greeks' as they are often labeled in the story, can live side-by-side drawing benefit from the *hagiasma*.

What's more, the story gave indications of divine validation of the site, not only with its preservation and rescue against all odds by the appearing of its divine protector, but also by pointing outside the

Plate 9.15 *Nature's witness to Michael: the mighty monolith.*
Plate 9.16 *Nature's witness to Michael, looking east: the monolith rising from the trees at centre left, with the chasm at right.*

story to verifying marks impressed on the landscape. Here were clearly visible the split monolith overlooking the site, the ravine lanced by the power of the archangel and the multiple smaller rocky outcrops of petrified forms—the ultimate end of the enemies in the story. These features still bear their testimony to the site of the healing waters today.

Plate 9.17

Such topographical features not only help to identify elements in the story but also to pinpoint the actual site, still known to local people who carry a memory of its healing properties. That site is known today as Göz Picnic Ground where voluminous flows of water still gush forth from various spots at the site. These natural features are thereby given an explanation in the story and lend their immense geological witness to the spring's sanctity and origins. For those who visited the site, already filled with the story, the grandeur of nature's testimony inspired hope and awe.

Plate 9.17 *Local Honaz resident, Mustafa Bayrak, indicates where the spring first emerges from the ground.*
Plate 9.18 *The modern structures of Göz Picnic Ground built to accommodate the springs.*
Plate 9.19 *One ancient constructed outlet for the underground spring still visible at the site.*

CHAPTER 9 - THE MIGHTY ARCHANGEL

The Waters and the Search for Ancient Colossae

One particular feature of the story attracted early travellers and interpreters of the story. To them the sudden evacuation of waters into a subterranean cavern had obvious resonance with a fantastic report given by the so-called father of history, Herodotos.

> Passing by the Phrygian town called Anaua, and the lake from which salt is obtained, Xerxes came to Colossae, a great city in Phrygia; there the river Lycus plunges into a cleft in the earth and disappears, until it reappears about five stadia away; this river issues into the Maeander.
>
> Herodotos, *The Histories*.

For eighteenth- and nineteenth-century explorers, this was *the* ancient literary text that could guide them (so they thought) to ancient Colossae, a city that had all but disappeared from European sight after the Seljuk takeover of the region in the thirteenth-century. Of course, they were expecting that the great classical historian Herodotos would be confirmed in what he wrote. The travelers took the Greek and Roman classics as well as the bible at face value as historically and geographically correct. Only later would these texts be understood to be more subtle and diverse.

One of the ways that early explorers tried to substantiate ancient texts was to find an inscription that carried the name of the city or its people—in this case, 'Colossae' or the 'Colossians'. So desperate were other early epigraphers to have 'Colossae' named on an inscription found on or near the site that one quite fragmentary inscription was heavily reconstructed in one of the major early collections of inscriptions, so that 'the Colossians' suddenly appeared in a published text. The journal note of the Rev'd Francis Arundell, the person who found the inscription, carried no indication that an epigraphical confirmation of a place-name had been found.

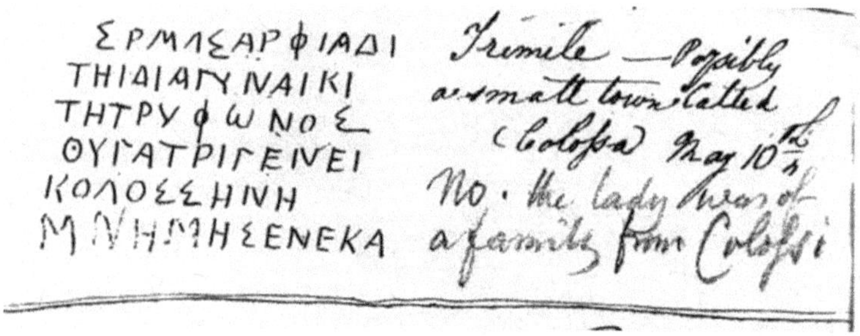

Plate 9.20 *Excerpt from the notebook of Edward Daniell recording his initial reading (with a later correction) of an inscription found at Trimile (=Altınyayla). The (corrected) inscription reads, "Hermas, for the sake of remembrance, erected this for his wife Apphia, who was the daughter of Tryphon and by birth a Colossian."*

Problems for this method arose when a place-name seemed to occur out-of-place. Considerable consternation beset the Rev'd Edward T Daniell in 1842 when he found an inscription that mentioned a certain Apphia, daughter of Tryphon, 'a Colossian'. The only trouble was, the river Lycus was nowhere to be seen in the part of the region of Caria where his expeditionary party (led by the English naval officer, Lieutenant Thomas Spratt and the naturalist Edward Forbes) was located—that is, between Boubon (near İbecik) and Balboura (=Çölkayiği). So he 'fudged' his initial report in his diary, so that this became a different 'Colossa', to him a small town near Trimile (=Dirmil).

Later it would be clarified that the woman Apphia had married and moved outside of Colossae but her home city and her father were so important to her that these details were, somewhat unusually, retained on the epitaph.

So this left the Lycus River as the means of pinpointing where Colossae was to be found. The problem was that a trek west along the Lycus from Denizli revealed no disappearing river. The old fallback explanation, that is, an earthquake had destroyed the evidence, came to be relied upon to argue that Herodotos was not wrong. It was proposed that the river, like other watercourses in the honey-combed limestone geology of Asia Minor, had originally disappeared into the ground only to re-appear a good length downstream. But that feature had since been seismically destroyed. This was the argument published by William Hamilton who surveyed the site around the höyük in 1836.

Plates 9.21–23 *The Lycus River at different times of the year, reveals its deep-pitted limestone course and the illusions of disappearing and appearing water flows.*

CHAPTER 9 - THE MIGHTY ARCHANGEL

Plate 9.24

His ideas were substantially accepted and promoted in the English-speaking world, at least until Georg Weber at the end of the nineteenth-century argued decisively that the other, perhaps shocking, option was the more likely—that Herodotos was wrong and had swallowed a fantastic story told to him.

The region around Honaz actually has a number of contenders for the Herodotos story. When the French explorer, Alexandre Laborde, travelled through the area in 1826, he made his way some kilometres further east of the höyük to a place that was then called, as he reports it, Suruksu. He felt that his discovery of a cave with flowing water that spills out and feeds into the Lycus was the exact confirmation that Herodotos needed, and sketched a fine drawing to substantiate his discovery (see Plate 9.25).

However, the ease with which Herodotos' dubious account was equated with the story of St Michael has misled commentators, even modern ones, into thinking that the ravine funnel of the archangel's effortless engineering referred to the Lycus River itself. Admittedly there are some steep cliffs that the Lycus has carved to the west of the höyük but there is nothing else (monolith, petrified boulders) that can corroborate the link. What appears to have diverted attention is that the traditional site of the church of St. Michael (yet to be confirmed by any archaeological excavation) lies across the modern (and partly ancient road) on the north side of the river.

By tying the St Michael story geographically to the church that celebrated it, the Christian narrative became a confirmation of Herodotos even if the evidence 'on the ground' was lacking. It seems that when Laborde passed through Denizli, some Greeks there had adjusted the story of St Michael's providential rescue so that the dramatic salvation was now of the church, not the *hagiasma*, named after the archangel who now wanted to prevent it from collapse into the raging, biting erosions of the 'wolf' (=Lycus) river. No longer was the healing spring the focus of his protective intervention. This version probably derived from an anonymous Byzantine historian, who added a postscript to the history written by John Scylitzes. He was pre-occupied with the focus of the invading Turks on the church of St Michael. By recalling the archangel's intervention by miraculous visitations in the past and now drawn to the site of the church, he probably hoped to revive Christian morale and perhaps even hoped to draw the archangel to make another epiphany.

Plate 9.24 *The travertine cliff overhangs to the west of the höyük formed by perennial tributaries flowing into the Lycus River may have influenced Hamilton into thinking that they at one stage completely covered the main water flow until the artificial arch was severed by an earthquake. His geological hypothesis lacked substance.*

But such a relocation required a dismissal of the constant refrain in the St Michael story, namely that it was set in a rural context strongly contrasted from the 'city' the place of subtle intrigue and political machinations. The traditional site of the St Michael church cannot claim to be anything other than 'city' in its current placement near the höyük; certainly Byzantine writers who mention the magnificent church are in no doubt that it is located at the city.

Rather the actual site appears to have been a sacred installation, rural in its origins but sufficiently close to the city of Colossae to be identified with it, especially under its 'new' name Chonai. In fact, the three kilometres distance between *hagiasma* and *höyük* would have lent itself very comfortably to a processional way where the god Zeus and later the archangel Michael and the God he served could be honoured with festival celebrations and liturgical re-enactments. These processions and celebrations are familiar enough at Ephesos for Artemis and from Miletos (=Balat) to Didyma (=Didim)—all 17 kilometres of it, for Apollo! Perhaps the most striking parallel is with the temple of Zeus Panamara, a rural site south of the city of Stratonikeia. An inscription of a long official city decree privileges the site because of a series of epiphanies of the mighty Zeus to defend the city against overwhelming odds in a siege laid against it by Labienus, a militant Roman usurper, in 40 BCE. The Zeus-Michael connection at Stratonikeia is remarkably parallel to the Colossian story.

Plate 9.25 *The sketch of 'Suruksou' by Alexandre Laborde. Today the site is a major tourist attraction for Honaz, albeit now known as the Kaklık cave complex.*
Plate 9.26 *The area traditionally labeled St Michael's Church retains a number of architectural fragments that lend some weight to the location. The area is now substantially under orchard. The twelfth century 'son of Chonai', named Nicetas Choniates, declaimed the church as the largest Michael church in Asia. Perhaps home-town bias coloured his description. The traditional site offers little to confirm his grandiose description, apart from wall blocks that line a space measuring approximately 100 metres by 40 metres.*

THE STORY AND THE ROMAN EMPEROR JULIAN 'THE APOSTATE'

But the extreme negativity shown by the story towards the female gods, especially given Phrygian devotion to the 'great mother', points to another moment of crisis that impacted Colossae and the entire Roman empire of the fourth century CE. This was the short-lived period of the reign of Julian, later dubbed 'the Apostate' by Christian writers of history.

This explains why the story includes a number of general references to 'the Greeks' not just 'pagans'. Julian's great ambition was to revive Greek religion and philosophy. There were a number of prongs to this policy—pagan temples were to be restored, refurbished, reopened and revived; Greek practices were to be encouraged and determined efforts in the realm of ideas and ascetic practice were to be made to win admiration for this return to past polytheistic world-views. Topping it all off was the re-appearance of sacrifices, so much so that Julian was lampooned as 'the butcher'.

A hint of the battle to revive these ancient religious practices is found in the story of St Michael. The inimical Greeks argue that they must eradicate the Christian site, saying that otherwise 'all our gods will amount to nothing'. The emperor lead the charge and added a certain touch of eastern flavor by accenting how important 'the great mother' was to this program. He wrote an extensive 'hymn', really a philosophical treatise, extolling her worth. He visited Cybele sites, providing munificently for their on-going viability. The feminine therefore became in the second half of the fourth century irrevocably connected with Julian's 'idolatrous' policies. In another story of the battle with heathen idolatry told by Gregory of Nyssa, a Christian soldier, Theodore (called 'the Recruit'), ridicules a pagan soldier's deity because it was prolifically female. Even though Theodore belongs to the period of Emperor Maximian (ruled 287–305 CE) at the beginning of the fourth century, by the time Gregory, a famous Bishop of Nyssa, shaped the story around 380 CE, it was clearly directed to damning the memory of a more recent emperor.

> 'You, however, o pitiable man with the intellect of a child, don't you blush or hide due to your confession in a female god and your veneration for her, a mother of twelve children, a kind of very fertile goddess who just like a hare or a sow effortlessly conceives and gives birth!'
>
> Gregory of Nyssa, *Panegyric on Theodore the Recruit*

Plate 9.27 *The bearded Emperor Julian (ruled 360–63 CE).*

Some accommodation to the old religious ideas was necessary for Christian productive and accepted continuity of such a healing site; but that continuity had to be male to remove any hint of influence of Julian's program. Zeus, not Cybele, provided the contours of the Christian god's providence—through his archangel. As for Julian, he is never mentioned explicitly in the story. However there are certain descriptions given to the devil that seem clearly to have the emperor and his practices in mind.

> It is he who is the murderer of saints and persecutor of divine churches, the terminator of wellbeing and tempter of the weak. He is the one who deceived the world and refused to be sated.
>
> *The Story of Michael of Chonai,*

It would not be the first time that religious groups have characterized their opponents as beings in league with the forces of darkness.

The complication comes with the naming of Laodikeia in none too flattering terms. The difficulty lies in the story portraying Laodikeia in terms of idolatry even though Laodikeia was clearly a well-credentialed Christian city by the fourth-century. It could boast a succession of martyrs for the faith, including the bishop Sagaris in the second century and the priest Artemon in the fourth century. From recent excavations directed by Professor Celal Şimşek, significant churches were built there from as early as the fourth century.

The hierarchical structures of early Christian administration imitated Roman models and made Laodikeia the centre (called 'the metropolitical diocese') of a group of regional dioceses. One of these regional dioceses was Colossae (as also was Hierapolis).

Given that the popular story of St Michael of Chonai has a substantial section that seems to reflect the

Plate 9.28 *A well-preserved cross-shaped baptistery from an early Byzantine church at Laodikeia.*

Plate 9.29

period of the emperor Julian, called the Apostate, in the fourth century, it appears strange that the story would label Laodikeia as 'idolatrous' without any redemptive Christian presence. The clue is to be found in a none-too-subtle attack on the St Michael cult that was passed at a special meeting (called a 'council' or 'synod') held at Laodikeia.

> Christians shall not forsake the Church of God and turn to the worship of angels, thus having gatherings in their honour. This is forbidden. Those who devote themselves to this hidden idolatry, let them be anathema, because they have forsaken our Lord Jesus Christ, the Son of God, and gone over to idolatry.
>
> *Canon 35, Council of Laodikeia, 365 CE*

Although Colossae is not expressly mentioned, later commentators, such as the fifth century Theodoret, the Bishop of Cyrrhus, were in no doubt— Colossae had been accused of idolatry because of the veneration of the archangel Michael at his healing spring. The church of Colossae was powerless to use administrative processes to defeat this attack on its acclaimed site. But what it did have was the sympathies of the people and of visitors who loved the archangel, his healing powers and the site where healing and epiphanies occurred. As it happened Laodikeia, right at this time, was suspected of harbouring its own false ideas, a Christian heresy called 'Arianism'. Those thought to have Arian leanings were also sometimes called 'idolaters'. This is exactly the term used for the enemies of the archangel's sacred place in the story and who 'gather' (another word in Canon 35) at Laodikeia. So a story moved from being a simple foundation story for a sacred site to being a conflict story, not against 'pagans' or 'Greeks' in reality, but against fellow Christians, positioning themselves against each other as a means of demonstrating they were standing against everything Julian the Apostate had promoted. As part of this struggle, Colossae began to call itself by the key event of the archangel's rescue in the story when the floods were funneled into the underground. Chonai means 'funnels'. Even the name of the guardian of the shrine, Archippos, may have been chosen because Laodikeia had claimed as its first bishop, the Archippos mentioned in the New Testament letter to Philemon. In every possible way, Colossae positioned itself against Laodikeia.

Plate 9.29 *A nineteenth century banner hanging in the Orthodox Church in the Fener district, İstanbul, shows a militaristic archangel, St Michael of Chonai, spearing a hole in the ground to funnel away the waters that threaten Archippos and the church/shrine (in the background).*

Eventually the popular story triumphed over the conciliar anathema. St Michael of Chonai became a champion of the late Byzantine emperors as they struggled to hold their empire. The archangel of Chonai even began to change in appearance to look more like a military general, just as was indicated by his title in the story 'archistrategos' (commander-in-chief). Unlike Julian who had used military force against the Christian god, Michael was a military general who was devoted to the service of that god.

The story and the battle over icons

This was not the only time that the St Michael story exerted an enormous influence in disputes between different Christian groups. In the ninth century, Colossae was gripped by its own heretical hierarchy. The local bishop became a champion of the rejection of icons and he was backed up by a high-ranking imperial administrator, called an exarch. This 'iconoclast crisis', as the period is called, again threatened not only the devotion to icons but also the site itself, as it had begun to inspire representation in icons. An old part of the story became critical to arguments in this new conflict. The propositions were presented by a learned monk, Theodore the Studite (who actually visited Chonai to dispute with the bishop), that the archangel had already made an enormous impact on the natural environment. If a spiritual being could do this to the material world, and leave a means of recognizing him in nature, then the material representation in icons of the angels (and saints and holy women and men) was equally legitimate. Theodore's argument won, but the popular story and its multitudes of readers and hearers provided the momentum. Colossae/Chonai was declared its own metropolitical diocese within a century, perhaps as a reward for eventually (in this case) taking a stand against what the wider church came to impugn as heresy.

Plate 9.30

So important did the story become that it was celebrated with a week-long festivity that attracted multitudes of pilgrims and merchants to the city. There are even reports that Seljuk business

Plate 9.30 *An illumination in a famous service book, called the Menologion of Basil (the emperor Basil II, who ruled 976–1025 CE) where Michael, whose wings link heaven and earth, dramatically impacts the environment. This service book (strictly a synaxarion) lists 430 illustrations for the feasts of saints throughout the year, each with a brief summary of the story line attached.*

families from Konya came to trade along with Christians when the Byzantines still controlled Colossae. In Ottoman times, the Greeks in Turkey were able to continue to celebrate the archangel's feast-day. In just over a century, most Greeks in Turkey could only speak Turkish even though they still used a Greek alphabet. A special language phenomenon, called *karamanlidika* (which put Turkish words in Greek letters), developed and was used in a service book. In this book of the feasts of a church's year (called a synaxarion), St Michael of Chonai has a special place. His feast-day by then was celebrated on September the 6th.

In one of the surviving churches of Honaz in the nineteenth-century, the icon of St Michael of Chonai held pride of place. The building is still in use as a mosque—the oldest active mosque in Honaz—having been retained as a religious building after Turks and Greeks were repatriated to their nominated homelands in the 1920s.

Plate 9.31 *A 1909 photograph (taken by George Lampakis) of the church at Honaz. It has been retained as a holy place today, in use as a mosque. Lampakis states that the icon of St Michael, dated to 1813, was located on the iconostatis (the main wall in the photograph).*

Select Bibliography - Chapter Nine: The Mighty Archangel

Apostolic Constitutions 7.46.12.

Bonnet, M, *Narratio de Miraculo a Michaele Archangelo Chonis Patrato*. Paris: Librairie Hachette, 1890.

Corpus Inscriptionum Graecarum. (= *CIG* I–IV). Edited by A. Boeckh;, 4 Vols; Berlin: Officina Academica, 1828–77, III.3956, 4380k³.

Eusebius *Ecclesiastical History* 4.26.3–4, 5.24.5.

Frontinus *On the Aqueducts of the City of Rome*, 4.

Grégoire, H, *Recueil des inscriptions grecques-chrétiennes d'Asie Mineure*. Repr. Amsterdam: AM Hakkert, 1968 [1922], no 341.

Joint Library of the Hellenic and Roman Societies (University of London), *The Wood Collection* Vol 6. Fol. 67.

Kokkinia, C (ed), *Boubon: The Inscriptions and Archaeological Remains: A Survey 2004–2006*. Paris: de Boccard, 2008.

Lampros, SP, *Μιχαὴλ Ἀκομινάτου τοῦ Χωνιάτου τὰ σωζόμενα*. Groningen: Bouma, 2 Vols, 1968 [1879].

Leemans, J, 'Gregory of Nyssa: a homily on Theodore the Recruit' in *'Let us die that we may live': Greek Homilies on Christian Martyrs from Asia Minor, Palestine and Syria c350–c450 AD*. Edited by J Leemans, W Mayer, P Allen and B Demandschutter; London, 2003, 82–90.

Pertusi, A, *Costantino Porfirogenito De Thematibus*. Vatican: Biblioteca Apostolica Vaticana, 1952, 68.

Stiltingo, J, C Suyskeno, J Periero, J Cleo (eds), *Acta Sanctorum: September*. Paris/Rome: Victor Palmé, 1869 [1762], volume 8, 41C–47C.

van Dieten, J-L (ed), *Nicetae Choniatae Historia*. Berlin: Walter de Gruyter, 1975.

Scylitzes, John, continuatus, 'History' in *Patrologia Graeca* (Migne) vol 122, 415–16.

Theodore of Studios *Epistles* 2.63; *Antirrhetici III*. 47 (*Patrologica Graeca* [Migne] vol. 99.411B).

Anderson, W, 'An Archaeology of Late Antique Pilgrim Flasks', in *Anatolian Studies* 54 (2004): 79–93.

Arnold, JC, *The Footprints of Michael the Archangel: The Formation and Diffusion of a Saintly Cult c 300–c 800*. New York: Palgrave, 2013.

Arundell, FVJ, *A Visit to the Seven Churches of Asia Minor with an excursion into Pisidia*. London: John Rodwell, 1828.

Ascough, RS, 'Religious Coexistence, Co-operation, Competition, and Conflict in Sardis and Smyrna', in *Religious Rivalries and the Struggle for Success in Sardis and Smyrna*. Edited by RS Ascough; ESCJ 14; Waterloo, Ont: Wilfrid Laurier University Press, 2005, 245–52.

Bouras, C, 'Aspects of the Byzantine City, Eighth–Fifteenth Centuries', in *The Economic History of Byzantium: from the Seventh through the Fifteenth Century*. Edited by A Laiou; Washington, DC: Dumbarton Oaks, 2002, 497–528.

Bouvier, B and F Amsler, 'Le Miracle de l'Archange Michel à Chonai: Introduction, Traduction, et Notes', in *Early Christian Voices: in texts, traditions and symbols: Essays in Honor of François Bovon*. Edited by DH Warren, AG Brock and DW Pao; Boston / Leiden: Brill Academic Publishers, 2003, 395–407.

Cadwallader, AH, 'Revisiting Calder on Colossae', in *Anatolian Studies* 56 (2006): 103–111.

— 'The Inversion of Slavery: The ascetic and the archistrategos at Chonai', in *Prayer & Spirituality in the Early Church V: Poverty and Riches*. Edited by GD Dunn, D Luckensmeyer, L Cross; Strathfield, NSW: St Pauls Publications, 2009, 215–36.

— 'A stratigraphy of an ancient city through its key story: the archistrategos of Chonai', in *Colossae in Space and Time: Linking with an Ancient City*. Edited by AH Cadwallader and M Trainor; Gottingen: Vandenhoeck and Ruprecht, 2011, 282–98.

— 'The Story of the Archistrategos, St Michael of Chonai', in *Colossae in Space and Time*. Göttingen: Vandenhoeck and Ruprecht, 2011, 323–30 [English translation of the popular version of the story].

— 'Inter-city Conflict in the Story of St Michael of Chonai', in *Religious Conflict from Early Christianity to the Rise of Islam*. Edited by W Mayer and B Neil; Arbeiten zur Kirchengeschichte 121; Tübingen: de Gruyter, 2013, 109–28.

— 'St Michael of Chonai and the Tenacity of Paganism', in, *Intercultural Transmission throughout the Medieval Mediterranean: 100–1600 CE*. Edited by D Kim and S Hathaway; London/NY: Continuum, 2012, 37–59.

Clines, R, *Ancient Angels: Conceptualizing Angeloi in the Roman Empire*. Leiden: Brill, 2011.

Cormack, R, 'The Wall-painting of St Michael in the Theatre', in *Aphrodisias Papers, 2: The theatre, a sculptor's workshop, philosophers and coin-types*. Edited by RRR Smith and KT Erim; Portsmouth, RI: Journal of Roman Archaeology Supplement, 1991, 109–22.

Cotsonis, J, 'Saints and Cult Centers: A Geographic and Administrative Perspective in Light of Byzantine Lead Seals', in *Studies in Byzantine Sigillography* 8. Edited by J-C Cheynet and C Sode; Munich: KG Saur, 2003, 9–26.

Foss, C, 'Pilgrimage in Medieval Asia Minor', in *Dumbarton Oaks Papers* 56 (2002): 129–51.

Fox, RL, *Pagans and Christians in the Mediterranean World from the second century AD to the conversion of Constantine*. Harmondsworth: Penguin, 1986.

Gerstel, SEJ and A-M Talbot, 'The culture of lay piety in medieval Byzantium 1054–1453,' in *The Cambridge History of Christianity, V, Eastern Christianity* Edited by M Angold; London: Cambridge University Press, 2006, 79–100.

Hoffmann, RJ, *Julian's 'Against the Galileans'*. Amherst, NY: Prometheus, 2004.

Jenkins, RJH and E Kitzinger, 'A Cross of the Patriarch Micahel Cerularius with an Art-Historical Comment', in *Dumbarton Oaks Papers* 21 (167): 233–50.

Jolivet-Lévy, C, *Études Cappadociennes*. London: Pindar, 2012.

Kokkinia, C (ed), *Boubon: The Inscriptions and Archaeological Remains: A Survey 2004–2006*. Athens: 2008.

Koloski-Ostrow, AO (ed), *Water Use and Hydraulics in the Roman City*. Dubuque, Iowa: Kendall/Hunt Publishing, 2001.

Laborde, ALJ de, *Voyage de l'Asie Mineure*. Paris: Firmin Didot, 1838.

Laiou, AE, 'Exchange and Trade, Seventh–Twelfth Centuries', in *The Economic History of Byzantium: from the Seventh through the Fifteenth Century*. Edited by AE Laiou; Washington, DC: Dumbarton Oaks, 3 vols, 2002, 697–756.

Lampakis, G, *Οἱ ἑπτὰ ἀστέρες τῆς Ἀποκαλύψεως*. Athens: 1909.

Liebeschuetz, JHWG, 'Julian's *Hymn to the Mother of the Gods*: The Revival and Justification of Traditional Religion', in *Emperor and Author: The Writings of Julian 'the Apostate'*. Edited by N Baker-Brian and S Tougher; Swansea: The Classical Press of Wales, 2012, 213–27.

Lupu, E, *Greek Sacred Law: a Collection of New Documents*. Leiden: Brill, 2005.

Martin-Hisard, B, 'Le culte de l'archange Michel dans l'empire byzantin (VIIIe–XIe siècles)', in *Culto e Inseiamenti Micaelici nell'Italia meridionale fra Tarda Antichità e Medioevo*. Edited by C Carletti and G Otranto; Bari: Edipuglia, 1994, 351–73.

Meinardus, OFA, 'St Michael's Miracle of Khonae and its Geographical Setting', in *Ekklesia kai Theologia* 1 (1980): 459–69.

Mullen, RL, *The Expansion of Christianity: A Gazetteer of its First Three Centuries*. Leiden: Brill, 2004.

Munn, M, 'Earth and Water: The Foundations of Sovereignty in Ancient Thought', in *The Nature and Function of Water, Baths, Bathing*. Edited by C. Kosso and A Scott; Leiden / New York: Brill, 2009, 191–210.

Niehwöhner, P *et al*, 'Bronze Age höyüks, Iron Age hilltop forts, Roman poleis and Byzantine pilgrimage in Germia and its vicinity. 'Connectivity' and a lack of 'definite places' on the central Anatolian high plateau', in *Anatolian Studies* 63 (2013): 97–113.

Peers, G, *Subtle Bodies: Representing Angels in Byzantium*. Berkeley: University of California Press, 2001.

Pritchett, WK, *The Greek State at War Vol 3: Religion*. Berkeley: University of California Press, 1979.

Ramsay, WM, *Historical Geography of Asia Minor*. London: John Murray, 1890.

Rohland, J, *Der Erzengel Michael. Arzt und Feldherr*. Leiden: Brill, 1977.

Sanders, GDR, 'The Sacred Spring: Landscape and Traditions', in *Corinth in Context: Comparative Studies on Religion and Society*. Edited by SJ Friesen, DN Schowalter and JC Walters; Leiden: Brill, 2010, 365–89.

Schaller, A, *Der Erzengel Michael im frühen Mittelalter: Ikonographie und Verehrung eines Heiligen ohne Vita*. Bern: Peter Lang, 2006.

Şimşek, C, *Laodikeia (Laodikeia ad Lycum)*. Istanbul: Ege Yayınları, 2007.

—*Church of Laodikeia: Christianity in the Lykos Valley*. Denizli: Denizli Belediyesi, 2015.

Smith, M, 'A Note on Some Jewish Assimilationists: The Angels (P. Berlin 5025b, P. Louvre 2391)', in *Janes* 17–18 (1984–5): 207–12.

Stengel, C, *S Michaelis Archangeli principatus, apparitions, templa cultus & miracula, ex sacris litteris, SS. PP. & histories ecclesiasticis eruta*. Augsburg: 1649.

Thonemann, P, *The Meander Valley: A Historical Geography from Antiquity to Byzantium*. Cambridge: Cambridge University Press, 2011.

Thomas, C, 'The 'Mountain Mother': the other Anatolian Goddess at Ephesos', in *Les Cultes Locaux dans les mondes Grec et Romain*. Edited by G Labarre and J-M Moret; Paris: de Boccard, 2004, 249–62.

Tougher, S, *Julian the Apostate*. Edinburgh: Edinburgh University Press, 2007.

Trombley, F, *Hellenic Religion and Christianization c370–529* vol 1. Leiden: Brill, 1993.

Vryonis, S, 'The Byzantine Legacy and Ottoman Forms', in *Dumbarton Oaks Papers* 23/24 (1969/70): 251–308.

— 'The Panegyris of the Byzantine Saint', in *The Byzantine Saint*. Edited by S Hackel; London: Fellowship of St Alban and St Sergius 1981, 196–226.

— *The Decline of Medieval Hellenism in Asia Minor and the Process of Islamization from the Eleventh through the Fifteenth Century*. Berkeley: University of California Press, 1971.

Zanetti, U, 'Fêtes des anges dans les calendrieres et synaxaires orientaux', in *Culto e Inseiamenti Micaelici nell'Italia meridionale fra Tarda Antichità e Medioevo*. Edited by C Carletti and G Otranto; Bari: Edipuglia, 1994, 323–49.

A Stylistic Map to Colossae and the Environs

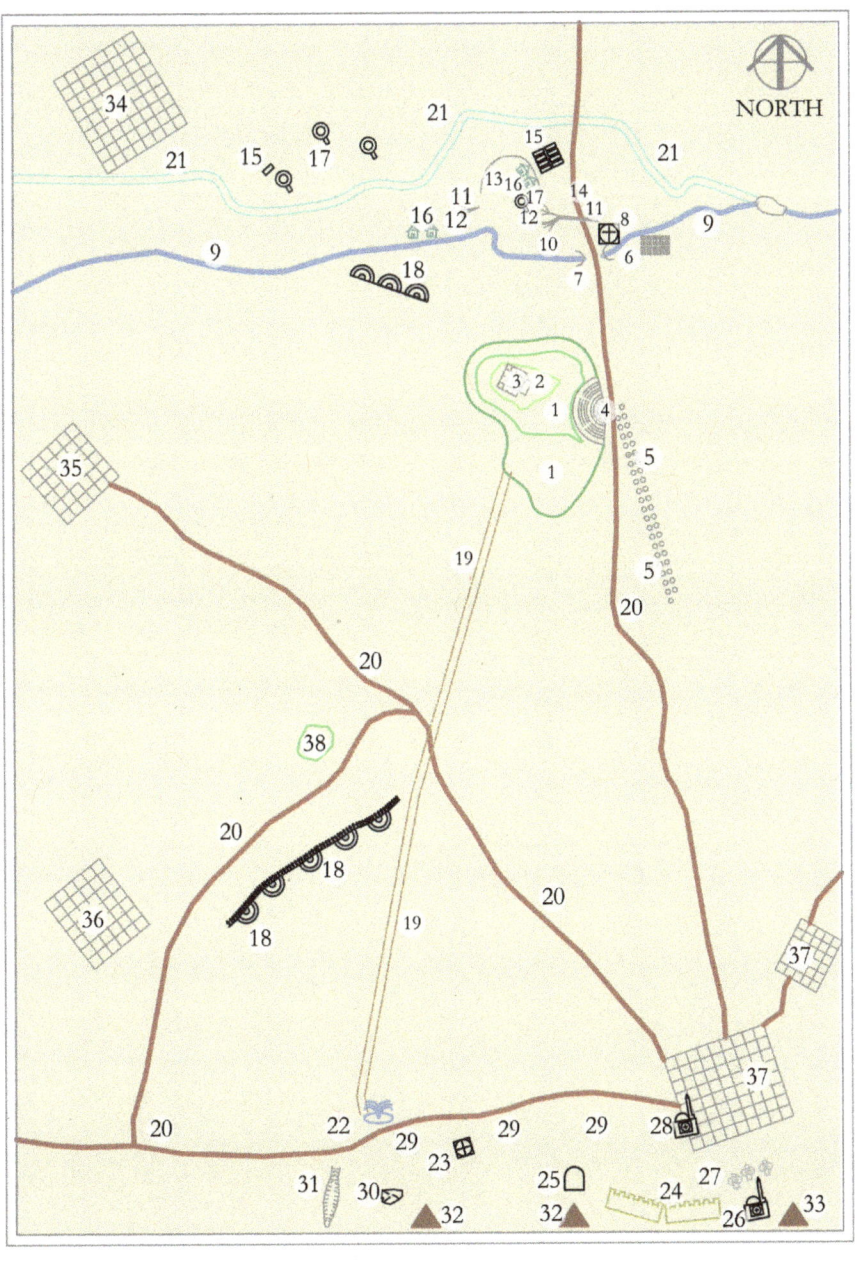

1. Biconical höyük
2. Acropolis
3. Temple of Zeus (?)
4. Theatre cavea
5. Colonnaded Way / Theatre Street (?)
6. Baths
7. Roman / Byzantine Bridge
8. St Michael's Church (?)
9. River Lycus
10. City wall (?)
11. Water Channel
12. Water Chutes
13. Necropolis basin
14. Bomos
15. Chamosorion tomb
16. Cliff tombs
17. Tumulus tomb
18. Caves
19. Sacred way (?)
20. Modern road
21. Modern watercourse
22. St Michael spring (Göz Picnic Ground)
23. Byzantine church remains
24. Medieval fortress
25. Medieval cistern
26. Sultan Murad cami (mosque)
27. Moslem old cemetery
28. Old cami, former Greek church
29. Ottoman Greek quarter
30. St Michael monolith
31. St Michael ravine
32. Taurus mountains
33. Mt Cadmus
34. Light industrial area
35. Pinarkent
36. Emirazizli

Map of Ancient Asia Minor

Map of Ancient Asia Minor - Western region

FRAGMENTS OF COLOSSAE
Glossary

On most occasions the text provides sufficient explanation for the meaning of technical terms. This glossary is for easy reference to cover those instances where no explanation occurs or where there is repeated mention of a technical term after the initial usage.

Achaemenid	The dynastic name that governs the terminology for the Persian empire.
Acroterion	Stone or terracotta decorations, often stylised palm branches, embellishing the lower extremities of the pediment on temples and funerary stelai.
Adventus	The visit of an emperor or his delegate to a city or other destination.
Agonothete	The financier and/or chief organiser/president of games, athletic contests and theatre performances. Originally the judge of a contest cf stephanophoros.
Agoranomos	Clerk of the market, regulating business transactions.
Amphora	A tall jar with narrow mouth and two handles designed for holding wine or oil. A wooden/stone plug set in place by wax sealed it.
Antrophulakes	Officials of the Dionysos cult who guarded cave entrances where special religious rites might be practiced or drinking festivities celebrated.
Architrave	Lowest portion of the entablature, which rests directly on the column capitals.
As	Standard unit of Roman bronze coinage (=4 bronze quadrantes).
Asclepeion	A religious centre, under the patronage of the god Asclepios, designed for healing and treatment for general health.
Asia	The name of the Roman province formed in 129 BCE ranging from the Mediterranean Sea to the Anatolian high plateau.
Asiarch	High official in the province of Asia, combining religious and/or political functions in the provincial assembly called the *koinon*.
Baptistery	The dedicated part of a Christian church where the rite of baptism is performed, whereby a person is declared to be a Christian.
Basilica	A large, colonnaded building where public affairs (eg court cases) were often heard.
Bema	A special, elevated seat, carved and placed in a place of honour, as in a theatre.
Biga	A chariot drawn by a team of two animals, usually horses.
Bishop	The overall leader of a group of churches in a designated area, supervising priests and deacons and other church officials and subject to a higher-ranked official called an archbishop or a metropolitan.
Bollard	A retaining or restraining post set up for public use (such as for tethering horses or boats).

Boss	A circular protrusion, often reminiscent of a Greek shield, used in architecture, on coins and even epitaphs.
Boule	Council of a city, composed of elders or elected or appointed representatives. Distinct from the *demos* (the assembly of all the citizens) and the *prytaneis* (the presiding officers of the city government).
Bouleuterion	Meeting hall or other dedicated space for the city council.
Bronze	Alloy of copper and tin (usually, though lead and zinc were sometimes used).
Bust	Portrait of person's head and shoulders.
Caduceus	The wand of Mercury, ornamented with snakes and wings.
Caravanserai/Akhan	A temporary dwelling and refreshment place for travellers in Ottoman times.
Cartography	The study and construction of maps.
Cavea	Rounded, often semi-circular section of the odeion or theatre containing seats for the spectators.
Cenotaph	Honorary tomb or monument for person whose remains are kept or buried elsewhere eg soldiers who died in foreign wars.
Chamosorion	A grave carved into the ground, similar in shape to the (above-ground) sarcophagus and sealed with a stone lid, often but not necessarily flat.
Chiton	Cloth foundation garment, an under-shirt, that, for women, could be full-length.
Chlamys	A cloak usually fastened by a clasp/brooch at the shoulder.
Cistophori	"Basket-bearing" — first rendered on coins in Pergamon but adopted under (Roman) imperial authority for silver tetradrachms of similar weight/design; common in Asia but intended as provincial not civic coinage. Often bearing a Latin legend, they added to the prestige of a minting city's status.
Cippus/cippa	A short, round pillar, often sepulchral.
Cista mystica	Basket from which snakes slide out; associated with Dionysos, Asclepios and Hygeia, the imagery frequently appears on early cistophoric coins.
Colonnade	Row of columns along a street or building, frequently demarcating a stoa.
Conventus juridicus	A Roman assize centre. The province of Asia was divided into a number of assize regions, each with a city designated as the centre for hearing legal cases affected by Roman law.
Corinthian order	Related to Ionic order in regard to its columns and entablature. Capitals and philasters are decorated with acanthus leaves.
Cornice	Projecting, upper part of entablature below the sima.
Cornucopia	The horn of plenty, usually overflowing with fruit.
Cunei/kerkides	Segments of the levels of theatre seating separated by steps.
Countermark	An extra figure/design, usually miniature, stamped into a coin's face, often indicating the nominated value and/or the re-striking city.

Cuirass	Piece of armour covering the body from neck to hips with a breastplate and back piece. Often elaborately embellished with various symbolic representations for emperors.
Daric	A Persian gold coin.
Decurion	A member of the local city administrative body with significant responsibilities for the functioning of public life, such as contracts, tax collection and the maintenance of order.
Dentils	Small rectangular cavities and abuttings adorning the lower edge of the cornice.
Distaff	A spindle used for spinning fleece into thread; also a symbol of conventional female domesticity.
Doric order	Doric columns stand directly on the stylobate without a base. Columns have 16 to 20 flutes separated by sharp arrises. Column capitals have two parts; a square abacus which supports the architrave, and a lower part, bell-shaped, called an echinus.
Drachm	Greek silver coin roughly equivalent to the Roman denarius (see Luke 15:8–9).
Drum	The name for a section of rounded stone making up a pillar, when the pillar is not carved as a single complete structure. Sometimes the separated drums were converted to farm rollers.
Entablature	Upper part of a building which rests on a wall or columns, consisting of architrave, frieze and cornice, and which carries the pediment and roof of the building.
Ephebe	Young man, aged 18–20 (though sometimes younger), undergoing military, gymnastic and oratorical training, organised by an 'ephebarch'.
Epigraphy	The classification and interpretation of inscriptions.
Equestrian	Mounted on horseback.
Euergetism	The provision of public constructions, services and support by wealthy members of a city, for which they gained status and influence.
Exergue	The small space on the reverse of a coin below the principal design, often filled with a name, mark or date.
Field	Smooth area around the main design on obverse and reverse side of the coin.
Flan	The flat, blank piece of metal prior to impression with a die.
Fillet	Narrow projecting vertical strip on an Ionic column which separates its concave flutes.
Fiskus	The Roman imperial treasury with branches in the cities of the empire for the collection of taxes, fines and other revenue.
Flute	Vertical channel on a column; flutes are separated from each other by an arris (Doric) or a fillet (Ionic).
Follis	A large bronze coin which in late Roman imperial times held a thin layer of silver. This overlay was not continued under Byzantine emperors.
Fresco	A technique of painting where the pigment is added to moist plaster, allowing it to set and dry in the surface.

Frieze	Part of the entablature above a colonnade or the uppermost part of a wall, usually decorated with reliefs.
Fuller	A labourer who cleans clothing whether in the manufacturing process or as a service to others.
Grammateus	The municipal secretary or scribe responsible for public records and ensuring the proper execution of public decisions.
Hagiasma	The dedicated, religious site of a healing spring.
Herm	Square pillar surmounted by a sculpted head. Male genitals (often erect penis) are the only fashioning on the pillar itself. Herms were commonly used as boundary markers, but also were incorporated, as indicators of gods, into household worship and other institutional buildings. The shape could also be used as decorative statues and memorials for famous persons.
Hero	Initially understood as a semi-divine figure, such as Herakles, the term came to be applied to as a mark of esteem for someone, especially a young deceased person.
Heroon	A cenotaph shrine or funerary monument to a hero/ine.
Himation	Flowing outer garment, which could be worn by both men and women.
Hippochamp	A horse-head serpentine creature associated with the god Poseidon and frequently used in funerary motifs.
Homonoia	= concordia, an expression of harmony and peaceful relationships often between different cities, frequently expressed on special coin mintings.
Höyük	Artificial mound (tell) that frequently contains archaeological evidence of different historical periods.
Incuse	An impression by stamping.
Iconoclast	One who destroys icons or religious paintings; frequently the name given to two main periods in the history of the Byzantine Empire where a major political and religious controversy occurred over the place of icons in Christian worship and devotion.
Iconostasis	The main wall of an Orthodox Church that separates the body of people (congregation) in the area called the 'nave' from the main altar area ('the snactuary') where the priest performs the Divine Liturgy. It is covered with different icons, or religious paintings.
Janissary	An Ottoman official who was the authorised guide for European travellers.
Kalathos	grain-measure (cf. modius).
Kantharos	A wide-mouthed, double-handle drinking vessel.
Karamanlidika	The linguistic phenomenon of the Ottoman period whereby Greek letters were used to transliterate Turkish words.

Kitharos/cithara	Musical stringed instrument similar to a lyre, usually having seven strings stretched between a cross-bar and the soundbox which were themselves held by a bracing rib on either side of the strings.
Kitharoedos	Lyre-player, an epithet usually applied to Apollo.
Knights of St John	A religious order established in Jerusalem c1023 CE with a commitment to medical care. It added a military focus after the first crusade.
Koinon	Provincial council of Asia.
Krater	A large, open-mouthed vessel used to mix wine and water.
Laodicena	A style of clothing made without any seams.
Laureate	Wearing a wreath of laurel.
Legend	Inscription on a coin (often abbreviated).
Legionary eagle	The principal standard of the Roman Legion, normally affixed to a spear, usually made of silver.
Lekythos	A long, narrow-necked jug containing wine or oil.
Levant Company	An English trading business with major centres in İstanbul, Smyrna and Aleppo. It provided major diplomatic representation for England.
Lintel	Horizontal architectural piece above a door or other opening.
Lituus	An augur's curved wand.
Loggia	Special separated section of a theatre for elite seating.
Madder root	The vegetable tuber from which is extracted a cheaper purple dye used in clothing.
Martyrion	The place, either a separate (sometimes octagonal) building, chapel, or a crypt inside a church under the altar or apse, where the relics of a martyr are kept.
Mausoleum	A building which is dedicated to housing the dead, usually of a family or a formal group, though sometimes for a wealthy or honoured individual.
Menologion	A collection of stories of Christian saints usually arranged by order of the month in which falls the service wherein the saint is remembered.
Mint	place where coins were made, usually under licence.
Modius	A measure of wheat or any dry or solid commodity, containing the third part of an amphora. In form it resembled an inverted bucket standing on three legs. The god Serapis is usually shown wearing it on his head, as the god of corn supply as well as of the underworld (cf. Hades-Persephone).
Moulding	Decorative horizontal bands used on buildings and columns. The designs can range from simple concave and convex bands to intricate egg-and-dart designs.
Murex	The mollusk shell creature from which is extracted the rare purple dye, so valued in the ancient world.

Neokoros	Temple warden/custodian. Used in early times for priestly officers of high rank; under the Roman emperors, the term became a title of dignity for cities which had received permission to erect temples for the imperial cult and were regarded as guardians of the official provincial cult of the emperor.
Numismatics	The study of coins and medals.
Nymphaeum	A public water fountain both for display and for the provision of water to the populace. Sometimes they were attached to sanctuaries and carried additional religious significance.
Obverse	The 'front' or main face of a coin ('head').
Odeion	Roofed concert or lecture hall, generally smaller than open-air theatres.
Officina	Monetary workshop within a mint.
Oikeus	Household slave as distinguished from common chattel slaves; nevertheless they remained the property of house owner.
Omphalos/baetylus	The representation of the boundaries of the centre of a particular focus (eg the religious focus on the centre or 'navel' [umbilicus] of the world or a sanctuary). Sometimes the symbolism was of the centre itself.
Orchestra	Originally "the space where the chorus danced." A circular or semicircular area between the front row of the cavea and the scaena.
Orichalcum	Ancient name for brass, an alloy of copper and zinc.
Osteoteks	Boxes designed to hold the bones of deceased persons after the flesh has decomposed away.
Palladium	An ancient sacred image of Athena (Minerva).
Palmette	A decorative carving often used on cornices and capitals, that draws on the shape of a fan palm.
Paludamentum	A cloak (often military) indicative of high office.
Parazonium	A short, sheathed sword.
Pareskon	The official responsible for civic grain organisation, stockpile and supply.
Patera	A broad flat bowl or dish for drinking or pouring libations.
Pedestal/plinth	A stone support (square or round) for a statue, bust or vase; sometimes it refers to the base section for a column.
Pediment	Triangular space in the gable of a building above the entablature, including the tympanum and cornice, usually decorated with sculpture in high relief. Also the miniature representation in funerary monuments.
Pedum	A crook, sheep hook, staff.
Peplos	A woman's large full robe, cf. himation, worn over the base garment.
Personification	The representation of an entity or institution as a person/being.

Plinth	Square block which serves as the bottom of an Ionic or Corinthian column base; also refers to the lowest portion of a pedestal.
Polos	A type of headdress, styled on the vault of heaven turning on an axis, often worn by goddesses.
Praecinctio/diazoma	Walkway that separated the levels of a theatre (for example the summa and ima cavea).
Quadriga	A chariot drawn by four animals, usually horses.
Quaestor	Roman financial officer in charge of public monies; also a public judge or prosecutor in criminal trials.
Radiate	Wearing a spiky crown, symbolic of the sun-god Helios.
Reverse	The opposite side of the obverse face of a coin ('tail').
Satrap	A regional governor and military commander in Persian administration.
Serration	The cross-cutting of the edge of a coin.
Sestertius	A bronze Roman coin, four of which made up a denarius (=two dupondii).
Sherd/potsherd	A fragment of a piece of pottery; sometimes such fragments were used for fill in buildings, for recording a vote (an ostracon) or for practicing writing.
Simpulum	A sacrificial vessel in the form of a ladle with a long handle.
Sistrum	A rattle, derived from its use in Egyptian worship of Isis.
Situla	A water pitcher.
Scaena	The entire stage construction of a theatre or odeion, especially the walled area that rises at the back of the stage.
Spolia	Building materials that have been used previously and are recycled in other uses, sometimes with added symbolic meanings.
Squeeze	A cast or impression (French: impressage; German: Abklatsch) made of an inscription and/or relief on a stone by the use of filter paper.
Stele	A carved, flat stone set up in a base to record special matters by inscription and/or carved relief, such as epitaphs, boundaries etc.
Stephanephoros	A high-ranking official permitted to wear a laurel wreath.
Stoa (portico)	Long covered colonnade or arcade, either freestanding or alongside a building.
Strategos	Originally meaning 'general', the term came to be used for the chief or leading magistrate in the political organisation of a city.
Synaxarion	A collection of saints' days for the year of services in the Orthodox Church. The days may be given a brief summary of the story of the saint.
Taenia	A band or ribbon worn as a hair-tie.
Talmud	The written collection (compiled c4–5th century CE) of the sayings and writings attributed to various rabbis regarding the interpretation of Jewish law. Sometimes the term can include the earlier collection of rabbinical sayings called the Mishnah.

Tambor	A hand-held circular drum with a narrow wooden frame and animal skin stretched across one side.
Tameion	The treasury for a city that collected civic dues and other revenue.
Temenos	Sacred precinct, cut off from common usage and dedicated to a god. It usually consists of land immediately surrounding a temple, often marked by a low wall.
Tessera	A square tablet marked with points representing gifts such as coin, oil or money. An attribute of the personification *Liberalitas*.
Tetradrachm	A large, silver coin worth four drachmas, and roughly equivalent to three-four denarii.
Tetrastyle	Construction with four columns, usually a temple.
Theme	The name for administrative regions in the organisation of the Byzantine empire.
Theonym	A name, usually of a person, that derives from the name of a god.
Togate	Wearing the Roman toga.
Tondo	Elaborate design forming an outer rim or border of a coin face.
Tourma	A key military garrison in the organisation of the Byzantine empire in the middle to late periods.
Tribune, military	Was a high-ranking Roman official in the army, subordinate to consuls and praetors. Tribunes frequently commanded cohorts, although sometimes elite troops acting as body-guards for the emperor; distinct from the plebeian tribunes, who monitored the power of the senate.
Triclinium	A dining arrangement for a banquet, usually in the shape of a squared horse-shoe. It can be used for funeral festivities at a grave, or even as an arrangement for laying out the dead in a large sepulchre.
Triga	Chariot drawn by three animals, usually horses.
Trimitos	A specially woven over-garment that, by a combination of three threads, produces a layered appearance.
Trophy	The arms of a vanquished enemy set up to commemorate victory over them.
Tumulus	A type of grave which has a burial room, an antechamber and an entrance way enveloped by earth in the shape of a mound.
Turreted	Descriptive of headpiece stylised as a defensive city wall, usually worn by the "city goddess".
Type	The main design on obverse/reverse side of a coin.
Unguentarium	Container for perfumed oil used in preparation of the body of the dead for burial.
Venator	A person who fought wild beasts in the arena or other suitable public entertainment space.
Vexillum	Military standard of a maniple, a subdivision of a legion.
Zeri	A gold Ottoman coin.

Index of Ancient and Modern Place-names

Map references follow after the place-names, where given. Note that the modern Turkish place-names give the nearest settlement to an ancient site. Bracketed names are alternate spellings or alternate names.

Aegean islands *A-4, B-6*, 99
Afyon 158, 161
Ağlasun / Sagalassos *D-5*, 88, 90
Aidin 9
Aigai (Vergina) 163
Aizanoi / Çavdarhisar *C-3*, 90, 160, 175
Ak Khan (Accan) 45, 106
Akhisar / Thyatira *B-3*, 12, 112, 121, 122
Aksu / Perge *D-5*, 76
Aksu River / Cadmus River 139
Alaşehir / Philadelphia *B-4*, 12, 112, 121, 129, 184
Alikel Yaila / Orcistus *D-3*, 149
Alsatia 76
Altınyayla / Trimile *C-5*, 190, 191
Amisos / Samsun 91, 92
Amorion / Hisarköy *D-3*, 115
Amphipolis 116, 163
Amsterdam 65
Anaua *C-5*, 190
Ankara / Ancyra 18, 22, 50, 117, 147, 150
Antalya / Attaleia *D-5*, 118
Antioch of Pisidia / Yalvaç *D-4*, 118
Antioch in Syria 63
Apa reservoir 141
Apameia (Kelenai) / Dinar *D-4*, 32, 101, 112, 136
Aphrodisias / Geyre *B-4*, 6, 34, 87, 90, 92, 98, 99, 118, 126, 168, 169, 175, 185
Apollonia Salbake / Tavas 119
Appa 20, 156

Appia / Pınarcık *C-3*, 29
Appian Way 36
Asia *A-3, D-5*, 8, 50, 52, 56, 112, 136–7, 138, 167, 193, 207
Asia Minor 5, 6, 7, 32, 45, 50, 52, 55, 59, 63, 65, 83, 92, 97, 119, 121, 126, 127, 136, 145, 146, 155, 168, 169, 184, 191
Aspendos / Belkiz *D-5*, 78, 82
Athens 36, 52, 60, 85, 111, 170, 185
Attaleia / Antalya *D-5*, 118
Aydin / Tralles *B-4*, 112, 121
Babadağ / Mt Salbakos 12, 111
Babylon 187
Ballıhisar / Pessinous *E-3*, 29, 50
Banias / Caesarea Philippi 78
Balat / Miletos *B-4*, 34, 112, 121, 193
Bay of Phineka 32
Bergama / Pergamon *B-3*, 12, 75, 81, 99, 112, 126, 141, 207
Belkiz / Aspendos *D-5*, 78, 82
Bithynia *C-2, D-2*, 169
Bodrum / Halicarnassos *B-5*, 182
Bolu / Trapezopolis *C-4*, 118
Bourdeaux 174
Cadmus River / Ak Su 139
Caesarea Philippi / Banias 78
Cambridge 8
Cappadocia 129, 161
Caria *B-5*, 114, 135, 137, 191

Carura / Tekkeköy *C-5*, 118
Chairetopa / Keretape *C-5*, 185
Chonai (Chonos, Khonos) / Honaz *C-4*, v, 3, 4, 5, 8, 12, 13, 14, 15, 16, 19, 20, 21, 32, 38, 39, 40, 45, 57, 78, 79, 84, 85, 88, 96, 100, 101, 102, 103, 104–5, 106, 139, 185, 187, 189, 192, 193, 198
Çinaraltı Restaurant 14, 139
Çivril / Eumeneia *C-4*, 157, 172
Colose (Cosole) 7
Coloso 7
Colossi 7
Colossae (Colosse) *C-4*, *passim*
Constantinople / İstanbul (İslâmbol) *C-2*, 7, 9, 10, 11, 15, 101, 103, 104, 186
Çürüksu / Lycus River River 2, 6, 8, 12, 18, 20, 29, 35, 38, 47, 48, 49, 53, 61, 78, 79, 107, 111, 115, 120, 138, 139, 140, 141, 148, 150, 155, 161, 181, 190–2
Cyme / Namurt Limani *B-3*, 123
Cyprus 7
Çavdarhisar / Aizanoi *C-3*, 90, 160, 175
Denizli (Denizley) *C-4*, v, 5, 10, 11, 12, 13, 14, 22, 40, 45, 104, 116, 158, 191, 192
Dinar / Apameia (Kelenai) *D-4*, 32, 101, 112, 136
Dionysopolis / Ortaköy *C-4*, 60, 115
Dublin 8
England 9, 11, 14, 147, 210
Ennaton 184
Ephesos / Selçuk *B-4*, 8, 11, 12, 36, 38, 46, 55, 56, 57, 58, 59, 62, 63, 64, 76, 78, 81, 87, 91, 92, 102, 112, 119, 121, 126, 167, 169, 173, 185, 187, 193
Erubris River 174

Eskihisar / Stratonikeia *B-5*, 34, 87, 92, 128, 169, 174, 175, 184, 185, 193
Eskişehir 161
Eumeneia / Çivril *C-4*, 157, 172
Euphrates River 32
Fener district 196
Fethiye / Telmessos *C-5*, 63
Galatia *E-3*, 184
Germia (Myriangeloi) / Günyüzü *E-2*, 184
Geyre / Aphrodisias *B-4*, 6, 34, 87, 90, 92, 98, 99, 118, 126, 168, 169, 175, 185
Gölhisar / Kibyra *C-5*, 34, 119, 170
Göz Picnic Ground 2, 189,
Güllübahçe / Priene *B-4*, 76, 78, 80, 81, 85, 86
Güllük / Termessos *D-5*, 83, 161, 170
Günyüzü / Germia (Myriangeloi) *E-2*, 184
Halicarnassos / Bodrum *B-5*, 182
Herakleia Salbake / Vakıf *C-5*, 118
Hierapolis / Pamukkale *C-4*, 1, 5, 6, 8, 10, 13, 20, 22, 34, 35, 36, 44, 45, 46, 49, 50, 68, 80, 87, 88, 111, 112, 113, 114, 115, 119, 120, 121, 122, 123, 125, 126, 127, 129, 130, 138, 142, 143, 160, 163, 164, 173, 175, 181, 185, 186, 195
Hisarköy / Amorion *D-3*, 115
Honaz / Chonai (Chonos) *C-4*, v, 3, 4, 5, 8, 12, 13, 14, 15, 16, 19, 20, 21, 32, 38, 39, 40, 45, 57, 78, 79, 84, 85, 88, 96, 100, 101, 102, 103, 104–5, 106, 139, 185, 187, 189, 192, 193, 198
Honazdağ / Mt Cadmus 4, 29, 38, 39, 52, 76, 77, 96, 99, 111, 113, 183
Hydriale / Sigma Kasabası 118
Hyrkanis / Saruhanli *B-4*, 64
Iconium / Konya *E-4*, 64, 99, 139, 198
Iguvium 81

İçikler / Sattai *C-3*, 122
İncealiler / Oinoanda *C-5*, 183
İstanbul (İslâmbol) / Constantinople *C-2*, 7, 9, 10, 11, 15, 101, 103, 104, 186
İzmir / Smyrna *B-4*, 8, 9, 11, 12, 14, 40, 118, 184
Jerusalem 7, 210
Jordan 58
Jordan Valley 129
Kaklık *C-4*, 158, 193
Kale / Myra *D-6*, 92
Kalkan / Tlos *C-6*, 161
Kalyvia Kuvara 185
Kapros River 49
Karateke 158
Keretape / Chairetopa *C-5*, 185
Kınık / Xanthus *C-6*, 14
Kibyra / Gölhisar *C-5*, 34, 119, 170
Konya / Iconium *E-4*, 64, 99, 139, 198
Kosovo 180
Laodikeia ad Lycum (Diospolis, Rhoas) / Gonçalı *C-4*, 1, 5, 6, 8, 10, 12, 13, 20, 21, 22, 34–5, 36, 38, 45, 46, 49, 65, 67, 68, 80, 81, 102, 104, 111, 112, 113, 114, 115, 116, 118, 120, 122, 126, 127, 128, 129, 130, 145, 149, 150, 163, 165, 170, 183, 186, 195, 196
Laodikeia Combusta (Katakekaumene) *E-4*, 8
Laodikeia in Lycia 186
Lycus / Cürüksu River 2, 6, 8, 12, 18, 20, 29, 35, 38, 47, 48, 49, 53, 61, 78, 79, 107, 111, 115, 120, 138, 139, 140, 141, 148, 150, 155, 161, 181, 190–2
Lycus Valley 3, 20, 35, 38, 61, 68, 75, 100, 101, 103, 107, 111, 112, 113, 114, 116, 118, 119, 124, 125, 126, 127, 128, 129, 130, 137, 145, 147
Lydia 122, 123, 135, 137

Maeander / Menderes River 6, 8, 38, 102, 112, 126, 181, 190
Magna Graeca 164
Magnesia-on-the-Maeander / Tekin *B-4*, *32*, 112
Malea 119
Manisa *B-4*, 88, 183
Menderes / Maeander River 6, 8, 38, 102, 112, 126, 181, 190
Milas / Mylasa *B-5*, 175
Miletos / Balat *B-4*, 34, 112, 121, 193
Mt Cadmus / Honazdağ 4, 29, 38, 39, 52, 76, 77, 96, 99, 111, 113, 183
Mt Salbakos / Babadağ 12, 111
Mt Vesuvius 51
Mylasa / Milas *B-5*, 175
Myra / Kale *D-6*, 92
Namurt Limani / Cyme *B-3*, 123
Oinoanda / İncealiler *C-5*, 183
Olympia 89
Orcistus / Alikel Yaila *D-3*, 149
Ortaköy / Dionysopolis 60, 115
Oxford 11
Pactolus River / Sart Çayı 136
Pambouk Kalesi / Cotton Castle 5
Pamphylia *D-5*, *E-5*, 161
Pamukkale / Hierapolis *C-4*, 1, 5, 6, 8, 10, 13, 20, 22, 34, 35, 36, 44, 45, 46, 49, 50, 68, 80, 87, 88, 111, 112, 113, 114, 115, 119, 120, 121, 122, 123, 125, 126, 127, 129, 130, 138, 142, 143, 160, 163, 164, 173, 175, 181, 185, 186, 195
Paphlagonia 161
Parsa 184
Pella, Greece 146

Pergamon / Bergama *B-3*, 12, 75, 81, 99, 112, 126, 141, 207
Perge / Aksu *D-5*, 76
Persepolis 31
Pessinous / Ballıhisar *E-3*, 29, 50
Philadelphia / Alaşehir *B-4*, 12, 112, 121, 129, 184
Philippi 57, 91
Phrygia *C-4*, *D-4*, 8, 29, 50, 51, 112, 115, 116, 136, 146, 150, 168, 190
Pınarcık / Appia *C-3*, 29
Pinarkent 21, 55
Pisidia *D-4*, *E-4*, 8, 118
Pompeii 51, 124
Praenesta 63
Priene / Güllübahçe *B-4*, 76, 78, 80, 81, 85, 86
Rhodes *B-6*, 6, 7, 39
Sagalassos / Ağlasun *D-5*, 88, 90
Samsun / Amisos 91, 92
Sardis / Sart *B-4*, 12, 30, 56, 112, 118, 136, 184
Sart / Sardis *B-4*, 12, 30, 56, 112, 118, 136, 184
Saruhanli / Hyrkanis *B-4*, 64
Sattai / İçikler *C-3*, 122
Sebaste / Selçikler 129
Selçikler / Sebaste 129
Selçuk / Ephesos *B-4*, 8, 11, 12, 36, 38, 46, 55, 56, 57, 58, 59, 62, 63, 64, 76, 78, 81, 87, 91, 92, 102, 112, 119, 121, 126, 167, 169, 173, 185, 187, 193
Selçuk Germiyan region 45, 105
Sigma Kasabası / Hydriale 118
Smyrna / İzmir *B-4*, 8, 9, 11, 12, 14, 40, 118, 184
Socnupaci Neos 129
Spoletum 81

Stratonikeia / Eskihisar *B-5*, 34, 87, 92, 128, 169, 174, 175, 184, 185, 193
Şuhut / Synnada *D-4*, 175
Suruksu (Suruksou) 192
Susa 30, 32, 101
Synnada / Şuhut *D-4*, 175
Tavas / Apollonia Salbake 119
Tcharshamba River 139
Tekin / Magnesia-on-the-Maeander 32, 112
Tekkeköy / Carura *C-5*, 118
Telmessos / Fethiye *C-5*, 63
Termessos / Güllük *D-5*, 83, 161, 170
Thessalonike 48, 68, 146
Thrace *B-1*, 161
Thrakesion *C-4*, 39, 102, 103
Thyatira / Akhisar *B-3*, 12, 112, 121, 122
Tlos / Kalkan *C-6*, 161
Tralles / Aydın *B-4*, 112, 121
Trapezopolis / Bolu *C-4*, 118
Trimile / Altınyayla *C-5*, 190, 191
Tripolis / Yenicekent *C-4*, 86, 112, 118
Turkey (Turky/Turkie) 5, 8, 9, 10, 11, 14, 97, 99, 100, 114, 139, 175, 183, 198
Vakıf / Herakleia Salbake *C-5*, 118
Vindolanda (Chesters) 147
Xanthus / Kınık *C-6*, 14
Yalvaç / Antioch of Pisidia *D-4*, 118
Yazilikaya 161
Yenicekent / Tripolis *C-4*, 86, 112, 118
Ziraat Bankasi, Denizli 22

Index of Ancient and Modern Persons

In the index, additional descriptions are only given when there is a need for distinction.

Achilles 121
   gladiator 88
Adrastos 117
Ailiane 117
Ainsworth, William 42, 75, 93, 138, 151, 155, 157, 176
Alcaeus of Messene 29, 42
Alexander Moschianos, Marcus Aurelius 125
Alexander the Great 32, 33, 75, 127, 135, 138, 163
Alexandros, son of Stephanos 116
Allom, Thomas 9, 12, 25
Ammas 124
Ammiane 15, 160
Ammianus, Marcus Aurelius 173, 174
Anderson, JCG 37, 42
Anderson, SP 25
Anderson, W 199
Androcles, Roman prefect 57
Androcles, founder of Ephesos 59
Anson, George 8
Antipater of Thessalonike 48
Antoninus Pius, Emperor 35, 48, 60, 63, 65, 138,
Apollonios 68, 124
Apphia 37, 57, 83
Apphia, daughter of Tryphon 190, 191
Apphia, Colossian priestess of Zeus 66
Archippos 37, 57, 83, 196
Archippos, custodian 186, 187, 196
Ariaios, satrap 33, 136, 137
Aristotle 31, 42

Artaxerxes II, King 32, 33, 135, 136
Artemidoros 164
Artemon 195
Arundell, Rev Francis 12, 14, 101, 108, 158, 176, 190, 199
Augustus, Emperor 50, 82, 83, 171, 172
Aurelius Tatianus 86
Ausonius, Decimus Magnus 47, 123, 174
Autokleides 118
Ayaz, Esedüddin 104
Bacchulis 55, 68
Barnes, Hugh 102, 108
Basil II, Emperor 57, 197
Bayrak, Mustafa 189
Baysal, Hüseyin vi, 84, 93
Beamont, William 9, 25, 99
Bell, Gertrude 20, 25, 156, 176
bin Abdullah, Seyfettin Karasungur 14, 45
Boas 125
Calder, William 15, 16, 18, 25, 70, 93, 122, 131, 159, 166, 169, 170, 176, 177
Caracalla, Emperor 49
Cellarius, Christopher 5, 6, 25
Ceylan, Ali vi, 22, 25, 166
Chandler, Richard 13, 14, 18, 25, 94, 108, 113, 132
Chares 33
Chishull, Edward 26, 105, 108
Cicero 34, 62, 70
Clarke, John 51, 71
Claudia, priestess of Cybele 52

Claudian 115, 131
Commodus, Emperor 35, 48, 57, 150
Constantius I, Emperor 15, 16
Constantine IX, Emperor, Monomachus 103
Cook, Stanley 59, 72
Corsten, Thomas 22, 25, 131
Covell, John 10, 25
Creophylos 58
Crispina 48
Cyrus the Younger 32, 33, 75, 111, 112, 136
Danford, CG 181
Daniell, Rev Edward T 190, 191
Darius I, King 32, 33
Davis, Rev Edmund 97, 142, 156, 157
de Tournefort, Pitton 13, 27, 40, 41, 100
Demas of Colossae 68
Demetrios 68, 92
Diocletian, Emperor 15, 16, 128, 175
Diodoros, gladiator 92
Diodoros of Colossae 68, 69
Diodorus Corescus, Marcus Aurelius 120
Diodorus Siculus 33, 42, 70
Diodotos 68
Diokles 117
Diokrates 68
Dion, leather-worker 37, 156, 169–70
Duman, Bahadır 18, 72, 94, 98, 103, 104, 109
Effendi, Mahmouz 14
Elagabalus, Emperor 63
Epaphras 69
Epictetus 149
Euthenia 164
Eutuches 68
Eutuches Pompeios 125, 126
Fagan, Garrett 94, 145, 152

Fellows, Sir Charles 5, 14, 16, 26
Foss, Clive 38, 43, 102, 108, 200
Frontinus 181, 199
Gadatas 32, 33
Geta, Emperor 56
Gluko, member of 'The Friends' 51, 83, 127
Glukona 51
Gluko, father of Aurelius Tatianus 86
Gregory of Nyssa, Saint 194
Hadaios 68
Hadrian, Emperor 35, 36–7, 46, 55, 58, 62, 63, 64, 65, 86, 147, 149, 183, 184
Hamilton, William 94, 141, 155, 191, 192
Hannibal 50
Heliodoros 68
Heraclius, Emperor 38
Herakles (Hercules) 32, 68, 121, 209
Herakleon 68
Herakleon, 'hero' of Colossae 15, 16, 160
Herakleon, father of priestess Apphia 66
Heraklides 68
Hermas 190
Herodotos 30, 111–2, 115, 137, 139, 141, 190–2
Hieronomos, Colossian magistrate 62
Hipponax 112, 131
Horace 150
Irby, Capt Charles 97, 108
Julian, Emperor, 'the Apostate' 15, 50–1, 173, 194–7
Julius Pollux 92, 93
Julius Vericundus 127
John Scylitzes 192, 199
Karabay, Nesrin 163
Karpio 15
Karpon 172
Karpos 164

Konakçi, Erim vi, 18–9, 55, 98, 103, 104
Korumbos 36, 54, 61, 69, 145, 146, 147, 168
Ktesas 168
Labienus 34, 193
Laborde, Alexandre 157, 177, 192, 193, 201
Lampakis, George 16, 18, 19, 26, 105, 109, 140, 152, 198, 201
Leake, Col William 14, 25
Lightfoot, Joseph Barber 19, 26
Livy 29, 42, 123, 131
Lewin, Thomas 78, 80, 94
Lucian of Samosata 93, 150, 151
Lucius Verus, Emperor 62
Lucretius 173, 176
Luke, Rev Dr John 10, 11, 15
Makedo, Loukios 36
Malay, Hasan 22, 26, 177
Mangles, Capt James 97, 108
Manius Aquilius 112
Mark Antony 34, 64
Markos, chief interpreter 18, 119, 120
Markos, father of Dionyseios 158, 172
Martial 124, 130, 150, 151
Maximian, Emperor 15, 16, 194
Mellaart, James 18, 26, 98, 109
Menas 68, 119, 168
Menogas 68, 69
Michael IV, Emperor, the Paphlagonian 103
Michael Choniates 185
Mithridates VI 34, 67
Morad, Inge 13
Nicetas, Archbishop of Chonai 185
Nicetas Choniates 3, 193
Nicholson, William 100, 109
Nympha 69

Ogle, Soley Bey 13, 40, 104
Oliver, Isaac 10
Onesimos 83
Ortelius, Abraham 7
Palladius 173, 176
Papias Klexos 118, 119
Parman, Ebru 18, 26
Parysatis 136
Paul, Saint, the Apostle 6, 19, 37, 57, 83, 87, 130, 185
Pausanias 55, 71, 80, 89, 93, 151
Petronius 93, 124, 131
Pharnabazus 136
Philemon 37, 57, 68, 83, 135, 185, 196
Philes, Manuel 6
Philopappos, Colossian magistrate 138
Picenini, Antonio 13, 26, 78, 93, 105, 109
Pliny the Elder 62, 71, 120, 131, 173, 176
Pliny the Younger 169, 176
Plutarch 64, 71, 93, 137, 151
Pococke, Rev Richard 13, 14, 24, 27, 45, 107, 109, 113, 133
Pomarede, Daniel 8
Pomeroy, Sarah 157, 178
Pseudo-Alexis 103
Pseudo-Quintilian 93, 169, 176
Pythotimos 78
Quandt, Wilhelm 54, 73
Queen Elizabeth I 9, 10
Quintilian 87, 88, 93
Quintus Oppius 34
Ramsay, Sir William 39, 43, 112, 118, 133, 141, 210
Renan, Ernst 19, 27, 30, 157
Ritti, Tullio 95, 116, 131, 133
Roger II, King 103
Rycaut, Paul 11, 27

Sabinus, Publius Vedius Antoninus 64
Sacerdos, (Tiberius) Claudius, Colossian magistrate and priest 63, 89–90
Sagaris, Bishop of Laodikeia 195
Sallares, Robert 123, 133
Salmon, Thomas 8, 27
Salter, Jerome 11, 27
Sennacherib, King 187
Septimus Severus, Emperor 59
Simeon Metaphrastes 186
Şimşek, Celal vi, 18, 27, 119, 133, 153, 158, 163, 178, 179, 195, 202
Sisinnius, Patriarch of Constantinople 186
Smith, Rev Dr Thomas ('Tograi'/'Rabbi') 10–13, 18, 27
Smith, Robert 94, 168, 178, 200
Söğüt, Bilal, Professor vi, 185
Somerville, Rev Alexander 155, 178
Sophocles 53, 71
Strabo 71, 113, 114, 132, 139, 151, 173, 176
Sultan Ahmed III 104
Sultan Ghiyath al-Din Kay-Khusraw I 104
Sultan Mehmet II 7
Sultan Mehmed III 10
Sultan Murad II 3, 101, 104, 105
Sultan Murad (Can) III 10
Sultan Suleyman the Lawgiver 39
Suetonius 83, 93, 124, 132, 169, 176
Tacitus 34, 35, 42
Tatas, wife of Alexandros 116
Tatas, wife of Karpon 172
Tatia 124
Tatia Attalis 169
Tatianos 171
Tertullian 91, 93
Texier, Charles 82, 84, 95, 160
Thallos 55, 68
Theodore I, Emperor 104
Theodore Mangaphas 103
Theodore, Saint, the Recruit 15, 194
Theodore the Studite 103, 108, 197, 199
Theodoret, Bishop of Cyrrhus 25, 196
Thomas, Professor Christine vi, 72, 73, 132, 169, 178, 202
Tissaphernes, Persian satrap 33, 134, 135–8
Tithraustes, Persian satrap 33, 136, 137
Truphon, grandson of Diodoros 69
Tychicus 69
van der Passe, Crispin 10
Ventidius 34
Virgil 71
Vitruvius 75, 93, 113, 132, 139, 142, 151, 173, 176
von Aulock, Hans 42, 56, 70
Weber, Georg 66, 71, 76, 77, 96, 169, 170, 179
Whittow, Mark 102, 108
Williamson, Sir Joseph 10
Wilson, Professor Andrew 76
Wood, Robert 5, 6, 27
Xenophon 3, 33, 42, 111, 132, 151
Xerxes 111, 112, 190
Yacut 103
Yıldız, Haşim vi, 27, 163, 166, 179
Zenon 86
Zeuxis, Titus Flavius 119
Zosimos, Colossian magistrate 28, 30, 35, 56, 62, 129, 146
Zotikos, Tiberius Claudius 125

Index of Subjects

In the index, additional descriptions are only given when there is a need for distinction.

A

Achilles, gladiator 88
Angels 3, 45, 180–98
    Gods 61
    History 183–4, 194–7
    Zeus and 66, 183
    See St Michael
Antipater of Thessalonike 48
Arabs / Arabic 11, 103
    incursions into Asia 38, 99, 100–1
    trade 11
Artefacts 3, 6, 46, 111, 166
    antiquities 13, 14, 24
    Byzantine 100
    Emperors 102
    re-location 14, 16, 20, 21, 22
    re-use 15, 16, 23, 44
    theft 22, 24
Asia 8, 50, 52, 56, 112, 136–7, 138, 167, 193, 207
    Asia Minor 5, 6, 7, 32, 45, 50, 52, 55, 59, 63, 65, 83, 92, 97, 119, 121, 126, 127, 136, 145, 146, 155, 168, 169, 184, 191
    Roman province of 11, 34, 46, 55, 64, 86, 87, 89, 145, 147, 162, 171, 206, 207, 208
    Seven Churches of 9, 10, 11–12
Associations 55, 115, 120–2, 125, 126–7, 130, 156, 171, 172
    dyers 120
    'the friends' 51, 83, 127
    leatherworkers 122, 156, 170
    purple-dyers 120, 125
Ausonius 47, 123, 174
    The Moselle 47, 174
    The Order of Famous Cities 47

B

Baths 35, 80, 117, 120, 122, 134–50, 168
    gymnasium 80, 146–7
    health 149–50
    parts 146
    repair 35, 54, 61, 69
    symbolism 149
    types 142–50
    water provision 143–5, 147

C

Caravanserai 14, 207
    Akkhan 14, 16, 45, 106
Challirhoe 82
Chonai v, 3, 38–9, 40, 57, 102–3, 104, 187
    Byzantine theme capital 39, 103
    Colossae alternate name 3, 15, 38, 39, 102, 103, 193
    hagiasma/healing spring 185–7, 188, 192, 193, 209, 211
    Honaz 8, 104–5, 198
    Iconoclasm 103, 197–8
    See St Michael of Chonai
Christianity v, 7, 9, 10, 15, 19, 56, 66, 90–1, 111, 127,

171, 172, 184, 192, 207, 210, 213
Angels 3, 180–98
Bishops, Archbishops, Patriarchs 38, 39, 91, 118, 185, 194, 195, 196, 197, 207
Churches 7, 11, 15, 16, 19, 37, 91, 102, 103, 105, 107, 120, 175, 184, 185, 192–3, 195
Colossae 37, 57, 130, 192
Emperor Julian 15, 50–1, 194–7
Feasts 45, 57, 102, 187, 193, 197, 198
Hierapolis 10, 130, 175, 185, 186, 195
Icons, battle over 103, 197–8, 210
Laodikeia 10, 12, 102, 130, 149, 150, 185–6, 195
Martyrion of St Philip 186, 211
paganism and 15, 44, 50, 91, 185, 186–7, 188, 194–6
popular 15, 66, 149, 150, 186, 187, 188, 197
seven churches of Asia 9, 10, 11–12
synods 150, 196
Clothing
See Textiles
Coins vi, 3, 19, 22, 24, 28, 30, 32, 33, 34, 35, 48, 56, 59, 86, 134, 135, 136, 138, 206, 207, 208, 209, 210, 211, 212, 213, 214
cistophoric 68
daric 135
follis 103
gods 35, 49, 50, 52, 53, 54, 55, 56–7, 58, 59–60, 62, 63, 65, 66, 67, 69, 150, 183, 184
homonoia 46, 59, 210
iconography 46, 58, 65, 135
legends 46, 62
magistrates 30, 62, 63, 89, 90
mints 34, 37, 65, 183
siglos 135

trade 30, 56, 65–6, 126, 128
zeri 104

D

Derveni Papyrus 50, 67

E

Earthquakes 141, 183, 191
Lycus Valley 1, 19, 20, 34, 35, 61, 141, 145, 191, 192
Edict of Prices 128–9, 174
clothing 128
Diocletian 128
inflation and 128
stoneworking 174
Stratonikeia odeion 128, 174, 175
Environment 3, 58, 137
agriculture and 18, 30, 34, 36, 49, 54, 65, 102, 103, 111, 115, 117, 137, 154, 173
earth and water 49–50, 137, 138, 139, 181
gods and 47–9, 54, 75
natural resources 58
topographical features 75–6, 197
European exploration 1, 10–11, 40, 75, 78, 82, 84, 100, 138, 142, 157, 160
collecting 11, 14, 24
confusion over Colossae 5–8, 140–1, 155, 190–1, 192
disappointment over Colossae 1
Franks 8, 11
Levant company 9–11, 12, 210
maps 5–8, 76–7, 112, 207
postcards 9, 99
records 5, 13, 14, 30, 105, 169, 190–1

Smyrna and 8–9, 11, 12, 14, 210
soldiers and 97
tourism 1, 16

F

Farming 18, 30, 34, 39, 49, 54, 65, 102, 103, 111, 115, 117, 137, 154, 173
    cherries 36
    dogs 35–6, 116, 117, 118, 159, 171
    goats 115, 117
    olives 36, 39
    pig 34, 116, 117, 159
    sheep 34, 111, 113, 115–18, 130, 212
    viticulture 36, 39, 47, 53, 54, 62, 115, 117, 129, 150, 157
Fortresses 97–107
    ancient 97
    cistern 105, 106
    Honaz 12, 13, 15, 41, 102, 105
    medieval / Byzantine 3, 15, 16, 29, 99–104
    position 38–9
    rebel outpost 40

G

Gladiators 83
    Colossian relief 87–92
    Diodoros the dejected 92
    oath 89
    rules 88
    types 88, 91
    venators 87, 214
Gods 45–69, 149, 167, 170, 183, 186, 194, 209
    acropolis 2, 3, 66, 76, 77
    Anahita 181

angels and 61, 66, 183
Aphrodite 65, 69
Apollo 46, 51, 52, 59, 68, 89, 135, 183, 193, 210
Artemis 51, 52, 65, 68, 185, 193
    Colossensis 59
    Ephesiaca 55, 56, 58, 59, 63, 187
    hunter 35, 55–9, 90
Asclepios 149, 150
Athena 48, 59, 68, 123, 212
Attis 50, 51, 52, 182
Christian god 186, 187, 188, 195, 197
Cybele 49, 50–2, 53, 68, 181, 182, 185, 194, 195
Demeter 48, 54, 60, 68
Dionysos/Bacchus 51, 53–5, 58, 68, 75, 86, 89, 206, 207
Echidna 51, 68, 185
Egyptian gods 22, 45, 65, 69, 213
Eros 166, 167
Hades 54, 68, 92, 211
Hecate 65
Helios 52, 58, 68, 212
Hera 50, 65
Hermes 89, 118
    Enagonios 89
Hygeia 149, 150
Imperial cult 56, 63, 89, 211
Ishtar 182
Isis 65, 68, 69, 213
Juno 64
Kybebe 181
Medusa 14, 44, 45, 68, 92, 107, 166, 167, 172
Mên 46, 49, 50, 51, 58, 68, 69
Mithras 51
Muse Melpomene 92, 166, 167

nature, connection with 47–55, 75–7
Nike 68, 166
Nymphs 48, 50, 60, 142, 174, 211
Persephone 54, 211
priesthood 50, 52, 54, 63, 66, 68, 78, 86, 89, 90, 122, 127, 150, 195, 207, 210, 211
ritual 47, 118, 127, 193, 206, 210
river god 35, 48–9, 68, 138
Roma 63, 65, 89
Sarapis 63, 65, 68, 69
theonyms 68–9, 170, 214
Tyche / Fortuna 35, 36, 52, 59–65, 68, 69
    Protogeneia 62, 63
Zeus (Dis, Dios) 37, 53, 60, 63, 68, 69, 75, 76, 89, 118, 149, 170, 183, 184, 188, 193, 195
    Aetophoros 46, 52, 65, 66, 67, 68, 183, 184
    Bronton 53, 65–8, 183, 184
    Ktesis Patrios 67, 118
    Laodikeus/Laodikensis 65, 67, 68, 183
    Panamara 193
Graves 16, 34, 105, 182
    city, relation to 155, 160, 165, 169, 175
    death rituals 125, 160, 162, 165, 166, 214
    epitaphs 21, 22, 37, 51, 87, 91–2, 116, 117, 127, 156, 163, 169–71, 172, 175, 191, 207, 213
    Greek 164
    Hellenistic 163–6
    location 105, 106, 107, 154
    manufacture 125, 158, 166, 173–5
    necropolis 3, 17, 18, 20, 34, 37, 47, 54, 66, 67, 110, 122, 126, 141, 142, 144, 155–75
    Phrygian 160–2
    protection 44, 167, 172–3
    reliefs 54, 117, 124, 125, 166–8, 171–2, 207, 213
    Roman 159, 168–9
    types 20, 54, 66, 155–9, 163–8, 169, 207, 214
Greece 50, 68, 86, 89, 146, 159
    artefacts 14
    repatriation v, 198
Greek Magical Papyri 61
Gregory of Nyssa *Panegyric on Theodore the Recruit* 194

H

Hadrian, Roman emperor 35, 46, 58, 62, 63, 64, 65, 149, 183, 184
    mint license at Colossae 34, 37, 65, 67, 68, 86, 183
    pan-hellenic tour 36–7, 55, 86, 147, 149, 183
Herodotos 30, 111–2, 115, 137, 139, 141, 190–2
    Histories 190
Heroes 33, 68–9, 89, 90, 120–1, 124, 169, 170, 209
    Achilles 88, 121
    Aeneas 50
    Cadmus (Kadmos) 52, 53
    change in concept 15, 119, 209
    Herakles (Hercules) 68, 121
    Semele 52
    young men 15, 160
Hippocratic Airs 137
Hittite 98, 111
    agriculture 111
    Colossae, name of 98
    dyes 115
Households 36, 166, 209, 211
    family 32, 69, 116, 117, 170
    imperial values 83, 171, 172
    society and 83, 126, 168, 169, 171
    structure 171

Höyük (tell, mound) 3, 4, 12, 17, 18, 19, 22, 23, 24, 38, 47, 53, 66, 96, 100, 102, 103, 105, 110, 137, 139, 140, 142, 155, 160, 165, 175, 191, 192, 193, 210
   stratigraphy 97–8, 104,
   theatre and 74–85, 98

I

Inscriptions vi, 3, 5, 13, 16, 21, 32, 33, 45, 54, 64, 8, 82, 83, 111, 115, 116–7, 123, 124, 125, 146, 159, 169–71, 183, 208, 210, 213
   Amisos 91, 92
   Aphrodisias 90, 126, 175
   Colossae 15, 16, 18, 19, 20, 22, 30, 35, 36, 37, 49, 51, 53, 54, 55, 56, 61, 62, 66, 68, 78, 83, 84, 86, 105, 119, 120, 122, 129, 145, 146, 157, 158, 160, 164, 166, 167, 168, 170, 171, 172, 173, 190, 191
   Ephesos 36
   Eumeneia 157, 172
   Hierapolis 116, 119, 121, 122, 125, 126, 175
   Laodikeia 22, 114, 115, 120–1, 122, 127,
   re-use 15, 16
   Stratonikeia 128, 174, 175, 193
Islam
   funerary practice 19
   mosques 9, 16, 20, 40, 55, 101, 104, 105, 107, 198

J

Julian, Emperor 15, 50–1, 194–7
   Edict against Tomb Desecration 173

L

Laodikeia 1, 5, 6, 8, 10, 12, 13, 20, 22, 36, 38, 45, 46, 49, 65, 80, 81, 102, 104, 111, 114, 145, 149, 163, 165, 170, 183
   textile industry 113, 114, 115, 116, 118, 120, 127–9, 130
   conflict with Colossae 34–5, 67–8, 112, 185–6, 195–6
   sieges of 34, 67–8, 193
   Synod of 150, 196
Leather 122, 123, 124, 130
   animal farming 116–7, 122, 130
   Dion leatherworker 37, 156, 169–70
Levant Company
   See European exploration
Livy 29
   History of Rome 123

M

Martial 124, 150
   Epigram 124
Mediterranean 9, 52, 81, 85, 187, 206
   trade 9, 30, 119, 124, 175
Menologion 57, 211
   of Basil 57, 197
Military 30, 32, 36, 37, 67, 97, 102, 103, 104, 136, 181, 196, 197, 208, 210, 214
   communication 30–1, 32, 38, 99
   garrisons 38–9, 40, 100–1, 214
   provisions 29–30, 36–7, 40, 129, 212
   stations 36, 38, 99
   transport 30, 32, 137

N

New Testament 7, 185
- Acts of the Apostles 82
- Colossians, letter to 45, 54, 57, 68–9, 90–1, 111, 135, 185, 186
- Corinthians, first letter to 87
- Ephesians, letter to 171
- Peter, first letter to 171
- Philemon 37, 57, 68–9, 83, 135, 185, 196
- Timothy, first letter to 90, 171
- Timothy, second letter to 90, 127
- Revelation (the Apocalypse) 184, 186

O

Ottoman Empire 7
- artefacts 10, 14, 105
- banditry 13, 40, 104
- diplomatic connections 9, 10, 210
- regional rule 10, 12–13,
- taxation 40

P

Persia 16, 30–3, 45, 111, 135–8, 180, 208
- Achaemenid dynasty 30, 32, 75, 135, 137, 138, 206
- army 32, 33, 38, 213
- Artaxerxes II 136,
- assassination of Tissaphernes 33, 135–7, 138
- conflict with Greeks 33–4
- estates 32, 58, 138
- Darius I 32,
- Parthians 34
- signal system 31, 32, 38
- template for satrapies 32

Philes, Manuel
- *Epigram* 6

Polis (city) 3, 4, 17, 20, 29, 30, 34, 36, 37, 38, 39, 49, 66, 80, 99, 102, 111, 112, 137, 141, 146, 149, 190, 191, 193, 195, 197, 206
- architecture/infrastructure 35, 47, 75–92, 105, 142–5, 147, 187, 214
- civic offices 30, 35, 56, 62, 63, 78, 86, 89, 90, 91, 129–30, 138, 146–7, 172, 206, 207, 208, 213
- euergetism 35, 54, 61, 89–90, 145, 168, 174, 209
- necropolis 155, 160, 163, 164, 169, 175
- religion 45–69

Pottery 1, 18, 24, 53, 97, 166, 213
- Bronze Age 18, 98
- Byzantine 103, 104
- Chalcolithic 98

R

Rhodes 39
- letter to the Rhodians 6
- St John Colossensis 7

Rome 11, 50, 52, 55, 64, 65, 68, 81, 82, 86, 89, 98, 111, 112, 123, 124, 138, 142, 145, 146, 147, 149, 162, 168, 172, 181, 182
- Fortuna / Tyche 36, 62, 63, 182
  - Redux 63–4
  - Mala 65
- pan-hellenic tour 36–7, 55, 86, 147, 149, 183
- neokoros status 46, 48, 55, 211
- Roman Empire 13, 15, 24, 37, 46, 50, 56, 66, 126, 127, 128, 149, 168, 170, 171, 194
- Roman Republic 34, 67–8, 112, 126, 145, 159, 162

S

Sophocles
   Antigone 53
St Michael 3, 180–98
   archangel 3, 66, 184–5, 187, 192
   archistrategos 197
   of Chonai 51, 57, 185–7, 195
   churches 102, 120, 135, 184, 192–3
   healing spring 3, 13, 186, 187, 189, 192
   icons 180, 187, 196, 197–8
   sanctuary 184, 185, 186, 188
   Zeus and 183, 184, 188, 193, 195
Stone 14, 15, 16, 17, 19, 37, 54, 55, 66, 89, 105, 107, 122, 142, 155, 158, 164, 166, 168, 173, 184, 185, 187, 206, 207, 208, 212
   inscriptions and 5, 10, 16, 21, 22
   limestone 14, 23, 85, 119, 140, 141, 158, 159, 169, 191
   marble 14, 16, 58, 107, 116, 119, 125, 127, 145, 158, 159, 166, 174
   stone cutters 16, 128, 159, 163, 168, 173, 174, 175
   stoneworking 48, 138, 156, 157, 164, 170, 171, 173,
Suetonius 124, 169
   Augustus 83

T

Temples 15, 16, 55, 56, 57, 59, 63, 64, 77, 82, 159, 160, 161, 163, 169, 194, 206, 211, 213, 214
   caves and 53,
   neokoros 46, 48, 55, 211
   of Zeus 66, 76, 193
Textiles 111–30
   animal farming 111, 112, 116–7, 122, 130
   clothing vi, 19, 36, 50, 51, 88, 111, 118, 120, 124, 127–30
   custom dues 126, 213
   divine backing 118
   dyeing 114, 115, 120, 121, 125, 211
   fleece 111, 113, 115, 118, 120, 123, 129, 139, 208
   labourers 121, 125, 126
   Laodicena 127, 128
   manufacture 121, 122, 123, 124, 125, 129, 209
   prices 128, 129
   shepherds 111, 113, 115–18, 120, 130
   styles 126, 127, 128, 207, 210
   symbolism 123–4, 130
   trade 112, 120
   and see leather
Theatre 3, 14, 55, 74–85, 98
   capacities 81, 82
   cavea 74, 75, 76, 77, 81, 82, 83, 84, 87, 98, 99, 207, 212
   civic use 82, 86, 91
   hierarchy 82–6
   Dionysos 86
   partisan colours 90
   parts 82
   religious use 54, 82
   seating 74, 78, 80, 82, 84, 85, 86, 87, 92
   site choice 75–80
   structures 82, 86–7
   'Theatre Street' 78, 80, 147
Trade 8, 46, 56, 111, 112, 113, 118–19, 120, 122, 123, 127, 128, 129, 130, 168, 175, 198
   routes 30, 102, 112, 113, 119, 126
   traders 8–9, 11, 119, 127, 129

W

Water 29, 32, 33, 75, 76, 80, 105, 113, 114, 120, 129, 134–50, 210, 211
    calcification 18, 114, 139, 141, 142, 143, 155
    healing and 3, 13, 186, 187, 188, 189, 192
    infrastructure 35, 47, 61, 122, 141–50, 154, 173, 174, 175, 183
    Lycus River 2, 6, 8, 12, 18, 20, 29, 35, 38, 47, 48, 49, 53, 61, 78, 79, 107, 111, 115, 120, 138, 139, 140, 141, 148, 150, 155, 161, 181, 190–2,
    religion and 47, 49–51, 63, 180, 182, 196
    river systems 34, 38, 49, 112, 138
    springs 34, 63, 181, 189
Women 37, 48, 51, 52, 62–3, 92, 197, 209
    conventions regarding 123–5, 137, 150, 159, 207, 208
    cottage industry 123, 126
    society 82–3, 117, 160, 191

Ingram Content Group UK Ltd.
Milton Keynes UK
UKHW050042100723
424739UK00008B/71